NOTES,

CRITICAL AND PRACTICAL,

ON THE BOOK OF

JOSHUA:

DESIGNED AS A GENERAL HELP TO

BIBLICAL READING AND INSTRUCTION

By GEORGE BUSH,

PROF. OF HEB. AND ORIENT. LIT. N. Y. CITY UNIVERSITY.

SECOND EDITION.

Wipf & Stock
PUBLISHERS
Eugene, Oregon

Wipf and Stock Publishers
199 W 8th Ave, Suite 3
Eugene, OR 97401

Notes, Critical and Practical, on the Book of Joshua
Designed as a General Help to Biblical Reading and Instruction
By Bush, George
ISBN: 1-59752-245-7
Publication date 6/8/2005
Previously published by Saxton & Miles, 1845

INTRODUCTION

TO THE

HISTORICAL BOOKS IN GENERAL.

THAT portion of the Old Testament which contains the history of the affairs of the Jewish nation, from the death of Moses to its conquest by the Chaldeans, is comprised in the books of Joshua, Judges, Samuel, and Kings. These, in the Hebrew classification, are termed the *Former Prophets,* The title *Prophets* is given them on the ground of the general belief, that they were written under the prompting of a Divine impulse; and the epithet *Former* is applied in reference to the place which they occupy in the Sacred Canon, as preceding the books of the *Latter Prophets,* an appellation bestowed upon those whose character is more strictly *prophetical,* viz., Isaiah, Jeremiah, Ezekiel, and the twelve Minor Prophets. The records of the nation from the time of the exile and the return thence, down to the close of the Persian empire, are contained in the books of Esther, Ezra, and Nehemiah, which the Hebrews attach to that part of the canon called the *Hagiographa,* in which are included also the books of Ruth and Chronicles. How ancient this division was, we cannot positively affirm; but it was current at least as early as the time of Jerome and the later Talmudists.

As to the sources from which these records were derived, there is a very great degree of uncertainty, although it is admitted that they are a species of compilation, made up, for the most part, from pre-existing documents, in the shape of annals or chronicles, which were doubtless co-eval with the events narrated. The evidence of such an origin discloses itself repeatedly in the texture of the records themselves, as we shall have occasion hereafter to notice, although it does not seem to have entered into the design of the writers to designate, by formal reference or citation, the sources from which they drew. The mere circumstance that we have, in the Sacred Canon, a number of books bearing the names of certain individuals, does not of itself prove that the books were originally written, or even subsequently compiled, by the persons whose names they bear. Thus, if we admit that Joshua wrote the book

much stress upon the passage, ch. 24. 26, in which Joshua is said to have 'written these words in the book of the law of God,' for it is not clear that any thing more is there intended than the words uttered on that occasion, and in which the people express their solemn engagements to be faithful to the covenant. See Note *in loc.* But the following considerations have more weight.

(1.) The style of the composition is remarkably pure, free from foreign words, forms, or idioms, and so strikingly conformed to that of the Pentateuch as to argue a date nearly co-eval with it.

(2.) The writer speaks of himself as one that participated in the transactions which he records, ch. 5. 1 : 'And it came to pass, when all the kings of the Amorites which were on the side of Jordan westward, and all the kings of the Canaanites which were by the sea, heard that the Lord had dried up the waters of Jordan from before the children of Israel, *until we were passed over,* that their heart melted; neither was there spirit in them any more, because of the children of Israel.' As it is said, moreover, ch. 6. 25, that 'Joshua saved Rahab the harlot alive, and her father's household, and all that she had; *and she dwelleth in Israel even unto this day,*' there is a strong presumption that this was not written later than near the close of Joshua's life; and if so, he would be as likely to have written it as any one else.

(3.) It is scarcely conceivable that so many names of persons and places as occur in this book, should have been preserved, unless in a cotemporary document; and from whom would such a document have been more likely to proceed than from Joshua himself? He might naturally be expected to record such transactions as went to illustrate the truth of the Divine promises made to his people.

(4.) The division of the land among the different tribes was doubtless recorded at the time it was made, and it was certainly made by Joshua in person, immediately after the conquest. The account of this division occupies a very considerable portion of the whole book (ch. 14–21.), and as it is difficult, in the absence of all testimony to the contrary, to assign a reason why Joshua should not have written the bulk of the other parts as well as this, the presumption undoubtedly is, especially as tradition affirms it, that he is the principal author. The truth of the tradition may fairly be taken for granted, unless the work itself can be shown to contain internal evidence against it.

(5.) In ch. 17. 13, it is said, 'It came to pass, when the children of Israel were waxen strong, that they put the Canaanites to tribute; but did not utterly drive them out.' This has the air of having been written shortly after the conquest. Had it been penned at a much later period, the writer would scarcely have failed to mention the well known fact, that the Israelites were soon seduced into idolatry by these very tributaries. The date of the writing was undoubtedly prior to this apostacy.

The principal objections against assigning the authorship of the book to Daniel, are the following:—

(1.) In ch. 10. 13, the circumstance of the sun and moon being stayed in their course is said to be written in the book of Jasher. This testimony, it is contended, would not have been quoted by Joshua, or any other contemporary writer, concerning transactions of recent occurrence and unusual notoriety. The inference therefore is, that the book entitled 'the Wars of the Lord' must have been written at a much earlier period than that in which it is cited. But there is no difficulty in supposing, that, as Joshua probably composed his book towards the latter part of his life, he might have introduced an apposite quotation from a history or poem containing a more minute or vivid description of the miracle, and written some years before his own.

(2.) The use of the phrase 'to this day' is supposed to indicate a period very considerably subsequent to the date of the events. Thus of the stones set up in the Jordan, ch. 4. 9, 'they are there *unto this day*;'—of the place where the reproach of Egypt was rolled away, ch. 5. 9, 'the name of the place is called Gilgal *unto this day*;'—of the valley of Achor, ch. 7. 26, 'it is so called *unto this day*;'—of the ruins of Ai, ch. 8. 28, 'it is a desolation *unto this day*;'—and so in other instances. In reply to this it can only be said, that the phrase does not necessarily imply any considerable length of time. If Washington had written annals of the American Revolution in the last year or two of his life, no one would have been surprised to hear him saying of certain monuments or memorials of battles and victories, that they remained 'unto this day.' In like manner Joshua might have expressed himself in the same language in similar circumstances.

(3.) An argument to the same effect is derived from the narrative ch. 19. 48, 49, of the taking of Leshem by the Danites. This event, it is said, appears from Judges 18. 27–29, to have occurred after the death of Joshua, and therefore the present account of it is inconsistent with the asserted authorship of the book. Hence some have attributed its composition to Eleazar, some to Samuel, and some to Isaiah or Ezra. But it is not necessary, on this account, to attempt to invalidate the claims of Joshua to the authorship of the substance of the book. It is not denied that occasional interpolations have been made by later hands, and this may safely be admitted to be one, although it is to be remarked, that Jahn and others express strong doubts whether the two narratives refer to the same expedition, as they they vary in several particulars.

(4.) It is objected that certain places are called in this book by names which they did not acquire till some ages afterwards. But as to 'the stray city Tyre,' ch. 19. 29, Bochart contends that this is not the celebrated city of that name, but an inland fortified place. So the Cabul mentioned ch. 19. 27, is affirmed by Reland not to have been the country to which that name was applied by Hiram in Solomon's time, but a city which in the age of Josephus had degenerated into a village. We may observe, too, in this connexion, that the expression 'house of God,' ch, 9. 23, is not exclusively applied to *the temple*, but also to *the tabernacle*, as the Bedouins apply the term to a *tent*.

On the whole, therefore, we feel little hesitation in refering the authorship of the book, as a whole, to Joshua, though we doubt not that certain isolated passages have been inserted by copyists or revisers at a subsequent period. We see no good reason to doubt that the history here given is his work, as truly as the Commentaries of Cæsar are his; and in this view we are confirmed by the *a priori* probabilities of the case. Moses, it is certain, kept an accurate register of the various events that took place during his administration in the wilderness; and as Joshua was his constant servant and companion, he could not but be aware of the importance of such historical memoranda, nor can it well be supposed that, having succeeded him in the same office, he should not have continued the same practice.

§ 2. *Contents, Scope, and Design.*

The book relates the history of Israel while under the command and government of Joshua; the entrance of the Hebrews into Canaan; their conquest of the greater part of the country; the division of the territory by lot among the several tribes; and the provision made for the settlement and establishment of the Jewish church in that country. The length of time embraced in this history is variously stated by chronologists, at seventeen, twenty-seven, and thirty years. Between twenty-six and twenty-seven years is the usually received and most probable period. The leading drift of the writer is to demonstrate the faithfulness of God in the perfect accomplishment of all his promises to the patriarchs, Abraham, Isaac, Jacob, and Joseph, and also to Moses, that the children of Israel should obtain possession of the land of Canaan. Viewed in this light, it is an invaluable appendage to the preceding five books of Moses, and indeed bears to them very much the same relation as does the Acts of the Apostles to the Gospels of the four Evangelists. The inspired historian relates, with all the animation of one who was an actual eye-witness and participator of the scenes described, the successive miracles that favored and secured the conquest of the country, the general zeal, activity, and obedience of Israel in prosecuting their wars, with the occasional lapses and transgressions that interrupted the career of their victories. We see the Divine power and faithfulness conspicuously displayed in guiding, cherishing, and defending the chosen people amidst all the trials to which they were exposed; and while the general tenor of the narrative affords a striking emblem of the warfare of the Christian in gaining possession of his heavenly inheritance, it ministers the most abundant encouragement to those who in sincerity and faith throw themselves upon the superintending care of that Being, who keepeth covenant and mercy for ever.

The following will serve as a synopsis of the contents of the several chapters:

PART I.—*The Entrance of the Israelites into Canaan.*

1. The appointment of Joshua as leader of Israel, ch. 1.
2. The spies sent out to view the land, ch. 2.
3. The miraculous passage of the Jordan, ch. 1. 10–18, ch. 2. 4
4. The renewal of the covenant, ch. 5. 1–13.

PART II.—*The Victories of the Israelites under Joshua.*

1. The conquest of Jericho, ch. 6.
2. The capture of Ai, ch. 7. 8.
3. Fraud of the Gibeonites—conquest of the five kings—miracle of the sun's standing still, ch. 9. 10.
4. Conquest of Canaan completed, ch. 11.
5. Recapitulation of the conquests of Israel, ch. 12. 13.

PART III.—*Division of the Country.*

1. Inheritance of the two tribes and a half, ch. 13.
2. General division of Canaan, ch. 14.
3. Inheritance of Caleb, ch. 14. 15.
4. Lot of Judah, ch. 15.
5. Lot of Joseph, ch. 16. 17.
6. The Tabernacle set up, ch. 18.
7. Lot of Benjamin and the remaining tribes, ch. 18. 19.
8. Inheritance of Joshua, ch. 19.
9. Cities of refuge and Levitical cities, ch. 20, 21.

PART IV.—*The last Exhortations and Death of Joshua.*

1. The assembling of the people and first address of Joshua, ch. 23.
2. The tribes again assembled and addressed by Joshua, ch. 24.
3. The death and burial of Joshua, ch. 24.
4. The death and burial of Eleazar, ch. 24.

INTRODUCTION.

§ 3. *Commentators.*

(1.) *Jewish.*

RABBI SCHELOMOH BEN JIZCHAK, commonly called RASCHE, or JARCHI; R. DAVID KIMCHI; and R. LEVI BEN GERSON, commonly denominated RALBAG, have each of them furnished commentaries on this book, which are found in the *Biblia Rabbinica* of Buxtorf, published A. D. 1618. For a character of Jarchi, see Introduction to Judges.

פירוש יהושע לרבי ישעיה *pirosh Yehoshua lerabbi Yeshayah*, i. e. *The Commentary of R. Isaiah on Joshua*, written out, translated, and illustrated with notes, from a Manuscript in the Library of the Senate of Leipsic, by D. GEORGE ABICHT. Leips. 1712. Republished in the *Thesaurus Novus Theologico-Philologico*, or Sylloge of Exegetical Dissertations on Select Passages of the Old and New Testament, from the *Museum* of Theod. Hase and Conrad Iken, Leyden, 1732, vol. i., p. 474, *seqq.* This Rabbi Isaiah, the son of Elias, who is called *Isaiah the latter*, flourished in the 13th century, and wrote commentaries on the books of Joshua, Judges, Samuel, and Ezra, which Masius says, in the catalogue of Jewish authors subjoined to his Commentary on Joshua, that he possessed in manuscript, and from which he often quotes. Comp. WOLFII *Biblioth. Hebr.* T. I., p. 705, *seqq.*

(2.) *Christian.*

MART. BORRHAI, called also CELLARIUS, *Commentarii in Libros Josuæ, Judicum, Samuelis, et Regum.* Basil. 1557. Fol.

VICTOR STRIGELII *Liber Josuæ, argumentis et scholiis illustratus.* Leips. 1570, 1575. 8 vo.

ANDREÆ MASII. *Josuæ Imperatoris Historia illustrata atque explicata.* Antverpiæ, 1574. Fol.

Masius, though a lawyer and a Catholic, has produced by far the most elaborate work ever published on the book of Joshua, and probably the most valuable commentary, with the single exception of that of Calmet, to which the Roman church can lay claim. Considering the age in which it was written, and the limited facilities which the author could have enjoyed for such a performance, it is truly a remarkable work; and it will rather enhance the reader's estimation of its merit to know, that it comes within the list of books prohibited by the Papal see —a fate which we might be certain *a priori* its excellence would secure to it. Pool, in the preface to his Synopsis, says of Masius, 'Vir longiore vita et immortali memoria dignus; interpres cui parem ingenio, judicio, rerum ac linguarum peritia, candore et modestia, haud facile reperies,'—*a man worthy of a longer life and of an undying celebrity;*

an interpreter, whose equal in talent, judgment, historical knowledge, skill in languages, candor and modesty, is not easily to be found. Similar commendation is bestowed by Buddeus, Walchius, and other bibliographers upon the commentary of Masius; and from having it constantly before me in the preparation of the ensuing notes, I feel no hesitation in subscribing to the general justice of these encomiums. The work contains, besides the commentary, the book of Joshua in the original Hebrew, with the Greek of the Septuagint, and a three-fold Latin translation, together with a preface containing valuable readings to the Greek, from a manuscript copy in his possession, which since his death has unfortunately been lost to the learned world.

DAVID CHYTRÆI *Prælectiones in librum Josuæ.* Rostochii. 1577. 8vo.

BENED. ARIÆ MONTANI *Liber de optimo Imperio, sive in Librum Josuæ Commentarius.* Antwerp. 1583. 4to.

NICOL. SERARII *Commentarius in Librum Josuæ.* Duob. Tom. Mogunt. 1609. Paris. 1610. Fol.

COSMÆ MAGALJANI *Commentarii in sacram Josuæ historiam, cum Appendice rerum ab eo gestarum ante ingressum terræ Sanctæ.* Turnoni. 1612. Tom. I., II. Fol.

Jo. DRUSII *ad loca difficiliora Josuæ, Judicum, et Samuelem Commentarius. Additur est Sixtini Amama Commentarius de Decimis Mosaicis.* Franeck. 1618. 4to.

JAC. BONFRERII *Josua, Judices, et Ruth Commentario illustrati.* Paris. 1631. Fol.

EMANUELIS DE NAXERA *Commentarii literales et morales in Josuam, hostilibus redimitum trophæis, cum appendice de Rahab et Arca figurata.* T. I. Antwerp. 1650, and T. II. Lugd. 1652. Fol.

HENR MARCELLI *Commentarius in librum Josuæ.* Herbipoli. 1665. 4to.

PHIL. LUD. HANNECKII *Adnotata philologica in Josuam.* Gissæ. 1665. 8vo.

Jo. ADAMI OSIANDRI *Commentarius in Josuam, exhibens sacrum cum exegesi textum, lectionum et versionum varietatem, conciliatas antilogias, chronologiam, utilium quæstionum solutionem, objectiones cum vindiciis, observationes philologicas, et locos cummunes doctrinales.* Tubing. 1681. Fol.

SEBAST. SCHMIDII *Prælectiones academicæ in octo priora libri Josuæ capita.* Hamburgi. 1693. 4to.

For the character of Schmid as a Scriptural critic, see the list of Commentators prefixed to the book of Judges. His Prelections on Joshua, which were arrested at the eighth chapter by the death of the author, are of similar character and value with those on the succeeding book. He affords very important aid to the commentator.

JAC. FELIBIEN *Pentateuchus historicus, sive quinque libri historici, Josua, Judices, Ruth, ac duo Regum (Samuelis), cum Commentariis, ex fonte Hebraica, versione Septuaginta Interpretum et variis auctoribus collectis.* Paris. 1704. 4to.

GOTTLOB WILH. MEYER *Ueber die Bestandtheile und die Œkonomie des Buchs Josua.* In the *Theolog. Krit. Journ.*, edited by Bertholdt, vol. II., Fasc. 4to. p. 337, *seqq.* Solisbach. 1815.

H. E. G. PAULUS *Blicke in das Buch Josua, als Vorgeschichte der Suffetin und Samuels*, in auctoris *Theologisch-Exegetischen Conservatorium*, P. II., p. 149, et seq. Heidelberg. 1822.

CLAUD. HENR. VAN HERWERDEN *Disputatio de Libro Josuæ, sive de diversis ex quibus constat Josuæ liber monumentis, deque ætate, qua eorum vixerint auctores.* Groning. 1826. 8vo.

The object of the author is to show that the book of Joshua is composed of ten different documents, each of which is clearly distinguished from the others in style, diction, and scope. These various portions he has designated, and contends that they are distinctly marked by certain peculiarities of verbal usage, running through them respectively. Rosenmueller, however, objects that this is very precarious ground on which to form a definite decision of this nature; and though he gives the author credit for great research and acumen, he evidently deems his conclusions of little value.

F. J. V. D. MAURER *Commentar uber das Buch Joshua.* Stuttgard. 1831. 8vo.

This is mainly a *verbo-critical* commentary, detailing the nice points of grammatical construction, and indicating the application of certain philological principles, fixed by Gesenius and Ewald, to the language of the book. In this respect it has some value, but very little in any other. The author belongs to the freest school of biblical criticism, and does not scruple to call all the supernatural events recorded *mythical*, and like De Wette and others, considers the book a sort of patchwork, made up of the shreds of pre-existing rhapsodies and fragments.

In the ensuing Commentary, as well as in all my former vols. on the Pentateuch, I have adopted the plan of giving the Hebrew without points, simply with a view to preserve uniformity in the appearance of the printed page; as the insertion of the points would necessarily throw the lines, between which they occurred, wider asunder than the rest. By way of compensation I have endeavored to express the pronunciation of the Hebrew words in English letters; and as for this purpose the sounds of the vowels have to be modified by accents, the reader will bear in mind that they are indicated as follows:—

$\check{a}=a$ in *hall*. $\check{e}=a$ in *hate*. $\check{\imath}=i$ in *shire*. $\bar{o}=o$ in *bone*. $\bar{u}=oo$ in *moon*.

THE BOOK OF JOSHUA.

CHAPTER I.

NOW after the death of Moses, the servant of the Lord, it came to pass that the Lord spake unto Joshua the son of Nun, Moses'ᵃ minister, saying,

ᵃ Exod. 24. 13. Deut. 1. 38.

1. *Now after the death of Moses, &c.* The literal rendering of the Heb. is, '*And* it was (or happened) after the death of Moses, *and* the Lord spake, &c.' This rendering discloses more perfectly the use of the copulative 'and' in the original, which is so employed as to bring this book into immediate connexion with the foregoing, and thus makes it a regular *continuation* of the sacred narrative begun and carried on by Moses in the five preceeding books. In like manner the book of Ruth commences with a similar phraseology, ויהי *And it came to pass*, &c., although it cannot be questioned that there are other instances, as in the opening of the books of Esther and Ezekiel, where the ו *v* cannot have a *copulative*, but merely a *conversive* sense; i. e., it *converts*, according to a peculiarity of the language, the future into the past or pretorite sense. —The *time* referred to at the opening of this book, was probably at the conclusion of the thirty day's mourning for Moses, spoken of Deut. 34, 8; or it might have been during that period; in which time also it is the opinion of some commentators that the spies (chap. 2, 1) were sent out. —¶ *The servant of the Lord.* A high and honorable title, applied to Moses, not merely in the sense in which it is applied to pious and good men generally, who may justly be styled *servants* of the Most High, inasmuch as it is the grand aim of their lives to *serve* and obey him; but in this connexion carrying with it a reference to the peculiar *nature of the service* in which Moses was employed, viz., that of a minister, mediator, deputy, or vicegerent of God, the honored organ through whom he communicated his will to his chosen people and managed all their varied interests. It is in this character that he stands so highly commended in the sacred volume, having received the divine testimony to his being 'found faithful in all God's house *as a servant*,' and being expressly distinguished by this title, not only here, where God himself is pleased so to denominate him, v. 2, but also in Rev. 15. 3, where it is said of the company standing upon the sea of glass, that they 'sing the song of Moses *the servant of God*.' On the sense of *ministerial ruling* oftentimes involved in the term *servant*, see Note Gen. 24. 2.——¶ *The Lord spake unto Joshua, &c.* The name of this illustrious leader of Israel appears in a

somewhat different form in several different connexions in which it occurs. In Num. 13. 16, we are informed that 'Moses called Oshea the son of Nun, Jehoshua,' where the original is in the first instance הושע *hoshëa*, the same name with that of the Prophet Hosea, and in the second יהושע *yehoshua*, having the first letter of 'Jehovah' (יהוה) appended. The first of these the Gr. of the Sept. represents by Αυση, *Ausè*, the other by Ιησους, *Jesus*. The Hebrew root of the name has the import of *salvation*, and from this the sense of *Saviour* has been transferred into the Greek Ιησους, *Jesus*. In Neh. 8. 17, we have still another form; ישוע *yeshua*, *Jeshua*, where the Gr. preserves the usual form Ιησους, *Jesus*. It was doubtless from this current usage of the Septuagint that the New Testament writers have in two instances applied to Joshua the name of the Saviour, of whom he was undoubtedly an eminent type. The first is Acts 7. 45, 'Which also our fathers, that came after, brought in with *Jesus*;' i. e. Joshua. The other is Heb. 4. 8, 'For if *Jesus* (Joshua) had given them rest, then would he not afterward have spoken of another day.' This change of names, in the case of various Scripture personages, appears to have been governed by a change of relations, either to God or to man, as in the case of Abraham, Sarah, Jacob, Daniel, Paul, and others. See Note on Gen. 17. 5. Of the *manner* of the communication now made to Joshua, we are not expressly informed. From the fact that Moses and Joshua, just before the death of the former, were summoned together into the 'tabernacle of the congregation,' Deut. 31. 14, that the dying charge of Moses might be given to his successor, it seems highly probable that the instructions and encouragements imparted on this occasion were delivered from the same place.——¶ *Moses' minister.* Heb. משרת משה *meshâreth Moshëh, he that served, or ministered to, Moses.* The original שרת *shârath, to minister*, is used with the accusative of the person ministered to, and is found for the most part in those connexions, where *the service of God* is spoken of, especially that which was rendered by the Priests and Levites. Joshua was Moses' minister in the sense of an immediate attendant, one who waited upon his person, and assisted him in business; one of whose services he availed himself in a variety of ways, as Elisha, of those of Gehazi. In Deut. 1. 38, it is expressed by a different, but equivalent phrase העמד לפניך *hâomëd lepânëkâ, who standeth before thee*, a usual mode of expressing the idea of *ministration*. The word is rendered in some copies of the Greek, υπεργος, an *under-workman*, in others, θεραπων, *one that waits, attends upon, ministers to.* Previous to the death of Moses, Joshua had been specially designated to the office which he is now called to assume, Deut. 1. 38; 31. 3, 6—8; and for which he was peculiarly qualified by his long familiarity with Moses, and by the training which he would naturally receive in the station occupied under him. An humble and devoted spirit, a willingness to serve God in the meanest employments, is the best preparative, and often the surest precursor to posts of honor and dignity in the church. Wherever this is the case, no previous lowness or obscurity of origin is, in

B. C. 1451.] CHAPTER I. 15

2 ᵇMoses my servant is dead; now therefore arise, go over this Jordan, thou and all this people, unto the land which I do give to them, *even* to the children of Israel.

ᵇ Deut. 34. 5.

God's sight, an obstacle to advancement. Persons of this character are often surprised to look back, and see from what small beginnings they have been raised step by step, under the guidance of Providence, to stations of the most extensive influence and usefulness.

2. *Moses my servant is dead.* As Joshua was of course aware of the *fact* of Moses' decease, these words could not be intended merely to announce to him that event. They are equivalent to saying, 'The death of my servant Moses has left the people without a leader and a head to conduct them into the promised land. It is necessary that his place should be immediately filled. Thou hast been selected for that office, and the time has now come for thee to enter upon the active discharge of its duties. Arise therefore, and go at once about the work of thy high calling.' Probably Joshua's deep sense of his own insufficiency and unworthiness, and of the many dangers and difficulties which encompassed his path, had caused him somewhat to despond and waver in spirit, and rendered necessary this direct and rousing summons, which, for the same reason, God was pleased to accompany with so many encouraging promises. When it is considered that Joshua was now ninety-three years of age, that he had to govern a very perverse and rebellious people, and was going to contend with a warlike and formidable enemy, it will perhaps appear, that nothing short of the divine assurance he now received, could have sustained his courage in such an arduous station.——¶ *Go over this Jordan.* This river, which you now have in full view before you, and on the banks of which you are encamped. For a description of the Jordan, see 'Illustrations of the Scriptures,' p. 20. It was doubtless a severe trial to Joshua's faith, to be thus called upon to make immediate preparation for crossing a river that was now overflowing its banks, chap. 3. 15, and for getting over which he was totally unprovided with the ordinary means, whether of boats or bridges. But as God had given the command, he must not doubt that he would open a way for his people, though it should be by cleaving the waters and repeating the miracle witnessed at the Red Sea. It was as certain that they should be conducted *over* the Jordan, as it was that they should be led *into* Canaan, and to *this* the Most High had pledged himself by the most solemn promises, renewed from age to age, from the time of Abraham down to that of Moses. With a 'thus saith the Lord' for our warrant, we may boldly go forth in the face of obstacles that are absolutely insuperable to human power.——¶ *Thou and all this people.* That is, with the exception of Reuben, Gad, and the half tribe of Manasseh, to whom was granted, at their own request, a possession on the eastern side of the Jordan, where they were now encamped, Num. 32. ——¶ *Unto the land which I do give*

3 ᶜEvery place that the sole of your foot shall tread upon, that have I given unto you, as I said unto Moses.

c Deut. 11. 24. ch. 14. 9.

4 ᵈFrom the wilderness and this Lebanon even unto the great river, the river Euphrates, all the land of the Hittites, and

d Gen. 15. 18. Exod. 23. 31. Num. 34. 3–12.

---

to them. Heb. אשר אנכי נתן להם *asher ănoki nothēn lăhem, which I am giving to them.* That is, the land of which I have long promised them the inheritance, and of which I am now *in the very act* of putting them in possession. Though the promises of God may be slow in fulfilling, yet the accomplishment will come at last; not one jot or tittle shall fail. Though 'the vision be for an appointed time, yet at the end it shall speak, it shall not lie; though it tarry, wait for it; because it will surely come, it will not tarry.'

3. *Every place that the sole of your foot shall tread upon.* That is, every place within the limits specified in the ensuing verse. The expression in this, as in innumerable other cases, must be qualified by the connexion. The extent of the grant is more expressly defined in the striking parallel passage, Deut. 11. 24, 'Every place whereon the soles of your feet shall tread, shall be yours; from the wilderness and Lebanon, from the river, the river Euphrates, even unto the uttermost sea, shall your coast be.' It is to these words spoken to Moses that allusion is made in the next clause. Indeed, nearly every sentence in this address to Joshua, occurs somewhere in the course of the foregoing history, especially in the book of Deuteronomy.

4: *From the wilderness, &c.* God here proceeds, in very brief terms, to mark out and define the boundaries of the land of promise. Its utmost limits should be from the wilderness of Sin, or the desert of Arabia Petræa on the South, to Lebanon on the North; and from the Euphrates on the East, to the great sea, or the Mediterranean, on the West. The Israelites did not indeed possess the full extent of this grant until the time of David, but their failure to do so was owing entirely to their own remissness, unbelief and disobedience, as was every reverse with which they met during the whole period of their history. They were not straitened in God, but in themselves; and the same remark holds good with regard to his people in all ages.——¶ *And this Lebanon.* That is, *unto* this Lebanon, which was the boundary *opposite* to that of the wilderness. See Note on Deut. 11. 24. The mountain range is thus particularized because it could doubtless be seen from the spot where Joshua now stood, rearing its lofty summits towards the clouds in the northern extremity of Canaan. For an account of this well-known range of mountains, any of the various works in sacred geography may be consulted. See also 'Illustrations of the Scriptures,' p. 103. The name 'Lebanon' comes from the Heb. root לבן *laban, white,* from its summits' being so constantly covered with snow.——¶ *All the land of the Hittites.* This clause is wanting in the Gr. version of the LXX, and in the Arabic it is rendered *upon* (i. e. beyond) *the land of the Hittites.* But as nothing is known tending to invali-

B. C. 1451.]   CHAPTER I.   17

unto the great sea *toward* the going down of the sun, shall be your coast.

5 ^e There shall not any man be able to stand before thee all the

e Deut. 7. 24.

date the reading of the text, we must presume it to be genuine, and leave it undisturbed. It is not the name of a region lying *without* the limits above specified, or of a country promised *in addition* to that which had been so long assigned, in the divine purpose, to Israel, but it was one of the seven nations of Canaan, so often alluded to in the books of Moses, and here probably mentioned by synecdoche, a figure of speech by which a part is put for the whole. In like manner, in other instances, the nation of the Amorites stands for the whole of the Canaanitish people. As a reason for the particular mention of the Hittites here, rather than any other of the devoted nations, it may be remarked, that it appears from the transaction of Abraham with the sons of Heth, or the Hittites, (Gen. 23,) that they inhabited the southern borders of the land about the region of Beersheba and Hebron, where subsequently the spies saw the gigantic Anakims, who inspired them with so much terror. It was natural, therefore, that they should regard these people as the most formidable enemies whom they would be likely to encounter, and equally natural that God, in assuring them of the complete conquest of all these nations, should specify that one which more than all others they dreaded. He would thus banish their fears where they would be most certain to rise, and by promising them a victory, where they might apprehend a defeat, inspire them with unwavering confidence of success in contending with

all the rest of their enemies.——¶ *The great sea.* The Mediterranean; so called as being the *greatest* in the vicinity of the land of promise, the *greatest* with which the Israelites were acquainted, and especially so termed in respect to the smaller seas in Judea, such as the sea of Gennesaret or Tiberias, and the Dead Sea, which were comparatively *mere lakes.* The Hebrews, however, were accustomed to give the name of ים *yâm, sea,* to every large collection of waters. ——¶ *Toward the going down of the sun.* Heb. מבוא השמש *mebō hashshēmesh,* lit. *the going in of the sun.* The Heb. usage is to speak of the sun's *going in* instead of *setting,* as is common with us. According to the usual analogy of rendering adopted by our version, the word *toward* should be printed in Italics, as there is nothing to answer to it in the original. So also in v. 15.——¶ *Shall be your coast.* Your border, your boundary, your limits. Thus Mat. 2. 16, 'Then Herod sent forth, and slew all the children that were in Bethlehem, *and in all the coasts thereof;*' i. e. in all the region or territory *bordering* upon it. Such also is the import of the word *coast,* as used by some of the early English writers.

5. *There shall not any man be able to stand before thee.* Heb. לא יתיצב איש *lo yithyatztzeb ish, a man shall not plant or station himself.* The form of the sentence in our version 'shall not be able to stand' comes from the Lat. Vulg., which has 'nullus poterit vobis resistere.' The Gr. has οὐκ ἀντιστήσεται, *shall not resist.* But the

2*

18 JOSHUA. [B. C. 1451.

days of thy life: ᶠas I was with Moses, so ᵍ I will be with thee: ʰ I will not fail thee nor forsake thee.

f Exod. 3. 12. g Deut. 31. 8, 23. ver. 9, 17. ch. 3. 7. and 6. 27. Isai. 43. 2, 5.

h Deut. 31. 6, 8. Hebr. 13. 5.

---

idea expressed in our version no doubt correctly represents the sense of the original, which is not so much to deny the fact that opposition would be made to Joshua and the Israelites, for we know that their enemies did often ' plant themselves' against them, but rather to assert the *inability* of their adversaries to make any successful resistance. No man shall be able effectually to withstand thee, to maintain his ground before thee, or to throw any serious obstacle in thy way. Joshua is, however, admonished that his sufficiency was not of himself. It was solely in consequence of God's *being with him*, upholding and prospering him, as he did Moses, that he was to be rendered thus invincible. Those that contended with him were contending with omnipotence, and in this unequal contest they must necessarily be worsted. ' If God be for us who can be against us?' What Joshua had himself, on another occasion, said to encourage the people, Num. 14. 9, God now says to him. This signal success, moreover, was not only to mark the commencement of his enterprises, but to attend him throughout his whole career. However it might be with Israel when he was gone, yet during his life-time he should be favored with a constant tide of triumphs. If it be asked how this assurance consists with the fact, that he met with such a serious repulse in one of his earliest expeditions, and that so many thousands of Israel were smitten and turned their backs before the men of Ai, the answer is that they failed in the *conditions* on which the promises of victory were suspended. These promises were not absolute. They were made with a proviso. They were to be fulfilled on condition of the implicit faith and obedience of the people, with the perfect understanding, at the same time, that God's grace was sufficient for them, and that if they sought him sincerely, they should never fail to receive an adequate measure of ability to enable them to comply with these conditions. On the occasion alluded to, they had grossly failed in duty, they had sinned and transgressed the covenant and were therefore smitten before the enemy, 'because they were accursed,' i. e. laboring under the Divine displeasure, Josh. 7. 12. ——¶ *As I was with Moses, so I will be with thee*. Chal. ' As my Word was for Moses' help, so shall my Word be for thy help.'——¶ I *will not fail thee nor forsake thee*. Heb. לא ארפך *lo arpekâ*. The original term here rendered 'fail' properly signifies to *let sink, to let grow slack and fall down*, being generally spoken of the hands, and implying *a loosing or relaxing* of one's grasp, and the consequent falling down of the hands, as in Josh. 10. 6, ' *Slack not thy hands* (אל תרף ידך) *al tĕreph yâdekâ*) from thy servants.' It has a meaning directly opposite to that of the word for *laying a firm hold, taking a vigorous grasp*, of any thing. The other is the usual word for *leave, forsake, abandon*. The sense clearly

CHAPTER I.

6 ᶦBe strong and of a good courage: for unto this people

ᶦ Deut. 31. 7, 23.

shalt thou divide for an inheritance the land which I sware unto their fathers to give them.

is, that God would *keep firm hold* of his servant, *would not let go of* him, *would not resign him up* to the power of his enemies. Moses had before given to Joshua the same assurance, couched almost in the express words of this passage, Deut. 31. 6–8; and here God is pleased, in accordance with the character which he elsewhere gives of himself, Is. 44. 26, to 'confirm the word of his servant,' and engages never to leave or be wanting to Joshua.

6. *Be strong and of a good courage.* Heb. חזק ואמץ *hazak vematz.* Gr. ἴσχυε καὶ ἀνδρίζου, *be strong and act the man.* The original terms, though nearly related, are not precisely synonymous with each other. They both occur, though under slightly different forms, Is. 35. 3: '*Strengthen ye* (חזקו *hazzekū*) the weak hands and *confirm* (אמצו *ammëtzu*) the feeble knees,' from which and from other passages, it is inferred that the first, 'be strong,' properly implies that strength which is in the *hands* for *grasping and holding firmly* any thing, while the latter points primarily to the strength of the *knees* in steadfastly maintaining one's position, and withstanding every aggressive assault of the enemy. From this view of the primary and literal acceptation of the words, we obtain a better idea of their import when applied metaphorically, as here, to the acts of the mind. They imply the utmost degree of vigorous and determined action, a spirit and energy directly the reverse of every thing imbecile and pusillanimous.——¶ *Unto this people shalt thou divide for an inheritance the land.* Heb. תנחיל *tanhīl, thou shalt cause to inherit.* Which supposes the previous entire conquest of the land; and in this respect a higher degree of honor was vouchsafed to Joshua than to Moses, for *he* was only permitted to conduct Israel through the wilderness, and bring them to the *borders* of the promised land, while Joshua had the glory of actually taking possession of, and distributing the land to his people as an inheritance. God is pleased, therefore, to make known to him his purposes concerning him, *as a reason* for his assuming all that strength and courage which he now enjoins upon him. Compare the parallel passage, Deut. 1. 37, 38: 'Also the Lord was angry with me, for your sakes, saying, Thou also shalt not go in thither. But Joshua the son of Nun, which standeth before thee, he shall go in thither. Encourage him : for he shall cause Israel to inherit it.' This 'encouragement' which Moses was to give to Joshua we find embodied in his farewell address, Deut. 31. 7, 8, 23: 'And Moses called unto Joshua, and said unto him in the sight of all Israel, Be strong and of a good courage: for thou must go with this people unto the land which the Lord hath sworn unto their fathers to give them; and thou shalt cause them to inherit it. And the Lord, he it is that doth go before thee; he will be with thee, he will not fail thee, neither forsake thee ; fear not, neither be dismayed. And

20   JOSHUA.   [B. C. 1451.

7 Only be thou strong and very courageous, that thou mayest observe to do according to all the law ᵏ which Moses my servant commanded thee; ˡ turn not from it *to* the right or *to* the left, that thou mayest

ᵏ Numb. 27. 23.   Deut. 31. 7.   ch. 11. 15.

ˡ Deut. 5. 32, and 28. 14.

he gave Joshua the son of Nun a charge, and said, Be strong and of a good courage: for thou shalt bring the children of Israel into the land which I sware unto them: and I will be with thee.' The Most High, therefore, in these words emphatically reminds Joshua of the solemn charge which Moses had given him. God will not fail to adopt and enforce as his own those commands which are uttered by his servants in accordance with his will.

7. *Only be thou strong and very courageous.* The Heb. term here employed רק *rak, only,* clearly indicates that a *condition* is stated on which the promise of the foregoing verse shall be made good. This condition is the constant and rigid observance of the Divine command, an inflexible firmness in adhering to that code of precepts contained in the law of Moses. This he was incessantly to make the man of his counsel and the theme of his daily and nightly study. It was in this respect mainly that his courage and fortitude were to be evinced. A steadfast obedience to the mandates of Jehovah would require a stronger principle of courage, than his anticipated conflicts with the most formidable enemies. The important lesson which we hence learn is, that in nothing is there more scope for the display of the highest moral heroism than in daring, in all circumstances, to cleave steadfastly to the word of God as the rule of our conduct. It is in this chiefly that the fortitude of the Christian soldier is to evince itself. He is not only to fight, but to 'fight lawfully,' that is, in conformity to that system of Divine instructions contained in the Scriptures. From this he is never to deviate, nor to turn away his eyes. However difficult or self-denying its injunctions, he must obey them, and rather die than depart from them. In so doing he will find the promises fulfilled, and the Divine blessings imparted as truly and as signally as did Joshua himself in his arduous warfare.——¶ *Which Moses my servant commanded thee.* The particular commands of Moses here referred to are to be found in Deut. 5. 32; 28. 14, and 31. 7, 8; and though originally delivered to all the congregation, yet here they are especially applied to Joshua, who, as leader, stood as the representative of the whole collective body of the people.——¶ *Turn not from it to the right hand or to the left.* Heb. אל תסור ממנו *al tâsur mimmenu, turn not from him;* i. e. from Moses; where his person stands for his writings. So our Saviour says, 'If they hear not Moses and the prophets,' i. e. the words of Moses. The metaphor is taken from a man's pursuing a journey, who goes straight forward in the direct road, if he knows it, without turning aside into by-paths that lead he knows not whither.——¶ *That thou mayest prosper.* Or, Heb. תשכיל *tashkil, mayest do wisely, mayest deal or behave under-*

B. C. 1451.]   CHAPTER I.   21

prosper whithersoever thou goest.

8 ᵐ This book of the law shall not depart out of thy mouth;

ᵐ Deut. 17. 18, 19.

---

standingly. The primary and most usual sense of the original is, *to direct one's self wisely, to act with prudence and discretion, to be wise, intelligent,* and thence secondarily, *to prosper, to have good success.* Thus 1 Sam. 18. 14, ' And David *behaved himself wisely* (משכיל *mashkîl*) in all his ways; and the Lord was with him.' These two senses of the word are so intimately connected, that it is often difficult to determine precisely which of them is intended in a given passage. This very uncertainty, however, proves it to be clearly intimated, in the native import of the term, that *real prosperity and success* in the affairs of life, is the result of a *wise, discreet,* and *prudent course of conduct,* and inseparable from it, and that it is vain to look for it from any other source. Those only can reasonably expect the blessing of God upon their temporal affairs, who make his word their rule, and conscientiously walk by it in all circumstances; and this is the way of true wisdom.

8. *This book of the law.* That is, by way of emphasis, '*the* book of the law,' the law of Moses, to which, as he well knew, God attached the utmost importance, and of which he speaks as if it were at that moment in Joshua's hand, or at his side, as it continually ought to be.——¶ *Shall not depart out of thy mouth.* Thou shalt constantly read and ponder it; it shall incessantly employ thy lips; thou shalt have thy heart so constantly imbued with its letter and spirit, that thy mouth shall, as it were, overflow with its rich contents, as 'out of the abundance of the heart the mouth speaketh.' The same phrase occurs but once elsewhere in the Scriptures, Is. 59. 21. 'As for me, this is my covenant with them, saith the Lord. My spirit that is upon thee and my words which I have put in thy mouth, *shall not depart out of thy mouth*, nor out of the mouth of thy seed, nor out of the mouth of thy seed's seed, saith the Lord, from henceforth and forever;' where it is implied that the covenant promise should be deemed so precious, that it should be a perpetual theme of meditation and discourse; that it should constantly dwell on the tongues of those interested in it. It is moreover implied, in this charge to Joshua, that he was not only to make the book of the law the subject of assiduous study for his own personal benefit, but also to make it the sole rule and standard of all his public and official proceedings; he was to issue orders and pronounce judgments according to its precepts, and that too without exception or reserve —he must 'do according to *all* that is written therein.' Though appointed to the rank of supreme head and magistrate of the nation, he was not to consider himself elevated in the slightest degree above the authority of the Divine law, or the necessity of consulting it; nor should any Christian magistrate at this day consider himself at liberty to dispense with the light which beams from the word of God, in regard to the great matters of his duty. The higher any

but ⁿ thou shalt meditate therein day and night, that thou mayest observe to do according to all that is written therein: for then thou shalt make thy way prosperous, and then thou shalt have good success.

9 ᵒ Have not I commanded thee? Be strong and of a good courage; ᵖ be not afraid, neither be thou dismayed: for the Lord thy God *is* with thee whithersoever thou goest.

10 ¶ Then Joshua commanded the officers of the people, saying,

ⁿ Ps. 1. 2.   ᵒ Deut. 31. 7, 8, 23.   ᵖ Ps. 27. 1. Jer. 1. 8.

---

man is raised in office, the more need has he of an acquaintance with the sacred oracles, and the better will he be qualified by the study of them for the discharge of his arduous duties. ——¶ *Thou shalt meditate therein day and night.* This is the character of the good man as described by the Psalmist, Ps. 1. 2, in words which are almost an exact transcript of those here employed. The Heb. term for 'meditate,' (הגה *hâgâh*) implies that kind of mental rumination which is apt to vent itself in an *audible sound* of the voice. See my Comment. on Ps. 1. 2.——¶ *Make thy way prosperous—have good success.* Two different words are here employed, the latter of which is the same with that remarked upon above, v. 7, and which should probably be rendered here also, 'do wisely,' 'conduct understandingly,' as otherwise it is little, if any thing, more than a bare repetition of the preceding phrase. The Arab. renders it, *and thy ways shall be directed.*

9. *Have not I commanded thee?* I, whose authority is paramount, whose power is infinite; who am able to carry thee through all difficulties and dangers, and whom thou art bound implicitly to obey. So in the Christian warfare, it is the God of heaven whose battles we fight, and in whose service we are engaged.

Were it only an earthly monarch to whom we had devoted ourselves, we ought to serve him with all fidelity; what then should we not do for the King of kings, who has not only chosen us to be his soldiers, but has himself taken the field for *our sakes*, to subdue *our* enemies, and to deliver *us* from their assaults?—It should be remarked, that the interrogative form of speech is often used, not as implying any thing doubtful, but as the most emphatic mode of expressing either a negation or affirmation, particularly when the speaker wishes to rouse and excite strongly the attention of the hearer. Instances are innumerable.——¶ *The Lord thy God is with thee.* Here is somewhat of a remarkable change in the persons, from the first to the third, but whether with any peculiar significancy it is not easy to determine. The Chaldee renders it in reference to the Son, 'The Word of the Lord thy God shall be with thee.' Considered as a pledge of the presence and support of the God of heaven with all his faithful people, in their trials and conflicts, the promise is full of precious meaning. He says to *us*, in effect, what he says to Joshua; and what encouragement can we desire more?

10. *Commanded the officers of the people.* Heb. שטרים *shoterim.* These

11 Pass through the host and command the people, saying, Prepare you victuals; for ᵠ within three days ye shall pass over

q ch. 3. 2. See Deut. 9. 1, and 11. 31.

were under-officers, subordinate to the שפטים *shophetim* or *judges*, whose duty it was to see to the execution of the orders of the heads of the people, whether Moses, Joshua, or his successors the Judges. Deut. 16. 18; 20. 5—9. The original is usually rendered γραμματεις, *scribes*, in the Gr. version. See Note on Ex. 5. 6, where the import of שטרים *shoterim* is more fully discussed.

11. *Prepare you victuals.* The Heb. term צדה *tzēdah, prey*, from צוד *tzūd, to hunt*, primarily and properly denotes that which is taken in *hunting*. But the usage in several places proves that it is taken with more latitude, and implies *provisions* in general. In the present instance it doubtless refers somewhat widely to the *subsistence*, technically termed *viaticum*, such as the corn, oxen, sheep, &c., which they were now enabled to obtain in the more inhabited region which they had reached. For although the manna was their main dependence during their sojourn in the wilderness, yet they do not appear to have been forbidden to supply themselves with other kinds of food when they had an opportunity, Deut. 2. 6, 28; and at this time, when they had come into a land inhabited, where they could procure such provisions, it is probable that the manna did not fall so plentifully, or they did not gather so much as previously, so that they were now commanded to lay in a store of other eatables to supply the deficiency. Certain it is, however, that the manna did not entirely cease falling till they had entered the land of Canaan, and eaten of the old corn of the land, ch. 5. 12.—¶ *Within three days.* Heb. בעוד שלשת ימים *within unto three days.* The exact import of the Hebrew is not easily determined, and it is variously rendered in the versions. The Chal. which Kimchi approves, has 'at the end of three days;' the Lat. Vulg. 'post triduum,' *after three days;* Luth. 'über drei Tage,' *over three days.* The prevailing sense of עוד, denoting time not yet elapsed, favors the rendering in our version, but Winer and others suppose the phrase will admit the sense of three days complete. The probability we think is, that the passage over the Jordan was not made till *after* the lapse of three days, and that it took place on the fourth : the three days, therefore, here mentioned, are to be reckoned exclusive of that on which the proclamation was made, ch. 2. 22; 3. 1. Or, as the original for 'shall pass,' is literally 'shall be passing,' it may mean simply, that within the space of three days they should have broken up from their present encampment, and commenced their march, although the actual passage of the Jordan may not have occurred till a day or two afterwards. The confidence with which Joshua speaks of the event, shows the undoubting character of his own faith in the promise of God. Augustin thinks that Joshua acted too much on his own responsibility in fixing the definite period of three days for passing the river. But it is not to be supposed that he would order a step

this Jordan, to go in to possess the land which the Lord your God giveth you to possess it.

12 ¶ And to the Reubenites, and to the Gadites, and to half the tribe of Manasseh, spake Joshua, saying,

13 Remember 'the word which Moses the servant of the Lord commanded you, saying, The Lord your God hath given you rest, and hath given you this land.

r Num. 32. 20-28. ch. 22. 2, 3, 4.

---

of this nature without being prompted by Divine dictation. This was no doubt a part of the instructions now given him, though not expressly recorded.——¶ *Which the Lord your God giveth you.* Heb. נֹתֵן *nothën,* is *giving;* i. e. is even now in the act of giving. It would tend greatly to animate the faith and zeal of the people, and to secure their vigorous co-operation, to see God, as it were, girding himself to the work, and actually putting forth his power in the execution of his promises. It would not do for them to be remiss when omnipotence was visibly engaged in their behalf. This language would teach them too that the result was not to be brought about by their own strength, and, consequently, that they could not take the glory of it to themselves.——¶ *To possess it.* Heb. לְרִשְׁתָּהּ *lerishtâh, to inherit it;* i. e. not only to *occupy* it as something which had happened to come into their possession, but deriving their right from the grant of the Supreme Proprietor of heaven and earth, to enter upon as if they had received it by *inheritance from their forefathers.* Viewed in this light the language is peculiarly expressive.

12. *To the Reubenites, and to the Gadites.* Heb. וְלָראוּבֵנִי וְלַגָּדִי *velâ-rubeni velaggâdi, to the Reubenite, and to the Gadite;* the collective singular for the plural, a very common idiom of the original, particularly in speaking of tribes and nations; as if the whole body, from their intimate union, were regarded as one person. This is a peculiarity of the Heb. language, which is of almost incessant occurrence, and as it necessarily escapes the notice of the English reader, though in many cases important to be known, we shall usually indicate it wherever met with.——¶ *Remember the word which Moses, &c.* This engagement on the part of the two tribes and a half, is detailed with all the circumstances attending it, Num. 32. 1—42; and it was proper here to remind them of it, as, otherwise, having arrived at the place of their settlement, they might be induced to seek their own ease, by remaining with their wives and families in the rich and fertile region of which they had come into possession. ——¶ *The Lord your God hath given you rest.* The two tribes and a half had *already* received their possessions on the East of Jordan, as we learn from Num. 32. 33. These precise words do not occur in the address of Moses to the two tribes and a half, but the sense of them does, and Joshua intended, doubtless, merely to quote the *substance* of what Moses said. The phrase 'hath given you rest,' perhaps merely implies that they were now brought to a *place of rest,* rather than a positive *state of*

CHAPTER I.

14 Your wives, your little ones, and your cattle shall remain in the land which Moses gave you on this side Jordan; but ye shall pass before your brethren ᵃ armed, all the mighty men of valor, and help them;

15 Until the LORD have given your brethren rest, as he hath given you, and they also have possessed the land which the LORD your God giveth them: ᵗ then ye shall return unto the land of your possession, and enjoy it, which Moses the LORD's servant gave you on this side Jordan *toward* the sun-rising.

16 ¶ And they answered Josh-

ᵃ Exod. 13. 18.   ᵗ ch. 22. 4, &c.

---

rest, which they could hardly be said to enjoy till they had subdued their enemies. They were at rest, however, in contradistinction from journeying, and in this sense the original word is often employed.

14. *Your wives, your little ones, &c.*, Heb. טפכם *tappekem, your babe*, collect. sing. for plural.——¶ *Ye shall pass before your brethren.* That is, as the original implies, ye shall pass or cross over before, or *in the presence of*, your brethren. It does not appear to signify that they should take the *front rank* or *lead the van*, for such an intimation respecting them is no where else clearly given; but simply that they should not absent themselves; that they should be present with their brethren, united with them in the expedition. The Heb. phrase is often used in this sense.——¶ *Armed.* Heb. המשים *hamashim, marshalled by five.* Of the import of this expression, see Note on Ex. 13. 18, where it is rendered *harnessed.*——¶ *All the mighty men of valor.* Not absolutely all the fighting men of these tribes, but the choice of them, the most active, bold and energetic; for as there were only forty thousand of them that passed over, ch. 4. 13, while the whole number of warriors was far greater, Num. 26, it is evident that a large body of them must have remained on the other side of the Jordan, to take care of the women, children, and flocks. Probably as many at least as seventy thousand, as the sum total of the men in those tribes able to bear arms was upwards of one hundred and ten thousand. See Num. 26. 7, 18, 37.

15. *Until the Lord have given your brethren rest, as he hath given you.* That is, until he hath brought them to their *place of rest;* for it could not strictly be said of either company, that the Lord had given them rest, until they had so far conquered their enemies as to be in no danger of being henceforth seriously molested by them. But that was, at this time, by no means the case with the two tribes and a half, nor have we reason to suppose, in respect to the others, that the mere putting them in possession of the promised territory would be 'giving them rest,' as long as their enemies remained in great numbers unsubdued. We are led therefore to understand from this expression, simply the bringing them to, or planting them in, *a place of rest.* The actual enjoyment of the rest was a matter of subsequent favor.——¶ *Toward the sun-rising.* The East; as 'toward the going down of the sun,' signifies the West.

16. *And they answered Joshua,*

ua saying, All that thou commandest us, we will do, and whithersoever thou sendest us, we will go.

17 According as we hearkened unto Moses in all things, so will we hearken unto thee: only the LORD thy God ᵘ be with thee, as he was with Moses.

18 Whosoever *he be* that doth rebel against thy commandment, and will not hearken unto thy

ᵘ ver. 5. 1 Sam. 20. 13. 1 Kings 1. 37.

This, as some conceive, was not the answer of the two tribes and a half only, but the response of the whole host, who thus concurred heartily with them in their solemn engagements. It is not unlikely that such were the real sentiments of the entire congregation; but it seems more natural, from the connexion, to understand it of those who were directly addressed. They afterwards received the testimony of Joshua, as having fully complied with all their stipulations, ch. 22. 2-4.——¶ *All that thou commandest us we will do,* &c. Thus are *we* required to swear allegiance to Christ, the Captain of our salvation, the Christian's Joshua, and to bind ourselves to do what he commands us by his word, and to go wheresoever he sends us by his providence.

17. *According as we hearkened unto Moses,* &c. As we obeyed Moses. Nothing is more common than this sense of the word 'hearken' in the sacred writers. If it be asked, how this language is to be reconciled with the declaration of Moses himself in regard to their conduct under him, Deut. 9. 24, 'Ye have been rebellious against the Lord from the day that I knew you,' we answer, that neither the words of Moses, nor of the people, are to be understood as holding good *universally, and without any exception.* They were sometimes rebellious, and sometimes obedient.

What they mean is, that they would be as obedient to Joshua as they ever were to Moses, *when they did obey him,* when they were in their best moods; as obedient, in fact, *as they should have been* to Moses, and as many of them generally were. The literal rendering of the original is, 'According to all (in) which we hearkened to Moses, so will we hearken to thee.' This perhaps limits the point of comparison to those cases in which they were *actually obedient,* and excludes those in which they rebelled.——¶ *Only the Lord thy God be with thee,* &c. Chal. 'The Word of the Lord thy God be for thy help, as he was for the help of Moses,' &c. This is not to be understood as a *condition,* or *limitation* of their promised obedience, as if they should say, 'We will obey thee as far as we perceive the Lord is with thee, but no farther,' but rather as an earnest prayer in behalf of Joshua, that he might constantly enjoy the Divine guidance, protection, and blessing; q. d. 'Do not fear for us. Be assured of our constant obedience. Be solicitous mainly for thyself. This is the matter of our anxiety, that the Lord would be with thee, and prosper thee in all things.' To pray fervently for those in authority over us, is the surest way to render them blessings to us and to the communities in which we live.

18. *That doth rebel against thy*

words in all that thou commandest him, he shall be put to death: only be strong and of a good courage.

CHAPTER II.

AND Joshua the son of Nun sent ^a out of Shittim two

^a Num. 25. 1.

commandment. Heb. אשר ימרה את *asher yamrëh eth pika, that doth rebel (against) thy mouth;* i. e. the word or commandment of thy mouth. Perhaps in this they had an eye to what Moses had said respecting the Lord's raising up a prophet like unto himself, and to whose word they were to hearken under the severest penalty, Deut. 18. 18, 19. They might have supposed this prediction to be fulfilled in the appointment of Joshua as Moses' successor, without knowing, at the same time, but that it might have an ulterior fulfilment at some subsequent period, in a yet more illustrious personage.——¶ *Only be strong and of good courage.* The original for 'only' (רק *rak*) might perhaps be better rendered 'therefore,' as it undoubtedly means, ch. 13. 6, when speaking of the land that remained to be possessed. God promises to drive out the inhabitants, and *therefore* commands Joshua to divide it to the Israelites for an inheritance.

CHAPTER II.

1. *And Joshua the son of Nun sent, &c.* Or, Heb. וישלח *vu-yishlah, had sent.* The original will well admit of this rendering, and it is adopted by the current of commentators. Luther's translation is very express in this sense; 'But Joshua the son of Nun had previously sent spies,' &c. And this seems, on the whole, the most probable construction. Nothing is more frequent in the sacred writings than such transpositions (technically termed *hysterology*), so that interpreters have felt warranted to state as a general canon, *that there is no certain order, no former nor latter, in the histories of the Scripture.* Masius contends that the whole series of events mentioned in this chapter occurred prior to the order given by Joshua, ch. 1. 10, for providing food and getting ready to cross the Jordan within three days. But even if this view be admitted, it is somewhat difficult to determine the precise date of the sending forth of the spies. Each of the following suppositions has its advocates. (1.) The spies were dispatched and returned to the camp before the order, ch. 1. 10, was issued. The objection which Schmid brings to this is, that it would suppose Joshua to have acted in this matter without Divine direction; for there is no hint in the narrative of his having received any express intimation relative to his movements prior to the instructions given in the first chapter, and it is quite improbable that Joshua would have decided upon such a step upon his own responsibility. He, therefore, with many others, adopts the following alternative. (2.) On the morning of the same day on which the breaking up of the encampment is announced, Joshua sends forth the spies. This he did in obedience to a Divine suggestion, which, though not recorded, is, like many other things, to be inferred from the execution. The spies came to Jericho in the afternoon of the same day,

which the distance, according to Josephus, would well admit, and intended to lodge with Rahab that night. But being alarmed on account of the search ordered by the king of Jericho, they fled to the mountains the same evening, and remained there in concealment that night and the whole of the next day, and in the early part of the third day returned to the camp east of the Jordan. It is indeed said, v. 22, that they 'abode three days' in the mountains; but this may properly be understood of one whole day, and parts of two others, as is evident from the case of our Saviour, who is said to have lain three days in the earth, Mat. 27. 63, which is obviously to be understood in the same way. Comp. Mat. 12. 40. If this be the right explanation, Joshua may be supposed to have commenced his march on the evening of the third day, or on the morning of the fourth, and still have accomplished his purpose of setting out within the time specified, as we have already remarked that the phrase 'within three days' may imply the period of three days complete. This is the solution maintained by Masius and most of the Jewish commentators, and is perhaps the most probable, although it is still liable to one objection. Joshua's sending out the spies implies that his movements would be governed by their reports. But he could have had no assurance that he should receive this report within the space of three days, and yet he gives peremptory orders for moving forward within that time. Of what use then was the information which was to be gained from the reports of the spies? To this it may be replied, that as the distance from the encampment to Jericho was but of a few hours' travel, three days' time was so large an allowance for the accomplishment of their mission, that he could not reasonably be supposed to run any risk in fixing the time of departure at the close of that period. This is perhaps sufficient, and as *every* mode of understanding the matter is clogged with some difficulty, we are content to abide by that now given.——¶ *Out of Shittim.* Called elsewhere *Abel-Shittim,* unless the latter were the name of the adjoining valley. Its precise location cannot now be identified, and nothing more is known of it than that it was situated in the extensive plain of the Jordan. It is supposed to be the *Abila* of Josephus, and lay, according to him, about sixty stadia, or little upwards of seven miles from the Jordan, within the boundaries assigned to the tribe of Reuben. See Note on Num. 25. 1. It is supposed to have derived its name from the great quantity of trees, called *Shittim-wood,* growing in the vicinity. ——¶ *Two men to spy secretly.* The Heb. term for 'spies' is מרגלים *meraggelīm,* from רגל *regel, a foot,* implying those *who travelled on foot,* for the purpose of espial. See Note on Gen. 42. 9. The original of 'secretly' is חרש *hëresh,* signifying in strictness *silently,* and has reference either to the manner of their being sent, viz. in a secret, silent way, without the privity of the people; or to the mode of discharging their duty, that is, noiselessly, stealthily. The former is probably the leading import, as it is a matter of course and unnecessary to be intimated, that spies should perform their errand in

men to spy secretly, saying, Go view the land, even Jericho.

a secret manner. But it was not superfluous to mention that the spies were sent out without the knowledge of the people, as from the recollection of his own case when dispatched by Moses, Joshua might have apprehended very disheartening effects upon the timid minds of the Israelites when they came to hear the reports brought back. On the general policy of sending these spies on this occasion, when an express assurance had been given to Joshua that every place on which the sole of his foot should tread should come into his possession, and that no man should be able to stand before him, we may remark, that it is but in accordance with the ordinary arrangements of infinite wisdom as displayed in the history of its dispensations; and we must consider Joshua, in all this transaction, as acting not from himself, but from the impulse or the express direction of a higher power. The certainty of a promised or predicted issue does not supersede the use of prudent means in the attempt to compass it. To neglect the use of the appropriate means is to contravene the established order of the Divine councils, and to tempt God rather than honor him. Even when a cloudy pillar was vouchsafed to the Israelites, to conduct their march through the wilderness, yet it would seem from Num. 10. 31, that scouts were employed who were to serve as 'eyes' to the congregation by going before and designating the proper places for encamping. In the present instance Joshua is prompted to do just what any discreet and skilful leader would have done in similar circumstances. Being about to besiege a fortified place, he takes the requisite measures for acquainting himself with its true position, its strong and its weak points, that he may order his tactics accordingly. He was indeed well aware that his victory was certain, and that it was the arm of Jehovah, and not his own, that would achieve it; but he was equally assured that faith did not preclude effort, and that he was to proceed in the enterprise just as if every thing depended on his unaided prowess and skill. This is ever the true mode of evincing a *believing dependence* on the Divine blessing; to *act* as if all were owing to ourselves, to *feel* and *acknowledge* that all is owing to the favor and effectual working of God himself.——¶ *View the land, even Jericho.* Heb. 'The land and Jericho.' Explore the land or country about Jericho, but more especially the city itself. Thus 1 Kings 11. 1, 'But king Solomon loved many strange women, *and the daughter of Pharaoh*,' i. e. especially the daughter of Pharaoh. 2 Sam. 2. 30, 'And when he had gathered all the people together, there lacked of David's servants nineteen men, *and Asahel*.' Mark 16. 7, 'Go your way, and tell his disciples *and Peter*,' &c., i. e. especially inform Peter. They were to observe its site, its various localities, its avenues of approach, its fortifications, the state of the inhabitants—every thing, in fine, which would be of service to them in concerting the best mode of attack. The Heb. form of the name of this city is יריחו *yeriho* (elsewhere יריחו *yerĕho* and יריחה *yerihoh*), and

And they went, and ᵇcame into a harlot's house, named ᶜRahab, and lodged there.

ᵇ Heb. 11. 31.   James 2. 25.   ᶜ Mat. 1. 5.

is derived, according to Gesenius, from ירח *yârëah, the moon,* from the shape of the plain on which it stood, or more probably according to others from ריח *riah, scent, smell,* from the sweet *smell* of the *balsam,* or palm-trees, the latter of which abounded there in such profusion that it is sometimes spoken of as the 'city of palm-trees,' Deut. 34. 3; Judg. 1. 16. It seems not to have been situated immediately upon the river, but at the distance of six or eight miles, at the base of the Quarantina range of mountains. The modern Jericho, now called *Rihah,* is a miserable village of about fifty dwellings and two hundred inhabitants; but according to the most intelligent travellers it does not occupy the site of the ancient city. The latter is believed to have stood at least four miles nearer Jerusalem, at the very foot of the mountains, although it is admitted to be impossible distinctly to identify it. The modern Jericho is thus described by Prof. Robinson (*Trav.,* Vol. II., p. 279): 'We now returned through the village, which bears the Arabic name of *Eriha,* or, as it is more commonly pronounced, *Riha,* a degenerate shoot both in name and character of the ancient Jericho. Situated in the midst of this vast plain, it reminded me much of an Egyptian village. The plain is rich and susceptible of easy tillage and abundant irrigation, with a climate to produce any thing. Yet it lies almost desert; and the village is the most miserable and filthy that we saw in Palestine. The houses or hovels are merely four walls of stones taken from ancient ruins, and loosely thrown together, with flat roofs of cornstalks or brushwood spread over with gravel. They stand quite irregularly, and with large intervals; and each has around it a yard enclosed by a hedge of the dry thorny boughs of the Nubk. In many of these yards are open sheds with similar roofs; and the flocks and herds are brought into them at night, and render them filthy in the extreme. A similar but stronger hedge of Nubk branches surrounds the whole village, forming an almost impenetrable barrier. The few gardens round about seemed to contain nothing but tobacco and cucumbers. One single solitary palm now timidly rears its head, where once stood the renowned "City of Palm-trees." Not an article of provision was to be bought here, except new wheat unground.' The plain upon which Jericho stood is very extensive, and as numerous ruins are strewed over at a greater or less distance from the fountain by which it was distinguished, it is probable that in consequence of the malediction denounced against him who should rebuild its gates, the location was subsequently changed, and perhaps more than once.——¶ *And came into a harlot's house.* The character of this woman has been a much disputed point among commentators. As she is commended by the apostle for her faith, Heb. 11. 31, and by her marriage with Salmon, Mat. 1. 5, subsequently came into the line of our Lord's progenitors, great anxiety has been evinced to clear her reputation, if possible, from the reproach of an infamous course of life. On this account, great pains have been taken to show that the original term may be properly rendered 'hostess,' and so does not necessarily convey the idea attached to the English word 'harlot.' But it is beyond all question, that the legitimate and uniform signification of the Heb. term is that of a 'harlot,' either literal or spiritual. Judg. 11. 1; 1 Kings 3. 16; Ezek. 23. 44. So also the word is rendered in the Sept., and this rendering is adopted by two apostles, Heb. 11. 31; James 2. 25; though we do not consider the latter circumstance by any means decisive as to the genuine import of the original; for as the Sept. was the translation at this time in common use, they adopted the expression as they found it, without claiming thereby to settle its propriety as a version of the original. It is moreover to be remembered, that Rahab lived in the midst of a people, corrupt, abandoned and profligate to the last degree. Vices of the most enormous and debasing character were practised without reserve, and received the sanction of every class of people. From repeated intimations in regard to the devoted nations, it appears that the Divine judgments were kindled against them more on account of the abominations of their lewdness than any thing else, as had been the case with Sodom and Gomorrah of old. As these sins pervaded all ranks, they would cease to be regarded as infamous, and the term applied to Rahab does not perhaps indicate a character degraded much below the ordinary standard. Suppose her, however, to have been a harlot in the worst sense of the word, the licentiousness of her life, besides being the natural product of the universal laxity of moral sentiment on the subject, may have been promoted by the false religion in which she was educated. All this is said, not to excuse or justify her iniquitous conduct, but to make it less surprising that the spies should have fallen in with a person of her character, and been entertained by her. As to her being a *hostess*, or *keeping an inn*, there is not a particle of evidence from the original that such was the case, nor have we any reason to suppose, from the known customs of oriental nations, that any such establishments as houses of public entertainment, *in our acceptation of the phrase*, existed among them. Caravanserais or khans are indeed found in most parts of the East, but they are very different from public houses, taverns or hotels, with us. *These* are the result of a much more advanced state of society than has ever prevailed in the East. The following description from Volney, will give the reader somewhat of a correct idea of oriental accommodations of this nature. 'There are no *inns* any where; but the cities, and commonly the villages, have a large building, called a *khan* or *caravanserai*, which serves as an asylum for all travellers. These houses of reception are always built without the precincts of towns, and consist of four wings round a square court, which serves by way of inclosure for the beasts of burden. The lodgings are cells, where you find nothing but bare walls, dust, and sometimes scorpions. The keeper of this khan gives the traveller the key and a mat; and he provides himself the rest. He must therefore carry with him his bed, his

2 And ᵈ it was told the king of Jericho, saying, Behold, there came men in hither to-night of the children of Israel, to search out the country.

ᵈ Ps. 127. 1. Prov. 21. 30.

3 And the king of Jericho sent unto Rahab, saying, Bring forth the men that are come to thee, which are entered into thine house: for they be come to search out all the country.

kitchen utensils, and even his provisions; for frequently *not even bread is to be found in the villages.*' That Rahab had charge of such an establishment is in the highest degree improbable. Far more likely is it that she was, or had been, a woman of loose morals, living in a private station, and that the spies came to her house, moved doubtless by a secret impulse from above, because from its appearance, locality, or other causes, which we cannot now ascertain, it seemed to them a stopping place best suited to the purpose in which they were now engaged; and in countries but little civilized, there is never much ceremony among travellers in applying for a night's lodging. Hospitality is almost a universal characteristic of such a state of society. But whatever may have been Rahab's character *previous* to the destruction of Jericho, there is no reason to suppose that *after* that event it was other than pious and exemplary, and such as became a true penitent. The *opprobrious appellation*, it is true, remained, and it was not unfitting that her name, in the providence of God, should descend to posterity with something of a stigma attached to it, especially as it is according to scriptural usage, that a person should be called by a former denomination, even after the grounds of it have ceased. Thus Matthew is called 'Matthew the publican,' Mat. 10. 3;

9. 9, after he had been chosen an apostle, and Simon is called 'Simon the leper,' Mat. 26. 6, though cleansed from his leprosy. But if she had truly repented and reformed, there is no more justice in charging the sins of her former life upon her, than in reproaching Abraham with the sin of idolatry, of which he was doubtless guilty before his call.——¶ *And lodged there.* Heb. וישכבו שמה *va-yishkebū shâmmâh, and lay down there.* That is, they went in with the *design* of lodging there, and probably had actually lain down and composed themselves to rest, when the arrival of the king's messengers defeated their purpose, interrupted their repose, and made it necessary for them to save themselves by flight. Thus Gen. 37. 21, 'And Reuben heard it, and he delivered him out of their hands,' i. e. he *purposed to* deliver him.

2. *Behold there came men—to search out the country.* This could have been only a conjecture, yet they affirm it as a matter of absolute certainty. As they could conceive of no *other* motive for which they had come, it was perhaps natural that they should confidently assign this as the true one.

3. *For they be come,* &c. This seems to have been said by way of answer to anticipated objections on her part, as if it were the height of treachery to her guests thus to deal with them. 'But no, you need have no scruples on this score, for the me;

B. C. 1451.]   CHAPTER II.   33

4 °And the woman took the two men, and hid them, and said thus, There came men unto me, but I wist not whence they *were*: 5 And it came to pass *about*

e See 2 Sam. 17. 19, 20.

the time of shutting of the gate, when it was dark, that the men went out: whither the men went I wot not: pursue after them quickly; for ye shall overtake them.

---

are not good men, as you may have supposed; they have come hither as enemies and spies, whom it will be no breach of the laws of hospitality to deliver up to justice.'

4. *And the woman took the two men and hid them.* Heb. ותצפנו *vattitzpeno, hid him*, i. e. each one of them; implying probably that she hid them separately, at some distance from each other. The original for 'took,' should probably be rendered 'had taken,' and the whole clause inclosed in a parenthesis. She had, in all likelihood, learnt soon after their arrival the object of their errand, and aware of the danger to which they would be exposed if discovered, she had, at an early hour, conveyed them to a place of concealment; not, however, before rumors of their presence began to circulate about the city. This is justly celebrated by the apostle as an instance of high and heroic faith, Heb. 11. 31. So strong was her persuasion of the truth of what had been announced to her, so fully was she convinced, from what she had heard of the wonders wrought for Israel, that their God was the only true God, and consequently that his declared purpose in regard to Canaan would surely come to pass, that she ventures her life upon her faith. She knew that harboring them was exposing herself to the death of a traitor to her country, and yet she runs the risk. 'She contemns her life for the present, that she may save it for the future; neglected her own king and country, for strangers which she never saw; and more feared the destruction of that city before it knew that it had an enemy, than the displeasure and mortal revenge of her king.' *Bp. Hall.* It was thus that her faith justified itself by works. Had she merely assured the spies, that though she believed that both Jericho and Canaan would fall into their hands, yet in her circumstances she could show them no kindness, her faith would have been dead and inactive, and would not have justified her. James 2. 25. But her conduct showed that it was active and lively, and the event proved that it was efficacious to her salvation. So, unless *our* faith leads us to incur hazards and make sacrifices for God, it is to be accounted of no avail.——¶ *There came men unto me, but I wist not whence they were.* Thus far, perhaps, her answer contains no violation of truth. She admits that two men came to her house, but *at the time of their coming*, she knew not whence they were. The verb in the original is in the past tense, and should be so rendered—'I knew not.'

5. *About the time of shutting of the gate.* The gate of the city.——¶ *The men went out, &c.* This is the part of Rahab's conduct most difficult to be accounted for, consistently with the commendations elsewhere bestowed upon her by the sacred writers. That she *deceived* the messen-

gers by a falsehood is indubitable. She said the spies had left her house when they were still in it. How is this to be reconciled with the workings of a heart made right in the sight of God? The question is certainly one of no easy solution; but in forming a judgment of her conduct, it is fair that Rahab should have the benefit of every extenuating circumstance that can be adduced in her favor; and such are the following.

(1.) Having been born and brought up among the depraved Canaanites, she had probably never been taught the evil of lying, and least of all where an apparently good end was to be answered by it. From the uniform testimony of travellers and missionaries, it is evident that among all heathen nations, particularly those of the East, lying ever has been, and still is, a practice of universal prevalence, and of the criminality of which they have scarcely any sense. So weak is the feeling of obligation, as to the observance of strict veracity, that even apparently sincere converts have the greatest difficulty in freeing themselves from the habit of equivocation, and need to be perpetually admonished on that score. (See Read's *Christian Brahmun.*) What wonder then that Rahab, a poor, ignorant, heathen woman, upon whose mind the light of a saving knowledge had just begun to dawn, should have prevaricated in the trying circumstances in which she was placed? How much allowance precisely is to be made for her on this ground *we* may not know, but *God* does. To him we may leave it. That it should go *somewhat* in abatement of her guilt, if guilty she were, we have no doubt.

(2.) Apart from the above consideration, it was truly a difficult problem to be solved, how she should, under the circumstances, *act according to her faith.* She fully believed that what the spies had told her was true. She says not, 'I fear,' or 'I believe,' but '*I know*, that the Lord hath given you the land.' She was satisfied that it was in vain to fight against God, and what could she do? If she had either told the truth or remained silent, she had betrayed the spies; but if she believed them sent of God, could she have done this without sin? She knew, moreover, very well, that if these two spies were put to death, it would make no difference whatever as to the issue of the contest. The whole city and its inhabitants would at any rate be destroyed. To what purpose then would it be to deliver up the spies? It would not save one single life; it would only be to continue fighting against God, and to bring on herself and her family that destruction which it was now in her power to avert. By concealing the spies she could in fact injure nobody, whereas by giving them up, she would sacrifice not them only, but also herself and her family. Was there then any other conceivable mode by which she could act *according to her faith*, than by practising an imposition upon the king's officers?

(3.) By the fact of her exercising a firm faith in the Divine testimony, she did *virtually* throw herself upon the side of Israel, and unite her interests with theirs. Henceforth *their* enemies were *hers*. If the Canaanites had no right to demand the truth of Israel, they had no right to demand it of her. If it would have been right for the Israelites to have

CHAPTER II.

6 But ᶠshe had brought them up to the roof of the house, and hid them with the stalks of flax, which she had laid in order upon the roof.

f See Exod. 1. 17. 2 Sam. 17. 19.

7 And the men pursued after them the way to Jordan unto the fords: and as soon as they which pursued after them were gone out, they shut the gate.

recourse to a stratagem to mislead an enemy in arms, we see not why it was not equally right for *her*. But that the Israelites often did resort to such expedients in carrying on their wars is beyond question, nor do the scriptures absolutely condemn them. They are certainly as lawful as war itself is. No one probably doubts that Elisha was justified in deceiving the Syrian army, and leading them blinded from Dothan, whither they had come to destroy him, to Samaria, where they were brought into the power of the king of Israel. Considering Rahab then as *really* leagued with Israel against her countrymen, why is she not equally to be justified with Elisha in imposing upon her enemies? If they will suffer themselves to be deceived by her direction to pursue the spies another way, let them be deceived. The fidelity that she owed to God was entirely paramount to that which she owed her country, and she was bound to act accordingly. But whether we justify or condemn her conduct, it can afford no precedent to us. Before we can plead her example in justification of treachery or falsehood, we must be circumstanced as she was. But this it is nearly impossible we ever should be.

6. *She had brought them up to the roof of the house.* This verse is also parenthetical, and designed to explain more particularly the circumstances of the concealment mentioned, v. 4.

The roofs of houses were then, as they still are in that country, flat, and being furnished with such battlements or parapets, as were commanded to the Jews, Deut. 22. 8, were made use of for walking or sleeping upon, or for depositing any kind of goods or chattels which could not be conveniently bestowed elsewhere. See my 'Illustrations of the Scriptures,' p. 159, 414, 461.——¶ *Hid them with the stalks of flax*, &c. This was probably laid upon the roof, in order to dry in the sun, preparatory to beating and dressing it for the wheel on which it was to be spun. Had she kept a public-house, as some have supposed, she would have been less likely to have had her roof spread over with such an article. The original is explicit in saying that the flax had been spread out or laid in order 'for herself,' as if for her own use; from which the inference is, we think, not inaptly drawn, that she possessed one at least of the characters of the virtuous woman, viz. that 'she sought wool and flax, and wrought willingly with her hands,' Prov. 31. 13, and perhaps, at this time, supported herself in a way of honest industry.

7. *Unto the fords.* Heb. על המעברות *al hammaberoth, at the passages,* or *crossing-places;* whether such places were crossed by boats, or bridges, or fording. Probably there were several such places, and the pursuers may have divided them-

8 ¶ And before they were laid down, she came up unto them upon the roof;

9 And she said unto the men, I know that the LORD hath given you the land, and that ᵍ your terror is fallen upon us, and that all the inhabitants of the land faint because of you.

10 For we have heard how the LORD ʰ dried up the waters of the Red sea for you, when ye came out of Egypt; and ⁱ what ye did unto the two kings of the Amorites that *were* on the other side Jordan, Sihon and Og, whom ye utterly destroyed.

ᵍ Gen. 35. 5.   Exod. 23. 27.   Deut. 2. 25, and 11. 25.

ʰ Exod. 14. 21.   ch. 4. 23.   ⁱ Num. 21. 24, 34, 35.

---

selves into different companies, and directed their course to each of them. ——¶ *Shut the gate.* Doubtless with especial care, and perhaps setting an extra guard, both to bar out enemies that might be lurking in the neighborhood, and to prevent the escape of the spies, if perchance they still remained in the city.

9. *I know that the Lord hath given,* &c. I know and am assured; I am perfectly satisfied; I have not a doubt. An emphatic declaration implying much more than a shrewd conjecture or strong suspicion from existing circumstances that such would be the result. The words are expressive of the strength of her faith. The sources from which she had obtained this information and assurance are sufficiently detailed in what follows, v. 9–12.——¶ *Your terror.* The dread of you. See Ex. 23. 27; 34. 24; Deut. 11. 25; 28. 7.——¶ *All the inhabitants of the land faint.* Heb. 'are melted, dissolved, liquefied.' Precisely the same expression is used, Ex. 15. 15, in reference to this very event: 'all the inhabitants of Canaan shall *melt away*.' It expresses, in the strongest manner, the effect of the general consternation which had seized upon the devoted nations, in view of contending with such a powerful foe—one which was under the special conduct and protection of an Almighty arm. Their very hearts quailed before the approach of Israel, in a certain fearful looking for of judgment and vengeance at their hands. It was probably something more than a mere natural dread of a formidable enemy; it was a supernatural panic sent upon their spirits by the immediate power of God, a fearful presage of the destruction that awaited them.

10. *For we have heard,* &c. The first of these events, the drying up of the Red Sea, had happened forty years before, and though it had produced a deep impression at the time, on all the surrounding nations, yet in the lapse of that long interval, which was a season granted them for repentance, it is not unlikely that their alarm had in great measure died away, till now it was revived again by their nearer approach, and by the recent overthrow of the two Amoritish kings. The convictions of sinners are apt to come and go with the alarming or afflictive dispensations of God's providence. So it is said of Israel of old, Ps. 78. 34–37, 'when he slew them, then they sought him and they returned (changed their mind) and inquired early after God,

CHAPTER II.

11 And as soon as we had ᵏheard *these things*, ¹our hearts did melt, neither did there remain any more courage in any man, because of you: for ᵐ the LORD your God, he *is* God in heaven above, and in earth beneath.

12 Now therefore, I pray you, ⁿ swear unto me by the LORD, since I have showed you kind-

k Exod. 15. 14, 15. l ch. 5. 1, and 7, 5. Isa. 13. 7. m Deut. 4. 39.

n See 1 Sam. 20. 14, 15, 17.

Nevertheless, they did flatter him with their mouth, and they lied unto him with their tongues; for their heart was not right with him, neither were they steadfast in his covenant.'

11. *And as soon as we had heard these things, our heart did melt.* Heb. ונשמע וימס לבבנו *vannishma vayimmas levâvěnu, and we heard, and our heart did melt ;* spoken as if the whole nation were one person, having one heart. The original word for 'melt,' though not precisely the same with that in v. 9, is yet of kindred import, the metaphor being taken from the melting of metals before the fire.——¶ *Neither did there remain any more courage in any man.* Heb. ולא קמה עוד רוח באיש *velo kâmâh ôd ruah bâish, neither any more stood there up spirit in any man.* That is, no man's spirit was erect within him; every one's courage failed, and he became cowering and faint-hearted.——¶ *Because of you.* Heb. מפניכם *mippenëkem, from before you;* i. e. by reason of your presence; a frequent idiom of the Hebrew.——¶ *He is God in heaven above, and in earth beneath.* As much as to say, 'The Lord your God is both omnipotent and omnipresent;' a remarkable confession considering the previous ignorance and darkness of her mind. It was at once an acknowledgment of the true God, and a condemnation of the false gods and idolatrous worship of her country-men, and showed a supernatural influence of God upon her soul. He can cause the rays of truth to penetrate the thickest shades of that moral midnight which broods over the minds of the unenlightened heathen, though we have no evidence that he ever does this, except *in connexion* with some kind of external instrumentality.

12. *Swear unto me by the Lord.* This proposal still further displays the sincerity and the strength of her faith. While the people of Israel, with the miracles of the Divine power constantly before their eyes, were incessantly prone to stagger at the promises and give way to unbelief, she, upon the mere hearsay report of these wonders, is so firmly persuaded of their truth, that she desires to enter covenant with the spies for her own preservation and that of her family. Though *they* were now in perilous circumstances, shut up within the walls of Jericho, and surrounded by enemies, yet she treats with them as if they had already stormed the city, and had the power of life and death in their hands. So earnest is she in this matter, that she would have them ratify by an oath their agreement to save her. In like manner, a deep-rooted conviction of the danger hanging over the head of the sinner from the curse of a violated law, will prompt him to give all diligence to flee from the wrath to come and lay hold on eternal life, by joining him-

4

ness, that ye will also show kindness unto °my father's house, and P give me a true token:

13 And *that* ye will save alive my father, and my mother, and my brethren, and my sisters, and

° See 1 Tim. 5. 8. P ver. 18.

all that they have, and deliver our lives from death.

14 And the men answered her, Our life for yours, if ye utter not this our business. And it shall be, when the LORD hath

---

self to God and his people.——¶ *Have showed you kindness.* Heb. עשיתי עמכם חסד *âsithi immâkem hesed, have done you kindness;* and so in the next clause, 'That ye will also do kindness,' &c.——¶ *Give me a true token.* Heb. אות אמת *ôth ĕmeth, a sign or token of truth*, well rendered according to the sense; 'a true token,' i. e. a token which shall not deceive me; one which I may produce as a witness of this agreement; one on the sight of which the Israelites shall forbear to hurt either me or mine.

13. *That ye will save alive my father and my mother.* Heb. החיתם *ha'hayithem, will make or cause to live.* On the peculiar import of this word, see Note on ch. 6. 25. It will be observed that she makes no mention of her husband, from which it is to be inferred that she was now a widow, or had never been married. In either case, the fact militates altogether against the hypothesis of her being a *hostess*, for nothing could be more abhorrent from Eastern notions and usages, than a single woman's following such an occupation, even had the occupation been known among them. But a practical remark of more importance suggests itself in this connexion. The same feelings which warn us to flee the coming wrath and make our own peace with God, will also incite us to do all in our power to promote the salvation of our families and kindred, by bringing them also within the bonds of the covenant. We shall feel that our work is but half done when *our own* souls are safe.

14. *Our life for yours.* Heb. נפשנו תחתיכם למות *naphshĕnu tahtĕkem lâmoth, let our soul be to die instead of you (pl.)* That is, we pawn and pledge our lives for the security of yours, and those of your relatives; may our lives be destroyed, if we suffer yours to be injured. This language affords no warrant for those thoughtless imprecations which are often introduced in discourse in order to give more emphasis to the speaker's promises or declarations. ——¶ *If ye utter not this our business.* That is, if neither thou nor any of thy kindred ('ye') betray us when we are gone, or divulge this agreement, so that others may avail themselves of its conditions. 'They that will be conscientious in keeping their promises, will be cautious in making them, and may perhaps insert conditions which others will think frivolous.' Henry.——¶ *And it shall be,* &c. The preceding clause is properly parenthetical, and these words should be read in immediate connexion with what goes before, translating 'that' instead of 'and'— 'Our life for yours (if ye utter not this our business), that it shall be, when the Lord hath given,' &c. The present mode of punctuation gives a wrong, or at least an inadequate view

B. C. 1451.]   CHAPTER II.   39

given us the land, that ᑫ we will deal kindly and truly with thee.

15 Then she ʳ let them down by a cord through the window: for her house *was* upon the town-wall, and she dwelt upon the wall.

16 And she said unto them, Get you to the mountain, lest the pursuers meet you; and hide yourselves there three

days, until the pursuers be returned: and afterward may ye go your way.

17 And the men said unto her, We *will be* ˢ blameless of this thine oath which thou hast made us swear.

18 'Behold, *when* we come into the land, thou shalt bind this line of scarlet thread in the window which thou didst let us

ᑫ Judg. 1. 24. Matt. 5. 7.   ʳ Acts 9. 25.   ˢ Exod. 20. 7.   ᵗ ver. 12.

---

of the precise scope of the passage under consideration.

15. *Then she let them down*, &c. That is, by the help of her friends or domestics. In like manner Paul made his escape from Damascus, 2 Cor. 11. 33. The conversation mentioned in the succeeding verses appears to have taken place *previous* to their being let down from the window; for which reason Adam Clarke remarks, that the natural place of this verse is immediately after the first clause of v. 21. It is very unlikely that she would dismiss them before the above-mentioned conditions were agreed upon; or that she would discourse with them of matters of so much moment *after* they were let down, and were standing under the window, where others might overhear them; or that she would commence speaking to them in her chamber, and not finish till they had left the house.

16. *Get you to the mountain.* Heb. ההרה לכו *hâhârâh lĕku, mountainwards go ye.* That is, to the *mountainous region* in the vicinity; not to any particular mountain. This is an extremely frequent sense of the word 'mountain' in Scripture. The Gr. has here εἰς τὴν ὀρεινήν, *to the moun-*

tainous region. Jericho, as we have seen, was encompassed by a range of high hills. In some of the caves of these they might conceal themselves for the time specified.

17. *We will be blameless of this thine oath.* It shall not be our fault if the said oath be not kept, provided the annexed conditions be punctually observed on thy part. We will be free from the reproach of being unfaithful to our engagements. These conditions they go on to state in the next verse.

18. *This line of scarlet thread.* Rather 'this cord,' i. e. a line or cord, consisting of such a number of threads or braids, that when twisted together, they should be capable of sustaining the weight of a man's body; for it seems to have been the very same cord with which they were let down from the window. This was to be a mark upon the house, of which the spies would inform the camp of Israel, so that no soldier, however fierce and eager he might be in the work of destruction, should offer any violence to the place thus distinguished. It answered, therefore, the same purpose with the blood sprinkled upon the door-posts in Egypt, which secured the first-born

down by: ᵘand thou shalt bring thy father, and thy mother, and thy brethren, and all thy father's household home unto thee.

19 And it shall be, *that* whosoever shall go out of the doors of thy house into the street, his blood *shall be* upon his head, and we *will be* guiltless: and whosoever shall be with thee in the house, ˣhis blood *shall be* on our head, if *any* hand be upon him.

20 And if thou utter this our business, then we will be quit of thine oath which thou hast made us to swear.

21 And she said, According unto your words, so *be* it. And she sent them away, and they departed: and she bound the scarlet line in the window.

22 And they went, and came unto the mountain, and abode there three days, until the pursuers were returned: and the pursuers sought *them* throughout all the way, but found *them* not.

23 ¶ So the two men returned, and descended from the moun-

ᵘ ch. 6. 23.   ˣ Matt. 27. 25.

---

from the destroying angel.——¶ *Thou shalt bring thy father and thy mother,* &c. Heb. תאספי *taasphi, thou shalt bring together, assemble.* In no other way could Rahab's kindred be distinguished from those who were to be devoted to the sword. If they would not 'perish with them that believed not,' they must convey themselves to the only place of safety. If any of them had been met in the streets by the slaughtering Israelites, it would have availed them nothing to say, 'We belong to the house of Rahab.' The answer would be, 'If you belong *to* the house, why are you not *in* the house? We know you not.' So those who professedly belong to the church of Christ, if they would be saved, must keep close to the society of the faithful. If they are found mingled with the world in spirit and pursuit, they have reason to fear being overwhelmed in its destruction.

19. *His blood shall be upon his head.* The guilt of his blood-shedding shall rest wholly upon himself. He shall have no one else to blame. He has failed to perform the conditions of the covenant, and so must suffer for it.——¶ *If any hand be upon him.* That is, so as to slay him. See a like phraseology, Deut. 17. 7. Est. 6. 2. Job. 1. 12.

21. *According to your words so be it.* I readily agree to the terms; they are reasonable, and I have nothing to say against them.——¶ *And she bound the scarlet line in the window.* Probably not immediately, for fear of exciting suspicion, but in season to avail herself of the benefit of it.

22. *Abode there three days.* Not three entire days, but one whole day and part of two others. They were sent out on the sixth day of the month Nisan, and escaped from Jericho the same night. The seventh day they spent in the mountains. On the eighth they returned to the camp. These three days are reckoned in the same manner as the three days of our Lord's burial. Matt. 27. 64.

23. *Passed over.* Over Jordan. ——¶ *Told him all things that befel them.* Heb. 'all things that found

B. C. 1451.] CHAPTER III. 41

tain, and passed over, and came to Joshua the son of Nun, and told him all *things* that befel them:

24 And they said unto Joshua, Truly ʸ the LORD hath delivered into our hands all the land; for even all the inhabitants of the country do faint because of us.

CHAPTER III.

AND Joshua rose early in the morning; and they re-

ʸ Exod. 23. 31. ch. 6. 2, and 21. 44.

moved ᵃ from Shittim, and came to Jordan, he and all the children of Israel, and lodged there before they passed over.

2 And it came to pass ᵇ after three days, that the officers went through the host;

3 And they commanded the people, saying, ᶜ When ye see the ark of the covenant of the LORD your God, ᵈ and the priests the Levites bearing it,

ᵃ ch. 2, 1. ᵇ ch. 1. 10, 11. ᶜ See Num. 10. 33. ᵈ Deut. 31. 9, 25.

---

them.' They probably made their report to Joshua alone, or to him in company with the elders, without whose concurrence no matter of importance seems to have been concerted or undertaken.

24. *Do faint because of us.* Heb. 'are melted before our faces.' From this they drew the assured conclusion, that God was about to deliver the country into their hands. Those that were then deprived of their courage, would soon be deprived of their possessions. 'Sinners' frights are sometimes sure presages of their fall.'—*Henry.*

CHAPTER III.

1. *Joshua rose early in the morning.* That is, doubtless, on the morning of the third or fourth day after the proclamation mentioned, ch. 1. 11. Whether the spies had at this time returned or not is uncertain, though most probable that they had.—— ¶ *Lodged there before they passed over.* That is, for one night. It would be more convenient for the congregation to pass over in the day-time; the miracle to be wrought would be more conspicuous; and a greater ter-

4*

ror would be struck into the minds of the Canaanites. There is no evidence that the Israelites were informed of the *manner* in which they were to cross the river, yet they went forward in faith, being assured that they should pass it, ch. 1. 11. Duty often calls us to take one step without knowing how we shall take the next; but if brought thus far by the leadings of Providence, and while engaged in his service, we may safely leave the event to him. He will cleave the flood or the rock rather than that the way of his servants should be obstructed.

2. *It came to pass after three days.* In exact fulfilment of Joshua's declaration, ch. 1. 10, 11.

3. *Commanded the people,* &c. In the name and by the authority of Joshua, not of their own motion. It is not unlikely that there is something of a transposition here, and that the portion from v. 7 to 14 properly belongs to this place.——¶ *The priests the Levites bearing it.* The priests who are Levites, who belong to the tribe of Levi. Although it was ordinarily the duty of the sons of Kohath, who were merely Levites and not

then ye shall remove from your place, and go after it.

4 ᵉ Yet there shall be a space between you and it, about two thousand cubits by measure: come not near unto it, that ye may know the way by which

ᵉ Exod. 19. 12.

ye must go; for ye have not passed *this* way heretofore.

5 And Joshua said unto the people, ᶠ Sanctify yourselves: for to-morrow the LORD will do wonders among you.

ᶠ Exod. 19. 10, 14, 15. Lev. 20. 7. Num. 11. 18. ch. 7. 13. 1 Sam. 16. 15. Joel 2. 16.

---

priests, to bear the ark, Num. 4. 15, yet it appears that on solemn occasions this arrangement might be departed from, and the office performed by the priests, Josh. 6. 6. The same measure was adopted when the ark was carried round Jericho—when Zadok and Abiathar brought it back to Jerusalem, at the time that David fled from Absalom, 2 Sam. 15. 29,— and when it was lodged in the temple of Solomon, 1 Kings 8. 6; the Levites not being permitted to enter the sanctuary.——¶ *Remove from your place.* That is, break up from your encampment, leave your tents, commence your march, v. 14.——¶ *Go after it.* Follow it. Go in the rear of it. Hitherto, under the conduct of Moses, the ark had held a different position. It was stationed in the centre while the host was encamped, and borne in the middle of the immense procession when it set forward. But they then had the pillar of cloud by day and of fire by night to precede them. Now the cloud is removed, and the ark is transferred to the vanguard of the army, to go before.

4. *There shall be a space—about two thousand cubits.* Two thousand cubits amounted to about one thousand yards, or three quarters of a mile, and this space was to intervene between them and the ark, in order that they might be impressed with a becoming awe and reverence of the symbol of the Divine presence. They would see, too, by this means, that instead of their protecting it, they owed all their protection to it. Another reason is expressed in the words immediately following.——¶ *That ye may know the way by which ye must go.* The ark was to be their pilot across the waters, and by being advanced so far ahead of them, would be more conspicuous than if the people had gathered and pressed close around it. As it was put at such a distance before them, they would all have the satisfaction of seeing it, and would be animated by the sight. This was the more necessary, as the passage of the Jordan was an untrodden way to them.——¶ *Ye have not passed this way heretofore.* Heb. מִתְּמוֹל שִׁלְשֹׁם *mittemōl shilshōm, since yesterday and the third day;* i. e. never hitherto. The same form of expression occurs, Gen. 31. 2. It is perhaps intimated, moreover, that they were now to cross the river, not at any usual fording place, but at some point entirely new, by a passage which should miraculously open before them as the priests and the ark advanced.

5. *And Joshua said unto the people, Sanctify yourselves.* Rather, 'had said,' for as he speaks of 'to-morrow,' the charge was probably given on the day previous to the one now

CHAPTER III.

6 And Joshua spake unto the priests, saying, ^g Take up the ark of the covenant, and pass over before the people. And they took up the ark of the covenant, and went before the people.

7 ¶ And the LORD said unto Joshua, This day will I begin to ^h magnify thee in the sight of all Israel, that they may know that ⁱ as I was with Moses, *so* I will be with thee.

8 And thou shalt command ^k the priests that bear the ark of the covenant, saying; When

g Num. 4. 15.   h ch. 4. 14. 1 Chron. 29. 25.   2 Chron. 1. 1.   i ch, 1. 5.   k ver. 3.

---

current, on which they were passing over Jordan. The command now given was undoubtedly of the same import with that given by Moses, on the eve of the delivery of the law upon mount Sinai, Ex. 19. 10-14. They were to wash their persons and their garments, and to abstain from every thing that might indispose their minds to a serious and devout attention to the miracle about to be wrought in their behalf. A similar command was generally given on great and solemn occasions. Lev. 20. 7, 8; Num. 11. 18; 1 Sam. 16. 5; Joel 2. 16. The special manifestations of God's presence should be awaited by his people in a posture of deep humiliation, and penitence, and prayer, and by diligent efforts to 'cleanse themselves from all filthiness of flesh and spirit.'

6. *Take up the ark of the covenant*, &c. Joshua in giving this command is not to be considered as acting on his own absolute authority, for it would have been too much for him to assume the responsibility of changing the usual order of march, without a Divine direction. He was merely the organ of announcing the will of God in respect to this matter. He obeyed the commands of Heaven as the priests did his.——¶ *They took up the ark of the covenant, and went before the people.* Heb. וישאו *vayisu*, they bore up, i. e. upon their shoulders, according to the direction, Num. 7. 9. 'A noble defiance of the enemies of Israel was thus given; who were challenged to attack the unarmed priests, or to attempt to seize the unattended ark.' *Scott.*

7. *And the Lord said unto Joshua*, &c. Or, 'for the Lord had said,' as in numberless cases elsewhere. It seems highly probable that these words were spoken to Joshua before the preceding charge was given to the people. That which constitutes the *ground* or *reason* of a particular order or statement, and which is properly antecedent to it, is often by the sacred writers placed last.——¶ *This day will I begin to magnify thee*, &c. To make thee great, to raise thee in the estimation of thy people, to confirm thine authority, and to clothe thee with honor. God had before put distinguished honor upon Joshua on several occasions, Ex. 24. 13; Deut. 31. 7, but it had not been in so public and solemn a manner; now he designs to magnify him as the successor of Moses in the government. He was to be the visible instrument of working a mighty miracle in the eyes of the nation; and from his circumstantially foretelling how the waters should be cut off, as

ye are come to the brink of the water of Jordan, ¹ye shall stand still in Jordan.

9 ¶ And Joshua said unto the children of Israel, Come hither, and hear the words of the LORD your God.

10 And Joshua said, Hereby ye shall know that ᵐthe living God *is* among you, and *that* he will without fail ⁿdrive out from before you the Canaanites, and the Hittites, and the Hivites, and the Perizzites, and the Girgashites, and the Amorites, and the Jebusites.

11 Behold, the ark of the covenant of °the Lord of all the earth passeth over before you into Jordan.

l ver. 17.   m Deut. 5. 26.   1 Sam. 17. 26.   2 Kings 19. 4.   Hosea 1. 10.   Matt. 16. 16.   1 Thess. 1. 9.

n Ex. 33. 2.   Deut. 7. 1.   Ps. 44. 2.   o ver. 13.   Mic. 4. 13.   Zech. 4. 14, and 6. 5.

---

soon as the feet of the priests should touch them, v. 13, it was *demonstrated* that the secret of the Lord was with him. True greatness belongs to those with whom God is, whom he employs in his service, and upon whom his blessing rests. The honor that comes from man may surround one with a temporary eclat, but let those that aspire to lasting and solid distinction seek it in the favor of God.

8. *Ye shall stand still in Jordan.* They were first required to pause on the brink of the stream, till the channel was laid dry, and then they seem to have advanced and took their station in the midst of it, till all the people had passed over. As the entire bed of the river *below* the resting point of the ark would become dry by the waters running off towards the Dead Sea, the congregation might pass over in that direction, having the ark on their right, and keeping at the prescribed distance of 2,000 cubits.

9. *Come hither.* Draw nigh towards me, as many as can come within hearing.

10. *That the living God is among you.* Not a dull, senseless, lifeless, inactive deity, like the gods of the heathen, but a God of life, power, and energy, able to work for you, and to put to confusion all your enemies.

11. *The ark of the covenant of the Lord of all the earth.* The original will admit of being rendered, 'The ark of the covenant, *even* the Lord of all the earth,' and as the Hebrew accents favor this sense, it is adopted by many of the Jewish commentators, although the current of versions is against it. Indeed it is not a little remarkable that the first edition of our present English version published in 1611, exhibits this very rendering. It was afterwards altered, but at what time, by what authority, or for what reasons, it is now impossible to determine. This usage, it is contended by Buxtorf and others, is by no means confined to this passage. In repeated instances, as they maintain, the appellation 'Lord' is bestowed upon the ark of the covenant. Thus it is said the address is to the ark, Num. 10. 35, 36; 'And it came to pass when the ark set forward, that Moses said, Rise up, Lord, and let thine enemies be scattered; and let them that hate thee flee before thee. And when it rested, he said, Return, O Lord, to the many thousands of Israel.' So also, 2 Sam. 6. 2, 'And David arose and went with all the peo-

B. C. 1451.] CHAPTER III. 45

12 Now therefore ᵖ take ye twelve men out of the tribes of Israel, out of every tribe a man.

13 And it shall come to pass, ᑫ as soon as the soles of the feet of the priests that bear the ark of the LORD, ʳ the Lord of all the earth, shall rest in the waters of Jordan, *that* the waters of Jordan shall be cut off *from* the waters that come down from above; and they ˢ shall stand upon an heap.

14 ¶ And it came to pass, when the people removed from their tents to pass over Jordan, and the priests bearing the ᵗ ark of the covenant before the people;

15 And as they that bare the ark were come unto Jordan, and ᵘ the feet of the priests that bare the ark were dipped in the brim of the water, (for ˣ Jordan overfloweth all his banks ʸ all the time of harvest,)

p ch. 4. 2. q ver. 15, 16. r ver. 11. s Ps. 78. 13, and 114. 3.

t Acts 7. 45. u ver. 13. x 1 Chron. 12. 15. Jer. 12. 5, and 49. 19. y ch. 4, 18, and 5. 10, 12.

ple that were with him, from Baale of Judah, to bring up from thence the ark of God, *whose name is called by the name of the Lord of hosts.* Comp. Ex. 16. 33; 1 Sam. 4. 7. Such a title, however, could only be applied on the ground of its being the visible symbol of the Divine presence, and of the close connexion subsisting between the sign and the thing signified.

12. *Take ye twelve men out of the tribes of Israel.* The object of this selection is afterwards explained, ch. 4. 4, 5. They were now to be chosen, and to stand ready at a moment's warning, for the service to which they were set apart.

13. *That bear the ark of the* LORD, *the Lord of all the earth.* The Heb. here exhibits two different words for 'Lord,' the first יהוה *Yehovah*, the second אדון. *adōn*, which is also the word occurring v. 11. This seems to countenance the idea that the ark itself is called by that title.——¶ *The waters of Jordan shall be cut off from the waters that come down from above.* More correctly rendered, 'the waters of Jordan shall be cut off, *even* the waters that descend from above;' but whether he speaks in these words of the mass of waters remaining *above* the ark, that *they* were to be cut off from those below, which would be speedily drained off, and leave the channel bare; or whether the 'waters that come down from above,' mean those that flowed downwards from the point where the ark stood *above*, while the rest stood as a heap, it is difficult to determine. Comparing this, however, with v. 16, the first interpretation we think the most probable. This seems to have been the first intimation given to the people as to the manner in which they were to cross the river, unless we suppose such a transposition as we have hinted at in the note above, on v. 5.

15. *Jordan overfloweth all his banks all the time of harvest.* That is, the time of the barley harvest; which began in that country in our March or April. 1 Chron. 12. 15. Prof. Robinson remarks that he could find no evidence that the Jordan ever now

16 That the waters which came down from above stood *and* rose up upon an heap very far from the city Adam, that is beside ᶻZaretan ; and those that came down ᵃ toward the sea of the plain *even* ᵇ the salt sea, failed, *and* were cut off: and the people passed over right against Jericho.

ᶻ 1 Kings 4: 12, and 7. 46.   ᵃ Deut. 3. 17.   ᵇ Gen. 14. 3.   Num. 34. 3.

---

overflows its banks in the manner that would be supposed from the rendering of this passage; and he adds, 'I apprehend that even the ancient rise of the river has been greatly exaggerated. The sole accounts we have of the annual increase of its waters are found in the earlier scriptural history of the Israelites; where, according to the English version, the Jordan is said to "overflow all its banks" in the first month, or all the time of harvest. But the original Hebrew expresses, in these passages, nothing more than that the Jordan "was full (or filled) up to all its banks," meaning the banks of its channel; it ran with full banks, or was brim-full. Thus understood, the Biblical account corresponds entirely to what we find to be the case at the present day.'—(*Research.*, Vol. II., p. 262). This annual swelling of the waters of the Jordan arises from the melting of the snows upon Mount Lebanon, in which the Jordan takes its rise. It probably took place on this occasion just before Israel was to pass over, and served to render the miracle far more stupendous and unquestionable. Indeed we may suppose that this season was chosen expressly, in order that God might have the better opportunity to convince his people of his Almighty power; that they were under his immediate care and protection; and that they might never cease to confide in him in view of the most appalling dangers. 'Though the opposition given to the salvation of God's people have all imaginable advantages, yet God can and will conquer it.'—*Henry*.

16. *Stood and rose up upon a heap*. Being checked in their course they continued to accumulate and swell higher and higher, till they filled up the channel to a great distance towards the source of the river. Probably another miracle was wrought in restraining the waters thus piled up from deluging the adjacent country.——¶ *From the city Adam, that is beside Zaretan*. The position of these cities is not easily ascertained. As to the first, nothing is known; and perhaps it was even then so obscure as to be described by its nearness to Zaretan, a place of more notoriety. This we learn from 1 Kings 4. 12, was situated below Jezreel, near Beth-shean or Scythopolis, and not far from Succoth; but Succoth, as appears from Gen. 33. 17; Josh. 13. 27, lay on the east of Jordan, not far from the lake of Gennesaret, and somewhere in this immediate vicinity, doubtless, was Adam situated. ——¶ *Passed over right against Jericho*. It is probable that the people crossed the river at what was afterwards called Beth-abara, or *house of passage*, which seems to have derived its name from this very circumstance. It was here that John baptized, John 1. 28, and that Jesus, as well as Joshua, began to be magnified.

17 And the priests that bare the ark of the covenant of the LORD stood firm on dry ground in the midst of Jordan, ᶜ and all the Israelites passed over on dry ground, until all the people were passed clean over Jordan.

CHAPTER IV.

AND it came to pass, when all the people were clean passed ᵃ over Jordan, that the LORD spake unto Joshua, saying,

2 ᵇ Take you twelve men out of the people, out of every tribe a man,

3 And command ye them, saying, Take you hence out of the midst of Jordan, out of the place where ᶜ the priests' feet stood firm, twelve stones, and ye shall carry them over with you, and leave them in ᵈ the lodging-place where ye shall lodge this night.

4 Then Joshua called the twelve men, whom he had prepared of the children of Israel, out of every tribe a man:

ᶜ See Exod. 14. 29. ᵃ Deut. 27. 2. ch. 3. 17. ᵇ ch. 3. 12.

ᶜ ch. 3. 13. ᵈ ver. 19, 20.

---

17. *And the priests—stood firm on dry ground.* Stood fixedly and immovably in the same place and posture, neither pressed upon by the waters, nor sinking in the mire, nor shifting their position. It is probable, too, that they continued bearing the ark on their shoulders during the whole time of their standing. The miracle recorded in this chapter was in some respects more striking than that which marked the passage of the Red Sea, as in this case it could not be pretended that the water had retired from any natural cause. There was here neither wind nor tide, to the agency of which the effect could be attributed; and if the river was actually passed, at a high stage of its waters, without boats or bridges, the evidence of the miracle was irresistible—the current must have been suspended by a supernatural power.

CHAPTER IV.

2. *Take you twelve men,* &c. Heb. קחו לכם *kehu lâkem, take ye for yourselves,* pl., though addressed to Joshua; an usage of speech founded upon the union between a leader or ruler, and his people. Nothing would appear from the phraseology itself to intimate that any such command had been before given, but as we know there had, ch. 3. 12, the twelve men here spoken of are to be understood of those *already* chosen to this service.

3. *Command ye them.* Another instance of the phraseology noticed above. Joshua is addressed conjointly with the people, or, perhaps, rather with the officers, and required to give the annexed order.——¶ *Leave them in the lodging-place where ye shall lodge this night.* This was Gilgal, as appears from v. 19, 20, a place somewhat more than six miles from the river Jordan.

4. *Whom he had prepared.* Whom he had before chosen and appointed to that work, with a command that they should hold themselves in readiness for it. The stones were probably each of them as large as one man could conveniently carry.

5. *Pass over before the ark.* These twelve men had probably hitherto

48   JOSHUA.   [B. C. 1451.

5 And Joshua said unto them, Pass over before the ark of the Lord your God into the midst of Jordan, and take you up every man of you a stone upon his shoulder, according unto the number of the tribes of the children of Israel:

6 That this may be a sign among you, *that* ᵉwhen your children ask *their fathers* in time to come, saying, What mean ye by these stones?

7 Then ye shall answer them, That ᶠthe waters of Jordan were

e ver. 21. Ex. 12. 26, and 13. 14. Deut. 6 20. Ps. 44. 1, and 78, 3–6. f ch. 3. 13, 16.

---

remained, from motives of reverence, somewhat behind the ark, perhaps near to the eastern bank of the river. They are now commanded to advance, and picking up the stones near the place where the priests stood, to 'pass over before the ark,' and thus emerge from the bed of Jordan, and when arrived to deposit the stones in the place commanded. Otherwise the words must be understood to imply, that after passing over with the congregation, the twelve men were to *pass back again* to the place where the ark stood, and thence transport the stones; which we cannot but regard as a violent construction.

6. *That this may be a sign among you.* A sign that shall permanently remain among you; a monument or memorial; a conspicuous object which shall be a standing witness of the wonderful event that has this day happened. Heaps, or pillars of stone, in commemoration of great events, such as covenants, victories, &c., have been common among all nations from the earliest ages. See Gen. 31: 46; Ex. 24. 4. In the present case, though there was no inscription on the stones, yet from the number of them, and from the place where they stood, it would be evident that they pointed to some memorable transaction, and of *this* it was to be the duty of each generation to keep its successors informed. It would likewise serve as a standing proof in corroboration of the matter of fact to those who might, in after ages, question the truth of the written history. The record of this great event might indeed be read in the sacred writings, but God, who knows the frame of his creatures, and how much they are influenced by the objects of sense, kindly ordered an expedient for keeping it in more lively remembrance from age to age. So he has provided the sacrament of the Lord's supper to aid our understandings and affect our hearts by sensible symbols, though the same great truths which they represent are plainly delivered in words in the inspired oracles.——¶ *When your children ask*, &c. Heb. כי ישאלון בניכם *ki yishâlun benĕkem, when your sons ask;* i. e. your descendants; not little children merely, but your posterity of whatever age Thus 'children of Israel' is equivalent to 'sons of Israel, or Israelites.' ——¶ *In time to come.* Heb. מחר *mâhâr, to-morrow,* often used in the original to signify indefinitely *all future time.* Gen 30. 33. In like manner 'yesterday' is used in a general sense for *all past time,* as Heb. 13. 8, 'Jesus Christ, the same *yesterday,* and to-day, and forever.'——¶ *What mean ye by these stones?* Heb. מה

CHAPTER IV.

cut off before the ark of the covenant of the LORD; when it passed over Jordan, the waters of Jordan were cut off: and these stones shall be for ᵍ a memorial unto the children of Israel for ever.

8 And the children of Israel did so as Joshua commanded, and took up twelve stones out

ᵍ Ex. 12. 14. Numb. 16. 40.

of the midst of Jordan, as the LORD spake unto Joshua, according to the number of the tribes of the children of Israel, and carried them over with them unto the place where they lodged, and laid them down there.

9 And Joshua set up twelve stones in the midst of Jordan, in

האבנים האלה לכם *mâh hâ-ebânim hâ-ĕlleh lâkim, what these stones to you?*

7. *Then shall ye answer them, That the waters*, &c. This clause, as appears from the original, requires to be supplied thus, 'Then shall ye answer, These stones are designed to commemorate the fact *that* the waters,' &c. Such is undoubtedly the true grammatical dependence of the conjunction *that*.——¶ *Cut off before the ark.* As it were, at the sight of it, at its first approach. The clause respecting the cutting off of the waters of Jordan occurs again in the same words towards the end of the verse, to intimate, perhaps, the wonderful character of the miracle, and that a fact of such a stupendous nature should be repeated again and again in the hearing of those who were to be instructed.——¶ *A memorial unto the children of Israel.* To them particularly and primarily, but not exclusively; for the monument was calculated to be a witness and a standing reproof also to the heathen nations around.——¶ *For ever.* For an indefinite period of time; as long as the nation should endure.

8. *The children of Israel did so.* That is, the twelve men, who acted as the representatives of the whole body of the children of Israel and

therefore bear their name. A company or community is often said in the Scriptures to do that which is done by their constituted agents.

9. *Joshua set up twelve stones in the midst of Jordan.* As it is evident from the connexion that this was actually done by the twelve selected persons above mentioned, it is ascribed to Joshua only as commanding and superintending it, just as the building of the temple is ascribed to Solomon. Two sets of stones therefore were erected in memory of this miraculous passage, one at Gilgal, the other in the bed of Jordan. Should it be asked how the latter could serve as a monument, placed as they were in the middle of the stream, and liable to be concealed below the surface, we answer, that as nothing is said of their being each of them, like the others, of a size suitable for one man to carry, they might have been vastly larger, and so based upon a lower heap as to be *generally* visible, and thus indicate the very spot where the priests stood with the ark; for it is to be remarked, that the Jordan, at its ordinary stages, is not a deep river, and that its waters are remarkably clear and transparent, so that an object like this might probably always be seen except in the time of a high

the place where the feet of the priests which bare the ark of the covenant stood: and they are there unto this day.

¶ 10 For the priests which bare the ark stood in the midst of Jordan, until every thing was finished that the Lord commanded Joshua to speak unto the people, according to all that Moses commanded Joshua: and the people hasted and passed over.

11 And it came to pass, when all the people were clean passed over, that the ark of the Lord passed over, and the priests in the presence of the people.

---

freshet. From the native force of the Heb. term for 'set up,' which is properly to 'rear up,' 'to erect,' i. e. to raise to a considerable height, it may be reasonably inferred that they were placed so as to be ordinarily visible.——¶ *In the place where the feet of the priests—stood.* Heb. תחת מצב רגלי הכנים *tahath matztzab ragle hakkohanim, under the standing-place of the feet of the priests.* It was here that the stones were to be *erected* but from whence they were taken is not said. From aught that appears in the text they might have been gathered in the adjacent fields, as some commentators have imagined. ——¶ *And they are there unto this day.* Either the words of Joshua, who wrote this history near the close of his life, and about twenty years after the event occurred, or added at a subsequent period by Samuel or Ezra, or some other inspired man by whom the sacred canon was revised.

10. *According to all that Moses commanded Joshua.* It does not appear that Moses any where gave Joshua a charge respecting this passage of Israel over the Jordan. The words therefore are to be understood of the *general instructions* given him by Moses, requiring him to follow the Divine conduct in all particulars, as made known to him through the agency of Eleazar the High Priest. Num. 27. 21-23. So he did on the present occasion,——¶ *The people hasted and passed over.* Perhaps under some apprehensions that the standing mass of waters on their right might be suffered to give way while they were crossing. Even where the general acting of faith is strong, the weakness of nature sometimes causes the spirit to waver.—This passage of the Israelites through the Jordan, is not improperly considered as an emblem of the Christian's transition from the dreary wilderness of this world to the Canaan that is above. When the time is arrived for passing by that unknown, untrodden path, we are apt to fear lest we should sink in the deep waters, and never attain the wished for end. But God has promised to be with us, to make 'the depths of the sea a way for the ransomed to pass over,' and to bring us in safety to the land that floweth with milk and honey. The ark of his covenant will go before, both for our guidance and protection, and under its conduct we may cheerfully bid adieu to the friends who stand weeping on the bank.

11. *In the presence of the people.* Who stood upon the bank beholding with admiration and awe the last act of this great miracle.

B. C. 1451.] CHAPTER IV. 51

12 And ^h the children of Reuben, and the children of Gad, and half the tribe of Manasseh, passed over armed before the children of Israel, as Moses spake unto them:

13 About forty thousand prepared for war, passed over before the LORD unto battle, to the plains of Jericho.

14 ¶ On that day the LORD ⁱ magnified Joshua in the sight of all Israel, and they feared him as they feared Moses, all the days of his life.

15 And the Lord spake unto Joshua, saying,

16 Command the priests that bear ^k the ark of the testimony, that they come up out of Jordan.

17 Joshua therefore commanded the priests, saying, Come ye up out of Jordan.

18 And it came to pass, when

- h Num. 32. 20, 27, 28. i ch. 3. 7. k Exod. 25. 16, 22.

12. *Passed over armed before the children of Israel.* The original phrase here is precisely the same with that rendered in the preceding verse, in 'the presence of;' and, as we conceive, does not clearly intimate that they led the van, for the order of marching of the different tribes had been expressly prescribed in the wilderness, Num. 10; and it is not probable that it was departed from on this occasion. According to this order the tribe of Judah had the precedence. What is affirmed of the two tribes and a half here, we suppose, is, that in pursuance of their promises, ch. 1. 16-18, they passed over ' in the presence ' of their brethren, who were thus all witnesses to their fidelity.

13. *Passed over before the Lord.* That is, probably, before the ark of the Lord, the symbol of the Divine presence. Otherwise it may imply ' as in the sight of the Lord,' 'religiously,' ' conscientiously.'

14. *Magnified Joshua.* Caused him to stand high in the esteem and respect of the people, so that they henceforth yielded to him the same reverential fear and ready obedience which they had done to Moses. God now fully confirmed his authority, and showed that He was with him. That honor is ever most to be desired which is the result of a strict, conscientious, and uniform observance of all the Divine precepts.——

——¶ *They feared him as they feared Moses, all the days of his life.* The ' his ' here may refer either to Joshua or to Moses. The latter is most accordant with the Heb. accents, and it avoids, moreover, a certain air of incongruity in the letter of the text, as if the Israelites *on that day* feared Joshua *all the days of his life.*

15. *The Lord spake unto Joshua, saying.* This may be rendered ' had spoken,' and the whole paragraph, v. 15-19, be considered as a detailed account of what is stated more generally, v. 11. These verses seem designed to acquaint us with the main *ground* or *reason* to which, under God, it was owing that Joshua was so signally magnified on that occasion. ' The priests did not quit their station till Joshua, who had commanded them thither, ordered them thence; nor did he thus order them till the Lord commanded him: so obedient were all parties to the word of God.' *Scott.*

the priests that bare the ark of the covenant of the Lord were come up out of the midst of Jordan, *and* the soles of the priests' feet were lifted up unto the dry land, that the waters of Jordan returned unto their place, ¹and flowed over all his banks, as *they did* before. .

19 ¶ And the people came up out of Jordan on the tenth *day* of the first month, and encamped ᵐ in Gilgal, in the east border of Jericho.

20 And ⁿ those twelve stones which they took out of Jordan, did Joshua pitch in Gilgal.

21 And he spake unto the children of Israel, saying, ᵒ When your children shall ask their fathers in time to come, saying, What *mean* these stones'?

1 ch. 3. 15.   m ch. 5. 9.   n ver. 3.   o ver. 6.

---

18. *The soles of the priests' feet were lifted up unto the dry land.* Heb. נתקו *nitteku, were plucked up.* As upon the entrance into the river, the stream was cut off as soon as the soles of the priests' feet touched the water, ch. 3. 15, so now as soon as they touched the dry land it again resumes its natural course. This would make it evident that the arrest of the river was the effect solely of Divine power, and not owing to any secret natural cause.——¶ *Flowed over all his banks as they did before.* Heb. כתמול שלשם *kithmōl shilshōm, as yesterday and the third day.*

19. *On the tenth day of the first month.* That is, of the month Nisan, just forty years, lacking five days, after their departure out of Egypt. This was four days before the annual feast of the Passover, and on the very day when the paschal Lamb was to be set apart for this purpose, Ex. 12. 3; God having so ordered it in his providence, that their entrance into the promised land should coincide with the period of that festival. ——¶ *And encamped in Gilgal.* In the place *afterwards* called Gilgal, ch. 5. 9, for here the name is given it by *anticipation.* It is doubtful whether there was either city or town in that place before the arrival of the Isráelites. It was situated near the Jordan, on the eastern extremity of the plain of Jericho. There are at present no certain traces of the name or the place in that region.

20. *Did Joshua pitch in Gilgal.* Heb. הקים *hēkim, erect, rear up.* A foundation of stone-work or a mound of earth, was probably first laid, of considerable height, and then the twelve stones placed on the top of it; for twelve such stones as a man could carry six miles on his shoulder, could scarcely have made any observable pile or pillar of memorial; but erected on such a base as we have supposed, they would be very conspicuous, and strikingly answer the purpose for which they were designed.

21. *Shall ask—in time to come.* Heb. מחר *mâhâr, to-morrow.* See v. 6, 7. From their number, size, position, &c., and from there not being any others near them of the same kind, they would naturally excite inquiries, 'How came these stones here? What is meant by them?' This would afford to parents an excellent opportunity to turn to account the inquisitiveness of their children, to make them early acquainted with the wonderful works

B. C. 1451.] CHAPTER V. 53

22 Then ye shall let your children know, saying, ᵖIsrael came over this Jordan on dry land.

23 For the LORD your God dried up the waters of Jordan from before you, until ye were passed over, as the LORD your God did to the Red Sea, ᑫwhich he dried up from before us, until we were gone over:

24 ʳThat all the people of the

p ch. 3. 17. q Exod. 14. 21.

earth might know the hand of the LORD, that it *is* ˢmighty: that ye might ᵗfear the LORD your God for ever.

CHAPTER V.

AND it came to pass, when all the kings of the Amorites which *were* on the side of Jordan westward, and all the

r 1 Kings 8. 42, 43. 2 Kings 19. 19. Ps. 106. 8. s Ex. 15. 16. 1 Chron. 29. 12. Ps. 89. 13. t Ex. 14. 31. Deut. 6. 2. Ps. 89. 7. Jer. 10. 7.

---

of God, and to train them up in his fear. We should encourage young people to seek instruction, and should be glad of every thing that may afford us an occasion of making known to them the wonders of redeeming love.

22. *Israel came over this Jordan on dry land.* In commemoration of which remarkable fact, these stones are placed here.

23. *For the Lord your God dried up the waters of Jordan from before you.* The parents are still supposed to be speaking to their children. It is remarkable that they address them as if they were living and present at the miraculous passage of the Jordan, whereas they then existed only in the loins of their fathers. But it is not uncommon for the sacred writers to speak of the nation of Israel, through every period of its existence, as if they were *but of one generation*, so that what really happened to those that lived at one age, is said to have happened to those that lived at another, perhaps far remote. This gives us a very impressive idea of the light in which God viewed that people, viz., as morally one, as one great collective person continually subsisting. Thus Ps. 66. 6, the writer speaks as

5*

if he and his contemporaries were personally present at the passage of the Red Sea, 'He turned the sea into dry land: they went through the flood on foot; *there did we rejoice in him*,' though this happened ages before their time. So also our Saviour speaks as if the Jews of his day were living in the days of Moses, John 6. 32, 'Verily I say unto you, Moses gave *you* not that bread from heaven.' On the same principle Joshua speaks here.——¶ *The Red Sea, which he dried up from before us.* This is another instance of the usage just adverted to. He speaks of the Red Sea's being dried up from before the people whom he then addressed, whereas none of that generation were now living except himself and Caleb; the rest of them having perished in the wilderness through unbelief and rebellion. It is also to be remarked, that this passage through the Jordan being here said to have been accomplished in the same manner with that through the Red Sea, the inference is legitimate, that the waters of that sea were actually divided like those of the river, and that they did not merely retire from the shore, as some have supposed.

kings of the Canaanites ᵃ which *were* by the sea, ᵇ heard that the

ᵃ Num. 13. 29. ᵇ Exod. 15. 14, 15. ch. 2. 9, 10, 11. Ps. 48. 6. Ezek. 21. 7.

CHAPTER V.

1. *And it came to pass*, &c. As this verse is much more intimately related to what goes before than to what follows, it would probably have been better to have joined it to the preceding chapter. The present would then have commenced with an entirely new subject.—— ¶ *All the kings of the Amorites—and of the Canaanites.* As the whole land of Canaan was of comparatively small extent, the several *nations*, as they are called, which inhabited it, must have been mere clans or hordes, and what are termed their *kings* nothing more than petty chieftains, ruling over territories scarcely larger than the counties in many of the states of the American union. The term *king*, in modern usage, conveys the idea of a power and dominion altogether more extensive than was possessed by these petty potentates. The Amorites and the Canaanites here mentioned probably stand for the whole of the devoted nations, they being specified on account of their superiority to the rest in numbers, power, and courage. The nation of the Amorites occupied both sides of the Jordan; two of their kings, Sihon and Og, had already been slain on the eastern side, Deut. 4. 46, 47.—— ¶ *Which were by the sea*. The Mediterranean sea; along the coasts of which the Canaanitish tribes, properly so called, were spread. This region was afterwards known by the name of Phœnicia, of which Tyre and Sidon were the principal cities.

Lord had dried up the waters of Jordan from before the children of Israel, until we were passed over, that their heart

On this account the same person who is called 'a woman of Canaan' by Matthew, 15. 22, is called by Luke, 7. 26, 'a Syro-Phœnician.'—— ¶ *Had dried up the waters of Jordan*. Which they regarded as the natural bulwark of their country, one too strong for the enemy to break through, especially during the season of its annual overflow. It should seem that the Canaanites, if they had acted according to the rules of war, would have opposed the Israelites in their passage. But the destruction of Pharaoh at the Red Sea, some time before, and the recent victories over Sihon and Og, had spread such a panic through the land, that they did not dare to avail themselves of any supposed advantage, lest they should perish after their example. The event, indeed, shows how vain any attempt on their part would have been. It shows, too, that when the measure of any people's iniquities is full, they shall in no wise escape the vengeance of God. Whatever obstacles may appear to lie in the way, and whatever barrier an ungodly world may have, or think they have, for their defence, God will surely make a way for his indignation. Opposing myriads shall be only as the stubble before the fire of his wrath.—— ¶ *Until we were passed over*. These words intimate the writer to have been one of the company.—— ¶ *Their heart melted*. In modern language we read of the heart melting with pity and being dissolved with grief. The sacred writers, on

melted; ^c neither was there spirit in them any more, because of the children of Israel.

2 ¶ At that time the LORD said unto Joshua, Make thee ^d sharp knives, and circumcise again the children of Israel the second time.

c 1 Kings 10. 5.   d Exod. 4. 25.

---

this and similar occasions, apply the same metaphor, with equal truth and beauty, to the operation of fear and terror.——¶ *Neither was there spirit in them any more.* The special providence of God is to be recognized in the panic which fell upon these nations at this particular juncture. It gave the Israelites just the opportunity they required, to administer the rite of circumcision, and to keep the Passover securely and without disturbance. Had it been otherwise, and had the Canaanites attacked them, as Simeon and Levi did the Shechemites *when they were sore*, they would have taken them at every disadvantage.

2. *At that time.* As if in allusion to the remarkable circumstances by which they were now surrounded; encamped in the midst of an enemy's country, and yet that enemy providentially restrained from harming them, so that they were commanded, as if in their very sight and presence, to reduce themselves to a condition of comparative weakness and helplessness. 'This formed a very great trial of their faith, and their prompt and universal obedience in such critical circumstances, manifested a confidence in the Lord's protection, and a submission to his will, which confirm the sentiment that this was the best of all the generations of Israel.' *Scott.*——¶ *Make thee sharp knives.* Heb. עשה לך חרבות צרים *esëh lekàh harbōth tzurim, prepare, make ready, knives of rock, stone, or flint.* Of such materials were the edge-tools of all nations made before the use of iron became common. At this day, among most of the savage tribes inhabiting the islands of the sea, or other barbarous climes, the same custom prevails. Their *knives*, and also their *arrow* and *spear-heads*, are made of stone; and similar relics of the aborigines of our own country are often turned up by the plough. It is not probable that the Israelites were altogether strangers to the use of iron, or were unfurnished with various metallic tools, as their different fabrications in the wilderness force upon us the belief that they must have employed both *iron* and *steel*; but from the case of Zipporah, Ex. 4. 25, it appears to have been unlawful to use any kind of *metal* in this religious rite, and this opinion is confirmed by the practice of a tribe in Ethiopia at this day, who, professing to follow the Mosaic institution, perform the rite of circumcision, according to Ludolf, *with knives of stone*. It is supposed too that such instruments were not so liable to cause inflammation, as knives or razors of metal.—— ¶*And circumcise again the children of Israel the second time.* Heb. ושוב מל *veshûb mōl, return (and) circumcise.* This is not to be understood as a command to *repeat* circumcision on those individuals who had already received it. This would have been at once unnecessary and impracticable. It merely implies that they were to *renew* the observ-

3 And Joshua made him sharp knives, and circumcised the children of Israel at the hill of the foreskins.

---

ance of a rite which had been neglected in their travels in the desert. The command was given now, at this early period after their entrance into the promised land, (1) That the reproach of Egypt might be rolled away; (2) That they might be duly prepared to celebrate the Passover, of which none might eat who were uncircumcised, Ex. 12. 48; and (3). As a trial of their faith under the circumstances in which they were now placed, surrounded by enemies intent upon their destruction, and who could desire no greater advantage than such a crippled state of their invaders would give them. 'There is a general circumcision now of the people, as there had been at their coming out of Egypt; and as God then closed the Egyptians in three days' darkness that they could not stir, so now he striketh the Canaanites with terror, that they dare not stir to hurt the people while they were sore. Circumcision sealed the lease of the land of Canaan; and therefore as soon as they set foot on it they must be circumcised.' *Lightfoot*. Had Joshua acted on the principles common to all other generals, when invading an enemy's country, he would either have prosecuted his advantages instantly, while his enemies were filled with terror, and crushed them before they had time to prepare for their defence; or he would have fortified his own camp to prevent surprise, and to be in constant readiness for any emergency that might arise. But instead of adopting any military plans whatever, the very day after he had invaded the country, without waiting to know what effect the invasion would have, he appoints nearly every male in the congregation to be circumcised ! Thus by one act disabling the greater part of his whole army from even standing in their own defence ! What but a principle of the most triumphant faith could have brought them to submit to such an injunction as this ?

3. *And Joshua made him sharp knives.* That is, he caused them to be made, they were made by his order.——¶ *Circumcised the children of Israel.* Meaning those of them who had not been already circumcised, those who had been born in the wilderness and were under forty years of age. This he did by means of his agents. As the number to whom the rite was to be administered was immensely large, and the time allotted for it short, a great many hands must necessarily have been engaged in it. Probably any one who was himself circumcised, was authorized to perform it. In ordinary circumstances it is proper to stand upon instituted observances with great exactness, and to have religious rites performed by appropriate officers, but when peculiar emergencies arise, such scrupulousness must sometimes be waived, and *rituals* give way to *essentials*. God will have mercy rather than sacrifice, when only one can be rendered him.——¶ *At the hill of the foreskins.* So called from the hillock of foreskins, the result of the transaction.

4. *And this is the cause*, &c. The omission in this case was probably

CHAPTER V.

4 And this *is* the cause why Joshua did circumcise : *e* All the people that came out of Egypt, *that were* males, *even* all the men of war died in the wilderness by the way, after they came out of Egypt.

5 Now all the people that came out were circumcised; but all the people *that were* born in the wilderness by the way as they came forth out of Egypt, *them* they had not circumcised.

6 For the children of Israel walked *f* forty years in the wilderness, till all the people *that* were men of war which came out of Egypt were consumed, because they obeyed not the voice of the LORD : unto whom the LORD sware that *g* he would not show them the land which the LORD sware unto their fathers that he would give us, *h* a land that floweth with milk and honey.

7 And *i* their children, *whom* he raised up in their stead, them Joshua circumcised: for they were uncircumcised, because they had not circumcised them by the way.

e Num. 14. 29 and 26. 64, 65. Deut. 2. 16.
f Num. 14. 33. Deut. 1. 3, and 2. 7, 14. Ps. 95. 10.
g Num. 14. 23. Ps. 95. 11. Heb. 3. 11.
h Exod. 3. 8. i Num. 14. 31. Deut. 1. 39.

---

with the Divine connivance, as the people knew not the precise times when they were to march, and a removal immediately after the operation might have been dangerous to tender infants. Moreover, as one design of this rite was to *distinguish* the Israelites from all other people, it was not so necessary to be administered while they were secluded from the world, for forty years in the wilderness. This instance, however, is not to be pleaded as authorizing the neglect or postponement of any Divine ordinance in common circumstances.

6. *Walked forty years.* Led for that time a wandering, unsettled life. ——¶ *Till the people—were consumed.* Heb. עד כי תם הגוי *ad ki' tōm haggoi.* It is not a little remarkable that the word here rendered *people* (גוי) is not the usual term employed to denote the *peculiar people*, but that which almost invariably designates the *Gentiles*, or *heathen*, in contradistinction from the race of Israel. We know of no reason for its adoption here, unless it be to intimate, that they had, by their deportment, rendered themselves unworthy the name and privileges of Israelites. They were doubtless those of whom it is elsewhere said, that ' their carcases fell in the wilderness,' a doom which befell them by reason of their rebellion.——¶ *Would not show them.* Heb. הראותם *harothâm, cause to see,* i. e. would not *permit them to enjoy.* Thus Eccles. 2. 24, ' There is nothing better for a man, than that he should eat and drink, and that he should make his soul enjoy (Heb. הראה את נפשׁו *herâh eth naphshō, cause his soul to see*) good in his labor.' Ps. 4. 6, ' Who will *show* us any good ?' (Heb. מי יראנו *mi yarēnu, who will cause us to see,* i. e. to enjoy, to have the fruition of good).

7. *Their children whom he raised up in their stead.* Or, Heb. הקים *hēkim, caused to stand, made to sur-*

8 And it came to pass when they had done circumcising all the people, that they abode in their places in the camp, ᵏ till they were whole.

9 And the Lord said unto Joshua, this day have I rolled away ˡ the reproach of Egypt

ᵏ See Gen. 34. 25. ˡ Gen. 34. 14. 1 Sam. 14. 6. See Lev 18. 3. ch. 24. 14. Ezek. 20. 7, and 23. 3, 8.

---

vive, preserved. The writer's design seems to be, to state a contrast in the lot of the fathers and the children, using the term 'raised up,' in opposition to 'consumed,' in the preceding verse. The one he *destroyed* for their rebellion, the other he graciously *preserved alive, established, caused to subsist.* See Note on Ex. 9. 16, where this sense of the term is amply confirmed. The words contain a fulfilment of the promise given in connexion with the threatening, Num. 14. 29-31.

8. *Till they were whole.* Till they were healed. Heb. עד היותם *ad hayothâm, until they lived.* The original is, in repeated instances, used to signify *being restored to health.* Thus Num. 21. 8, 'Every one that is bitten, when he looketh upon it, *shall live,*' i. e. be recovered. 2 Kings 8. 8, 'Shall I *recover* of this disease?' Heb. 'shall I *live?*' Is. 38. 21, 'Lay it for a plaster on the boil, and he shall recover;' Heb. 'shall *live.*' The particle 'till' does not imply that they abode in their tents *no longer* than during the time of their recovery; for they remained there while keeping the Passover. The same remark is to be made of the import of this word in numerous other instances.

9. *This day have I rolled away the reproach of Egypt.* It has been much disputed by commentators what is meant by 'the reproach of Egypt.' We take the expression, in a very full sense, to mean *the reproach con-* nected *with Egypt,* in whatever way, whether actively or passively. (1) Actively; inasmuch as the Israelites themselves, while in the wilderness, did virtually reproach the Most High *in respect to the land of Egypt,* grieving that they had left it, wishing that they had died there, charging him with leading them out thence to slay them in the desert, and proposing to appoint a leader and to return thither. The 14th chapter of Numbers details these murmuring complaints, and shows that God was exceedingly angry with the people on this account, and would have destroyed them but for the intercession of Moses. But now the guilt of that conduct was to be rolled away or pardoned, they were no longer on account of it to be kept out of possession of the promised land; and not only so, they should never have any more the least occasion or inducement to vent such groundless reproaches. By being brought into Canaan in so gracious and glorious a manner, and having every promise fulfilled to them, all occasion of complaint was for ever cut off. (2) Passively; their bondage in Egypt was, in a sense, a reproach and a disgrace to them; it would be so accounted by other nations, while it continued, and they would be disparaged by reason of it. It is probable also that the Egyptians themselves, seeing them wander so long in the wilderness, reproached and taunted them, as if brought there to be de-

B. C. 1451.] CHAPTER V. 59

from off you: wherefore the name of the place is called ^m Gilgal unto this day.

10 ¶ And the children of Israel encamped in Gilgal, and kept the passover ⁿ on the fourteenth day of the month at even, in the plains of Jericho.

m ch. 4. 19. n Exod. 12. 6. Num. 9. 5.

stroyed; but now, having entered Canaan in triumph, and being put in possession of all the covenanted blessings promised to the seed of Abraham, of which circumcision was the seal, this reproach was henceforth done away. Both the disgrace of their bondage and the contemptuous aspersions of their oppressors, should cease from this time forward for ever. ——¶ *Wherefore the name of the place is called Gilgal unto this day.* That is, 'rolling,' 'rolling away.' Gilgal was situated between Jericho and the river Jordan, about one mile and a half, or two miles, from the former, and six from the latter. Nothing of this city now remains; but travellers are shown a pile of stones denominated *Galgala*, which, though at a considerable distance from the site of the ancient Gilgal, is supposed by some to be the monument erected by Joshua. The clause ' unto this day,' sufficiently indicates that the events related in the book of Joshua, or at least in this part of it, were not consigned to writing immediately upon their occurrence, but after the lapse of some considerable time.

10. *And kept the passover.* Heb. ' and made the passover.' The third from its institution. The first was observed in Egypt on the eve of their departure, the second at Sinai on the following year, Num. 9. 1, 2, while during the long interval down to the present time it had been wholly suspended. Amos 5. 25.——¶ *On the*

fourteenth day of the month. That is, the fourteenth day of the first month, or Nisan.—From this remarkable portion of the sacred narrative we may learn, (1.) That in whatever circumstances we are placed, religion should be our first concern. If ever there were circumstances which would seem to justify the postponement of religious duties, one would think they were those of Joshua on this occasion, when he had but just set foot on the land where great and powerful nations were prepared to combat for their very existence. Yet we behold him calmly and sedately engaging in the duties of religion, as if it were of vastly more consequence that God should be honored and served in the way of his appointment, than that the preservation or triumph of Israel should be secured. (2.) To place implicit confidence in God, even in the midst of the most appalling dangers. Nothing, to human view, could have been more rash or perilous than for the chosen people, just at this juncture, to suspend all their military preparations, and give themselves to the celebration of a religious festival. But conscious of being in the way of duty, they reposed so strong a confidence in the protecting power of Jehovah, that they gave themselves no concern as to the many dangers by which they were surrounded. Provided our motives and our conduct are right, we can be in no hazard of confiding too implicitly in God.

11 And they did eat of the old corn of the land on the morrow after the passover, unleavened cakes and parched *corn* in the self-same day.

12 ¶ And ᵒ the manna ceased on the morrow after they had eaten of the old corn of the land; neither had the children of Israel manna any more; but they did eat of the fruit of the land of Canaan that year.

13 ¶ And it came to pass when Joshua was by Jericho,

ᵒ Exod. 16. 33.

---

11. *And they did eat of the old corn of the land.* Of the old *grain*, of whatever kind it were. This they probably found in abundance in the deserted granaries of the inhabitants, who had fled away, and betaken themselves for safety to the defenced city of Jericho. The original phrase, however, may be rendered simply, ' They did eat of the *product* or *yielding* of the earth,' in contradistinction from the manna which came from heaven.——¶ *And parched corn.* That is, the new corn of the present year, which they found standing in the fields. The new or green corn was parched to enable them more easily to grind it for food. This would not be necessary in respect to old corn.——¶ *On the morrow after the passover.* Meaning, probably, on the sixteenth day of the month; for the paschal lamb was killed and roasted on the fourteenth, and the feast began that night, which, according to their reckoning, formed a part of the fifteenth day, through the whole of which the feast continued, so that the sixteenth day was the *morrow after the passover*, when they were required by the Law (Lev. 23. 10, 11) to offer to God the wave-sheaf of the first fruits, and then were allowed to eat the rest.——¶ *In the self-same day.* Perhaps importing the very great eagerness of the people to feast upon the fruits of the land as soon as they might lawfully do it. Having previously renewed their covenant with God and partaken of its seals, circumcision and the passover, they wished at once to enter upon the enjoyment of all the rights and privileges thereby confirmed to them.

12. *And the manna ceased on the morrow.* Because it was now no longer necessary. God would not have us expect extraordinary or miraculous supplies when they may be procured by ordinary means. The sudden cessation of the manna would teach the people also very impressively that it was not an ordinary production of nature, that it had not fallen for so long a time by chance, or, like the dew, in consequence of fixed laws, but that it was a special and preternatural gift of the Divine goodness. We are prone to look upon our common mercies as *matters of course*, and God sometimes withdraws them to teach us our dependence more effectually.—' The word and ordinances of God are spiritual manna, with which God nourishes his people in this wilderness, but when we come to the heavenly Canaan, this manna will cease, for we shall then no longer have need of it.' *Henry.*

13. *When Joshua was by Jericho.* Heb. בריחו *beriho, in Jericho;* i. e. in the plains of Jericho, in the coun-

that he lifted up his eyes and looked, and behold, there stood p a man over against him q with his sword drawn in his hand:

p Gen. 18. 2, and 32. 24. Ex. 23 23. Zech. 1. 8. Acts 1. 10. q Numb. 22. 23.

try or territory immediately adjoining Jericho, and called by the same name probably at some distance from the camp, whither he may have repaired for the purpose of observing in person the position of the city and the most favorable point of attack. The sixth chapter ought certainly to have commenced here, as the subject now entered upon is entirely new, and the present arrangement most unnaturally divides the communication which Joshua had with the angel, and which is continued to ch. 6. 5. ¶ *There stood a man.* One in the appearance of a man, one whom Joshua at first took for a man. That he was a superhuman being, however, is evident from what follows; and there seems no good reason to dissent from the established opinion of both ancient and modern expositors that this was no other than the Son of God, the Eternal Word, appearing in that form which he was afterwards to assume for the redemption of men. The reasons for this opinion are, (1) The title which he here gives himself, 'Captain of the host of the Lord,' which is but another form of the name 'Lord of hosts,' implying the ruler of all the heavenly hosts, and which is evidently the appropriate title of Jehovah-Jesus. (2) His acceptance of the worship or adoration which Joshua here pays him. This an angel or any created being would undoubtedly have refused. Comp. Rev. 19. 10; 22. 9; Judg. 13. 16. Here, however, instead of reproving Joshua for doing him too much honor, he commands him to do still more, by 'loosing his shoes from off his feet;' thus insisting upon the highest acknowledgment of the Divine presence which was in use among the eastern nations. (3) From the place being made holy by his presence, which was the special prerogative of God, Ex. 3, 5; and (4) From his being expressly called 'Jehovah,' ch. 6. 2, which passage undoubtedly forms a part of the present narrative, as otherwise he must have appeared without any ostensible object, neither delivering any message, making any promise, nor uttering any command, except merely that Joshua should loose his shoes from his feet.——¶ *Over against him.* As if with a hostile intent, in somewhat of a threatening attitude. The same phrase in the original occurs Dan. 10. 13, 'The prince of the kingdom of Persia *withstood* me (Heb. ' stood over against me.')——¶ *With his drawn sword in his hand.* As a symbol of the character in which he was now to manifest himself in behalf of Joshua and Israel. So he is elsewhere termed, 'A man of war,' Ex. 15. 3. His appearing in this form would serve also not only to justify the war in which Joshua was now engaged, to show him that it was of God, who had given him his commission to kill and slay, but to encourage him to prosecute it with vigor. If God was for him, who could be against him? He had indeed previously received many promises of success, but God is often graciously pleased to confirm and follow up his promises, by signal manifestations of

and Joshua went unto him, and said unto him, Art thou for us, or for our adversaries?

14 And he said, Nay; but as ʳcaptain of the host of the Lord am I now come. And Joshua ᵃfell on his face to the earth, and did worship, and said unto him, What saith my lord unto his servant?

15 And the captain of the Lord's host said unto Joshua,

ʳ See Ex. 23. 20. Dan. 10. 13, 21, and 12. 1. Rev. 12. 7, and 19. 11, 14.

ᵃ Gen. 17. 3.

his presence and favor: 'Thou meetest him that rejoiceth and worketh righteousness, those that remember thee in thy ways.'——¶ *And Joshua went unto him.* Displaying herein a remarkable courage and intrepidity. Instead of turning away from the formidable personage before him, and seeking hastily to regain the camp, he walks boldly up, and demands of him whether he be a friend or a foe. This undaunted bearing was the fruit of his strong confidence in God. No face of clay will intimidate him who looks upon God as his friend and protector, and who is found in the way of duty. It is the disobedient, the obstinate, the rebellious spirit, in which cowardice dwells. The good man is ever the true hero.

14. *And he said, Nay, but as captain of the host of the Lord am I now come.* 'I am neither Israelite nor Canaanite, neither friend nor foe in your sense of the words, for I am not a mortal man, but as prince and leader of the Lord's host, of the angels in heaven, and even of that very power of which you are commander, have I now come, to instruct and aid thee in the great undertaking in which thou art engaged.' There seems to be a peculiar emphasis in the word *now* (עתה *attâh*), as if he had said, 'I who formerly appeared as the Jehovah of the burning bush (Ex. 3.), and who was announced as the tutelary Angel of the travelling hosts (Ex. 23. 23), now appear in the different character of the Divine Defender of the covenant nation; and as my presence formerly made Sinai holy (Ex. 19. 20), so now doth it sanctify the spot upon which my footsteps tread.' He probably at the same moment put forth some visible demonstration of his true character, which at once satisfied Joshua, and filled him with an overwhelming sense of his majesty and glory, so that he instinctively fell on his face to the earth, and offered him those tokens of worship which a mortal is bound to pay to his Creator. How much reason he had for this is evident from ch. 6. 2, where the august stranger expressly denominates himself *Jehovah*.——¶ *What saith my Lord unto his servant?* With the profoundest reverence I acknowledge thee as my Lord and leader, I subject myself to thy sovereign will, and humbly wait for the orders it may seem good to thee to issue.

15. *Loose thy shoe from off thy foot.* This was a token of respect and reverence usual in the east, and equivalent to uncovering the head with us. (See Illustrations of the Scriptures, p. 129.) These are the same words which the angel of the burning bush spake to Moses, Ex. 3. 5. from which, and other circumstances, it is probable that it was the same person who

B. C. 1451.]   CHAPTER VI.   63

ᵃ Loose thy shoe from off thy foot, for the place whereon thou standest is holy: and Joshua did so.

ᵃ Ex. 3. 5.   Acts 7. 33.

CHAPTER VI.

NOW Jericho was straitly shut up, because of the children of Israel : none went out, and none came in.

---

appeared in both places. That great and glorious Being, who knows fully his own infinite perfections, which we are very inadequate to comprehend, knows what external manifestations of respect they justly claim of his creatures. 'Outward expressions of inward reverence, and a religious awe of God, well become us, and are required of us, whenever we approach to him in solemn ordinances.' *Henry.*——¶ *The place whereon thou standest is holy.* Heb. קדש *kodesh, is holiness.* It was for the time made holy, or consecrated by the Divine presence. As soon as that was withdrawn, its peculiar sacredness also forsook it, and it was no more holy than any other place. Yet with the pious heart there will naturally be, from the laws of association, a feeling of reverence for any place where God has been pleased to vouchsafe the special manifestation of himself. Such a sentiment, however, should be guarded from degenerating into superstition.

CHAPTER VI.

We fully assent to the remark of Dr. Adam Clarke, that there is scarcely a more unfortunate division of chapters in the whole Bible than here. According to the present arrangement, the reader is greatly at a loss to know what is intended by this extraordinary appearance of the Son of God, as it would seem that the whole account of his visit is closed with the foregoing chapter, whereas in fact it is continued in the present. The first verse of ch. 6, is a mere parenthesis, relating the state of Jericho at the time Joshua was favored by this encouraging vision. The thread of the narrative respecting this Divine personage, commenced in the preceding chapter, is then resumed, and continued to v. 5.

1. *Now Jericho was straitly shut up.* Strictly, closely shut up. Heb. סגרת ומסגרת *sogereth u-mesugereth, did shut up and was shut up,* or *closing and was closed.* The original expression is peculiar and emphatic, and was doubtless designed to imply the extreme care and vigilance with which the gates had been closed and were watched, not only by night, as when the spies came, ch. 2. 5, but also by day. Accordingly the Chal. renders it, 'And Jericho was shut up with iron doors and fortified with brazen bolts, so that none came out either to combat or to make offers of peace.' The language also intimates, that the city was not only effectually shut up and made secure from within, but was also so closely blockaded by the Israelites from without, that there was no going out or coming in even to its own citizens.——¶ *Because of the children of Israel.* 'Methinks I see how they called their council of war, debated of all means of defence, gathered their forces, trained their soldiers, set strong guards to the gates and walls; and now would persuade one another that unless Israel could fly into their city, the siege

2 And the LORD said unto Joshua, See, ᵃ I have given into thine hand Jericho, and the ᵇking thereof, *and* the mighty men of valor.

3 And ye shall compass the city, all *ye* men of war, *and* go round about the city once: thus shalt thou do six days.

a ch. 2. 9, 24, and 8. 1. b Deut. 7. 24.

was vain. (So) vain worldlings think their ramparts and barricadoes can keep out the vengeance of God; their blindness suffers them to look no further than the means; the supreme hand of the Almighty comes not within the compass of their fears. Every carnal heart is a Jericho shut up; God sits down before it, and displays mercy and judgment in sight of the walls thereof: it hardens itself in a wilful security, and saith, "Aha, I shall never be moved." ' *Bp. Hall.*

2. *And the Lord said unto Joshua.* That is, after Joshua had loosed his shoes from off his feet, as commanded above, ch. 5. 15. He who was before called the 'Captain of the Lord's host,' is here called 'Lord,' or 'Jehovah,' thus clearly proving that it was a Divine personage; for who else could promise and perform what follows?——¶ *I have given into thy hand Jericho.* Not only 1 *will* do it, but I *have* done it; it is all thine own, as surely as if it were even now in thy possession.——¶ *And the mighty men of valor.* The copulative 'and' does not occur here in the Hebrew. The proper rendering is, 'I have given into thy hand Jericho and the king thereof, (who are, or, although they are) mighty men of valor,' i. e. experienced and powerful warriors, men with whom, if you were to contend on ordinary terms, you would be unable to cope; but whom, through my assistance, you shall utterly overthrow. A city, in Scripture style, is often taken, not for a *collection of houses and walls,* but for the *inhabitants, an assemblage of people dwelling together in a corporate capacity.* The same distinction holds between the Latin *urbs* and *civitas.* By Jericho and its king, is here meant the inhabitants and their king, and they are spoken of collectively as 'mighty men of valor.'

3. *And ye shall compass—thus shall thou do six days.* The address is made in the latter clause to Joshua, in the singular number, as the commander and representative of the people. In the former clause the plural is used. Such changes of person are frequent, and always worthy of attention, as showing the constructive unity of people and their leaders. —It seemed good to Infinite Wisdom to appoint this method of besieging the city, (1) To magnify his power, to show in a convincing manner, both to the Canaanites and to Israel, that Omnipotence alone had achieved the work, that he was infinitely above the need of the ordinary means of obtaining a victory, and to render those of his enemies entirely inexcusable who should presume to withstand his resistless arm. (2) To try the faith and obedience of Joshua and his people, by prescribing a course of conduct that seemed to human wisdom the height of folly and absurdity, and also to secure a profound respect to all his subsequent institutions, however simple or contemptible they might seem to the eye of carnal reason. (3) To put honor

CHAPTER VI.

4 And seven priests shall bear before the ark seven ᶜtrumpets of rams' horns: and the seventh day ye shall compass the city seven times, and ᵈthe priests shall blow with the trumpets.

c See Judg. 7. 16, 22.   d Num. 10. 8.

5 And it shall come to pass, that when they make a long *blast* with the ram's horn, *and* when ye hear the sound of the trumpet, all the people shall shout with a great shout: and the wall of the city shall fall

---

upon the ark as the appointed token of his presence, and to confirm still more fully that veneration and awe, with which they had always been taught to regard it.

4. *Seven trumpets of rams' horns.* Heb. שופרות יובלים *shoperoth yobelim, trumpets of the jubilee*, i.e. such trumpets as used to be blown in the year of jubilee, implying, perhaps, that the entrance of Israel into Canaan was a kind of jubilee to them, an occasion that called rather for the sound of the trumpet of joy, than the dreadful notes of the trumpet of war. No other scriptural instance is adduced, in which the word יובל *yobël* is translated *ram*, though it be true that the Chaldee paraphrase favors that rendering. But its single authority on the point is not conclusive. The like phrase in v. 5, is, in the original קרן יובל *keren yobël, horn of jubilee*, and proves only that *horns* were used, without restricting the meaning to *rams' horns*. Still the sense of *rams' horns*, as a traditionary sense, seems for ages to have connected itself with the phrase, grounded, we presume, on the fact, that the trumpets in question were made in the *shape* of the horns of this animal, and the appellation 'horn of jubilee' may be used figuratively for *trumpet* of jubilee, just as with us a well known musical instrument of brass is called 'a horn,' from its form, and another called 'a serpent,'

for the same reason.——¶ *The seventh day ye shall compass the city seven times.* The time was thus lengthened out, both to afford a continued exercise of the faith and patience of the people, and that the besieged and besiegers might be the more deeply impressed with that supernatural power by which the result was to be accomplished. Men are usually prone to precipitate measures. God moves deliberately, and he would have his people wait his time. 'He that believeth shall not make haste.' 'It is the pleasure of God to hold us both in work and in expectation, and though he require our continual endeavors for the subduing of our corruptions, during the six days of our life, yet we shall never find it perfectly effected till the very evening of our last day.' *Bp. Hall.* The repeated mention of the number *seven* in this connexion, is worthy of notice. It has been suggested that it might have a latent reference to the creation of the world in six days, and God's resting on the seventh, which completed the first week, and in the present case, that it may convey an allusion to the preaching of the gospel for a limited period of time, at the close of which, perhaps early in the seventh thousand years, all Satan's remaining bulwarks shall fall to the ground, and the kingdoms of this world become the kingdoms of the Lord and of his Christ.

6*

down flat, and the people shall ascend up every man straight before him.

6 ¶ And Joshua the son of Nun called the priests, and said unto them, Take up the ark of the covenant, and let seven priests bear seven trumpets of rams' horns before the ark of the Lord.

7 And he said unto the people, Pass on, and compass the city, and let him that is armed pass on before the ark of the Lord.

8 ¶ And it came to pass, when Joshua had spoken unto the people, that the seven priests bearing the seven trumpets of rams' horns passed on before the Lord, and blew with the trumpets: and the ark of the covenant of the Lord followed them.

9 ¶ And the armed men went

---

5. *The wall of the city shall fall down flat.* Not absolutely *all* the wall in the whole extent of its compass, since that would have involved the house of Rahab in the destruction, which, it is plain, was not intended, nor did it happen, v. 22. As the city was completely surrounded by the Israelites, the falling of the wall would give the inhabitants no opportunity of escape. They could not break through the array of armed men that hemmed them in. The original for 'fall down flat' is 'fall down under itself,' or 'in its place,' which appears to mean simply, that the wall should fall down to its very foundations.——¶ *Ascend up every man straight before him.* The obstruction of the wall being removed, nothing stood in the way of the people's advancing in a direct line, as if from the circumference to the centre of a circle, and meeting in the heart of the city. This is called 'going up,' or 'ascending,' from the necessity there was of *climbing* over the ruins of the walls on their way. Besides which it is common, in nearly all languages, to d scribe the approach to a city as a 'g ing u ' to it. After giving these directions, the Angel-Jehovah no doubt departed.

6. *And Joshua the son of Nun called the priests,* &c. Although the charge which he now received relative to the manner of besieging the city was highly calculated to put his faith to the test, yet he falters not in the least, but complies as readily as if human reason had nothing to object to so strange a procedure. We cannot but be admonished, by his example, of the necessity of always subordinating our shallow wisdom to the plain mandates of Omnipotence.

7. *And he said unto the people.* Heb. ויאמרו *va-yomeru, and they said;* i. e. the officers acting under the general orders of Joshua. But the Masorites have indicated a doubtful reading, and the Chal., the Lat. Vulg., and most of the versions, have rendered it in the singular—'he said.' We see no reason, however, to question the correctness of the Hebrew text.

8. *Passed on before the Lord.* That is, as we suppose, before the ark of the Lord, v. 4, and ch. 3. 11.——¶ *The ark of the covenant.* The ark in which were deposited the two tables whereon the covenant was written.

9. *And the armed men.* Heb. החלוץ *hahalūtz, the armed man,* i. e. each armed man, collect. sing. for

B. C. 1451.] CHAPTER VI. 67

before the priests that blew with the trumpets, ᵉ and the rere-ward came after the ark, *the priests* going on, and blowing with the trumpets.

10 And Joshua had commanded the people, saying, Ye shall not shout, nor make any noise

ᵉ Num. 10. 25.

with your voice; neither shall *any* word proceed out of your mouth, until the day I bid you shout, then shall ye shout.

11 So the ark of the LORD compassed the city, going about it once: and they came into the camp, and lodged in the camp.

12 ¶ And Joshua rose early

---

plur.——¶ *The rere-ward.* The hinder part. The original מאסף *meassëph*, comes from אסף *asaph, to collect, to gather up*, and is equivalent to our military phrase *bringing up the rear*, and not improperly rendered in the margin, 'gathering host.' It implies a kind and protecting care towards those who are its objects. The same phraseology occurs, Is. 52. 12, 'The Lord will go before you, and the God of Israel will be your *rere-ward.*' (Heb. מאספכם *meassiphkim, your gatherer.*) Ps. 27. 10. 'When my father and my mother forsake me, then the Lord will *take me up.*' (Heb. יאספני *yaasphëni, will gather me.*) Judg. 19. 18, 'I am now going to the house of the Lord, and there is no man that *receiveth* (מאסף *meassëph*) me to house.' A rere-ward, therefore, is that portion of an army which, moving behind the main body, *gathers up* all the stragglers, takes care of any that may faint and fall by the way, sees that neither cattle nor baggage are missing, and protects or covers the rear of the host from the assault of enemies. The Jews think the division of Dan is meant, which always brought up the rear. Num. 10.

10. *Nor make any noise with your voice.* They were not only required to abstain from shouting, but to observe a profound silence in every respect. This would be expressive of a reverent awe in anticipation of the event; and would preclude all danger of mistake as to the precise time when they were required to shout. If noise of any kind had been allowed, they might have taken it for the signal of a general acclamation. This would not only have been ineffectual before the appointed time, but would have rendered them the derision of their enemies.

11. *So the ark of the Lord compassed the city.* Or, 'so he caused the ark of the Lord to compass the city.' The original will admit of this rendering, and, indeed, rather requires it, as the Hephil form of the verb (יסב *yassëb*) is no where used in an intransitive sense, excepting Ps. 140. 9. The procession undoubtedly moved at a sufficient distance to be out of the reach of the enemy's arrows, and out of the hearing of their scoffs. *They* must have looked with a very contemptuous eye upon such an unwarlike mode of assault, and when day after day passed, and no effect followed, would naturally become hardened in security, and think the whole the mere mockery of a siege, a senseless and childish parade. Thus they would cry 'peace and safety,' while sudden destruction was coming upon them. 'There was never so strange a siege as this of Jericho: here was no

in the morning, ᶠand the priests took up the ark of the Lord.

13 And seven priests bearing seven trumpets of rams' horns before the ark of the Lord went on continually, and blew with the trumpets: and the armed men went before them; but the rere-ward came after the ark of the Lord, *the priests* going on, and blowing with the trumpets.

14 And the second day they compassed the city once, and

ᶠ Deut. 31. 25.

returned into the camp. So they did six days.

15 And it came to pass on the seventh day, that they rose early about the dawning of the day, and compassed the city after the same manner seven times: only on that day they compassed the city seven times.

16 And it came to pass at the seventh time, when the priests blew with the trumpets, Joshua said unto the people, Shout; for the Lord hath given you the city.

---

mound raised, no sword drawn, no engine planted, no pioneers undermining; here were trumpets sounded, but no enemy seen; here were armed men, but no stroke given; they must walk, and not fight; seven several days must they pace about the walls, which they may not once look over to see what was within. Doubtless these inhabitants of Jericho made themselves merry with this sight. When they had stood six days on their walls, and beheld nothing but a walking enemy, "What," say they, "could Israel find no walk to breathe them with, but about our walls? Have they not travelled enough in their forty years' pilgrimage, but they must stretch their limbs in this circle? We see they are good footmen, but when shall we try their hands? Do these vain men think Jericho will be won by looking at? Or do they only come to count how many paces it is about our city? If this be their manner of siege, we shall have no great cause to fear the sword of Israel." Wicked men think God in jest when he is preparing for their judgment.' *Bp. Hall.*

15. *The seventh day—they rose early.* Because on this day they had to encompass the city seven times; a proof that the city could not have been very large, and also that the *whole* Israelitish host could not have been employed in going round it; for as the fighting men alone amounted to 600,000, independently of the mass of the people, who made a total of at least two millions more, the thing is utterly inconceivable. A select number, sufficient for the occasion, was doubtless all that were employed. It is evident that in the course of these seven days there must have been a *sabbath*. This the Jewish writers say was the last, the day on which the city was taken; but this is not certain. It is not material, however, which day it was. That God, who commanded the sabbath to be set apart for rest and religious purposes, has a right to suspend or alter the usual modes of its observance when he sees fit, and his command is sufficient to make any action lawful at any time.

16. *Shout; for the Lord hath given you the city.* As before it does not appear that the people were informed

B. C. 1451.]   CHAPTER VI.   69

17 ¶ And the city shall be ᵍ accursed, *even* it, and all that *are* therein, to the Lord : only Rahab the harlot shall live, she and all that *are* with her in the house, because ʰ she hid the messengers that we sent.

18 And ye, ⁱ in any wise keep *yourselves* from the accursed thing, lest ye make *yourselves* accursed, when ye take of the accursed thing, and make the camp of Israel a curse, ʲ and trouble it.

---

g Lev. 27. 28.   Mic. 4. 13.   h ch. 2. 4.

i Deut. 7. 26, and 13. 17.   ch. 7. 1, 11, 12.
j ch. 7. 25.   1 Kings 18. 17, 18.   Jonah 1. 12.

---

how they were to cross the Jordan till they came to the river's brink, so on this occasion Joshua seems to have forborne telling them how they were to become masters of the city, till they had compassed it six times. Their implicit obedience in this, as in the former instance, strikingly evinced their faith, which is commended by the apostle, Heb. 11. 30. 'By faith the walls of Jericho fell down after they were compassed about seven days.'

17. *And the city shall be accursed.* Heb. הָיְתָה חרם *hâyithâh 'hërem, shall be a curse, an anathema ;* i. e. devoted to utter destruction; no spoils were to be taken, no lives to be spared, except those of Rahab and her family. All was to be, if we may so say, *consecrated to a curse.* For an account of the *'hërem* or *anathema*, see on Lev. 27. 21, 28, 29. It is plain from 1 Kings, 16. 34, that Joshua spake this by Divine direction; and though to human view it may carry the aspect of undue severity, yet considered as the enactment of Him whose judgments are righteous altogether, we cannot question its perfect equity. Jericho belonged to a nation which had filled up the measure of its iniquities, and its guilt was peculiarly enhanced by reason of the amazing display of divine power which it had recently witnessed and against which it had hardened itself. It was just, therefore, that the vengeance taken should be in proportion to the light resisted. The severe judgment upon Jericho, moreover, would tend to strike terror into the hearts of the rest of the devoted nations, and make them an easier conquest.——¶ *Only Rahab shall live,* &c. The Most High never forgets his people. When he maketh inquisition for blood, he remembereth *them*, whoever else may be overlooked.——¶ *Because she hid.* The original has an extraordinary and emphatic form, implying that she *carefully and diligently hid them.*

18. *In any wise keep yourselves.* That is, by all means, most carefully, studiously, vigilantly. This city was as it were, the first fruits of Canaan, and as such wholly devoted to the Lord. The spoil of other cities, subsequently taken, was allowed to be divided among the captors, but this was to be an exception to the general rule.——¶ *And make the camp of Israel a curse.* Heb. 'put, or place the camp a curse.' The Heb. word for 'put' has often the signification of 'make, constitute, render.' The meaning is, that they would thereby render themselves obnoxious to the curse denounced upon the city.——¶ *And trouble it.* Bring distress upon it by provoking the Divine displeas-

19 But all the silver, and gold, and vessels of brass and iron, *are* consecrated unto the Lord: they shall come into the treasury of the Lord.

20 So the people shouted when *the priests* blew with the trumpets: and it came to pass, when the people heard the sound of the trumpet, and the people shouted with a great shout, that ᵏthe wall fell down flat, so that the people went up into the city, every man straight before him, and they took the city.

k ver. 5. Heb. 11. 30

---

ure, and interrupting the prosperous course of your victories. Heb. עכרתם *achartem*, from עכר *achar, to trouble.* See note on Gen. 34. 30, 31. This is spoken as if in foresight of the sin of Achan, to whom Joshua afterwards said, ch. 7. 25, 'Why hast thou *troubled* us? The Lord shall *trouble* thee this day.' From hence he is called *Achar,* or *trouble.* 1 Chron. 2. 7.

19. *All the silver and gold.* Except those portions of these metals which were formed into idols or their appendages, in respect to which the law was express, Deut. 7. 25, ' The graven images of their gods shall ye burn with fire: thou shalt not desire the silver or gold that is on them, nor take it unto thee, lest thou be snared therein; for it is an abomination to the Lord thy God.' Comp. 1 Chron. 14. 12.—¶ *Consecrated unto the Lord.* Heb. קדש ליהוה *kodesh lahovah, holiness to the Lord,* i. e. dedicated exclusively to him; being first legally purified by passing through the fire, according to the ordinance, Num. 32. 21—23.——¶ *Shall come into the treasury of the Lord.* To be employed wholly for the service of the sanctuary, and not to be appropriated in any manner to the use of any private person or priest. The place of deposit was the tabernacle of the congregation, where the spoils of the Midianites were laid up. Num. 31. 54.

20. *So the people shouted,* &c. More literally rendered from the Heb., ' So the people shouted and blew with the trumpets (i. e. the priests blew in the name of the people,) and it came to pass when the people heard the sound of the trumpets, that the people shouted with a great shout, and the wall fell down flat, and the people went up,' &c. The latter clause is merely a more detailed and exact account of what is contained in the first. Probably great numbers were killed by the falling of the wall. We are not warranted, perhaps, to speak of this event as *typical.* Nevertheless it was doubtless intended to convey most important instruction to all succeeding ages. It was peculiarly calculated to show how easily God can make a way for the accomplishment of his own purposes, and for the salvation of his people. If it did not *typify,* it certainly well *illustrates,* the victories which the gospel was to obtain over all the principalities and powers of earth and hell. No human force was to be used. Nothing but the simple announcement of the truth, and that by the instrumentality of weak and sinful men—men unlearned, unskilled in logic, and unfurnished with eloquence—was the means chosen for the destruction of

CHAPTER VI.

21 And they [1] utterly destroyed all that *was* in the city, both man and woman, young and old, and ox, and sheep, and ass, with the edge of the sword.

22 But Joshua had said unto the two men that had spied out the country, Go into the harlot's house, and bring out thence the woman and all that she hath, [m] as ye sware unto her.

23 And the young men that

[1] Deut. 7. 2.   [m] ch 2. 14. Heb. 11. 31.

---

idolatry, and the establishment of the Redeemer's kingdom over the earth. Yet how mightily has the bare sound of the gospel trumpet prevailed for the overthrow of Satan's empire in the world!'

21. *And they utterly destroyed.* Heb. יחרימו *ya'harimu, made a curse, devoted to destruction.*—— ¶ *Both man and woman, young and old,* &c. In all this the Israelites acted strictly according to their orders, Deut. 20. 16, 17, so that whatever charge of cruelty or barbarity may be brought against *them* in view of their conduct on this occasion, it strikes directly at the rectitude of the Divine judgments. That the Canaanites were a nation of incorrigible idolaters, whose morals, from the most remote periods, were polluted to the utmost degree, we have the highest authority for asserting. Had Jehovah, after bearing with such a people for no less than four centuries, sent upon them at last a famine or a pestilence, and cut them off from the face of the earth, who could deny that he had acted with perfect justice? Had he again caused fire to fall upon them from heaven, or overwhelmed them by the waters of a flood, the same admission must have been made. Why then should it be urged that he acted in opposition to any one of his known attributes, because he let loose another of his judgments upon them, namely war? For such, as far as they were affected, was really the case. The Israelites were towards them neither more nor less than instruments of punishment in the hands of the great Ruler of the universe, who chose to slay them by the edge of the sword, rather than by earthquakes, famine, or plague. Towards the Canaanites themselves, we must admit that there was great severity in the order for their extermination. But there was goodness in it, yea great goodness, towards the world at large; for it has shown the danger of unbelief and impenitence in such awful colors, that the proudest and most obdurate must tremble. If it be urged that to subject women and unoffending children to the horrors of war, is inconsistent with our ideas of Divine justice, we reply, that the very same observation might be made in the case of a plague or a deluge. In all public calamities infants are involved, and tens of thousands die in great agony every year. If God is the agent in these calamities, they must consist with the most perfect justice and goodness, and on the same ground is the present order, fearful as it was, to be vindicated.

22. *Go into the harlot's house.* Which had been miraculously preserved in the general overthrow.

23. *The young men.* These persons have all along hitherto been called simply 'men,' and no intimation given of their having been

were spies went in, and brought out Rahab, ⁿand her father, and her mother, and her brethren, and all that she had; and they brought out all her kindred, and left them without the camp of Israel.

24 And they burnt the city with fire, and all that *was* therein: °only the silver, and the gold, and the vessels of brass

and of iron, they put into the treasury of the house of the LORD.

25 And Joshua saved Rahab the harlot alive, and her father's household, and all that she had; and ᵖshe dwelleth in Israel *even* unto this day; because she hid the messengers which Joshua sent to spy out Jericho.

n ch. 2. 13.   o ver. 19.

p See Matt. 1. 5.

---

young. For an explanation of the Scriptural import of the phrase 'young men,' see Note on Gen. 14. 24.——¶ *All her kindred.* Heb. משפחותיה *mishpe'holhëyàh, all her families.*——¶ *And left them without the camp*—and made them to stay or abide, till they were cleansed from the impurities of their Gentile superstition, and prepared, by suitable instruction, for admission as proselytes into the Israelitish church.

25. *Saved alive.* Heb. החיה *hehëyàh, vivified, made to live.* The usage of the original is peculiar. It seems to imply that Rahab and her kindred were *as good as dead,* that they had *virtually* perished in the general destruction, but by being preserved through it, had had, as it were, their lives restored to them. See the Note on Pharaoh's being preserved, Ex. 9. 14-16.——¶ *Dwelleth in Israel even unto this day.* Heb. בקרב ישראל *bekereb Yisrăĕl, in the midst of Israel,* i. e. as a communicant and partaker of all the distinguishing privileges of the chosen seed. It is, however, contended by Masius and others, that this phrase implies that Rahab *lived in her posterity* in the midst of Israel, and that this clause was added by Ezra or some late reviser of the history. Rahab married Salmon, the son of Nahshon, a prince of the tribe of Judah, and thus became one of the ancestors of David and of Christ. Mat. 1. 5.——¶ *Unto this day.* A strong proof that the book was written *in or near the time* to which it refers, and in all probability by Joshua himself.——¶ *Because she hid the messengers.* This is repeated, as if the spirit of inspiration delighted to dwell on the act which redounded so signally to her credit and to her salvation. God takes pleasure in reciting the good deeds of his people.—From the various particulars recorded in the sacred narrative respecting Rahab, we may learn, (1) That there is no person so vile but that he may become an eminent saint. Would that all abandoned women in the world might hear of the mercy shown towards this harlot of Jericho! Despised and outcast as they are by their fellow-creatures, would that they knew what compassion for them exists in the bosom of God! They usually persist in their wickedness, through an utter despair of obtaining the mercy and grace which they need. But here they might see that there was hope for the vilest of the vile. (2) Faith, if gen-

B. C. 1451.] CHAPTER VI. 73

26 ¶ And Joshua adjured *them* at that time, saying, ^qCursed *be* the man before the LORD, that riseth up and buildeth this city Jericho: he shall lay the foundation thereof in his first-born, and in his youngest *son* shall he set up the gates of it.

q 1 Kings 16. 34.

uine, will uniformly produce good works. (3) Whatever we do for God or for his people, because they *are* his people, shall most assuredly be richly rewarded.

26. *Joshua adjured them.* Made them to swear, caused them to bind themselves by a solemn oath, confirmed by an imprecation upon themselves and their posterity, if they broke it, that they would never rebuild the city. This he did, not on his own responsibility, but by a Divine impulse, 1 Kings 16. 34. From the remarkable manner in which Jericho was taken and destroyed, it appears to have been the design of God to preserve such a memorial of the event, as would teach to the latest posterity, his detestation of idolatry and the vices that grow out of it. Accordingly Joshua here adjures the people by a solemn oath, and binds it upon them and their posterity, to leave the ruins of the city as a perpetual warning to after ages against the commission of those crimes. It would thus serve also as a precaution to Israel to abstain from worshiping the idol deities of the surrounding nations.——¶ *Cursed be the man before the Lord.* That is, from God's presence and by his sentence. Thus Joshua is said, ch. 18. 8, to have 'cast lots before the Lord,' i. e. as under his sanction and expecting the decision from him. This was what gave its terror to the penalty. As to what is implied in the curse of God, see on Gen. 3. 14.——¶ *That riseth up and buildeth.* That is, that attempts to build, that enters upon the work of building, that engages in it. This is often the sense of 'rise' in the sacred writers. The denunciation is here limited to the builder, and extends not to those who should *inhabit* the city after it was built, for that it was subsequently rebuilt and inhabited is evident. See below.——¶ *Shall lay the foundation thereof in his first-born,* &c. That is, shall lose all his children in the interval between laying the foundation and completing the walls; he shall, as it were, lay the first stone on the dead body of his eldest son, and the last on that of his youngest. This is said to have been fulfilled in Hiel, the Bethelite, 1 Kings 16. 34, who rebuilt Jericho in the reign of Ahaz, and 'laid the foundation thereof in Abiram, his first-born, and set up the gates thereof in his youngest son Segub.' This was 550 years after the utterance of the curse. The city does not appear, however, to have lain in ruins during the whole period from Joshua to Hiel, at least if the 'city of palm trees,' mentioned Deut. 34. 3, be, as is generally supposed, the same with Jericho, for we find this an inhabited place in the beginning of Judges, ch. 1. 16, a short time after the death of Joshua, and the same city appears to have been taken from the Israelites by Eglon, king of Moab, Judg. 3. 13. Moreover, the ambassadors of David, who were maltreated by Hanan, king of the Ammonites,

27 ʳSo the LORD was with Joshua; and ˢhis fame was *noised* throughout all the country.

CHAPTER VII.

BUT the children of Israel committed a trespass in the accursed thing: for ᵃAchan, the son of Carmi, the son of Zabdi, the son of Zerah, of the tribe of Judah, took of the accursed thing; and the anger of the LORD was kindled against the children of Israel.

ʳ ch. 1. 5.   ˢ ch. 9. 1, 3.

ᵃ ch. 22. 20.   1 Chron. 2. 6. 7.

were commanded to tarry at Jericho till their beards were grown, 2 Sam. 10. 4. 5. It appears, therefore, that there was a city which went under this name long before the time of Hiel, unless it be supposed that the 'city of palm trees' was a different place from the ancient Jericho, though standing in its neighborhood, and sometimes called by its name, which we think not improbable, especially as Josephus speaks of the site of the *old* city of Jericho, as if to distinguish it from a more modern one.

¶ 27. *The Lord was with Joshua*, &c. That is, by his powerful aid, giving him miraculous assistance, magnifying him and raising his reputation, making him acceptable to Israel, and formidable to the Canaanites. 'Nothing can more raise a man's reputation, nor make him appear more truly great, than to have the evidence of God's presence with him.' *Henry*.

CHAPTER VII.

1. *Committed a trespass.* Heb. רמעלו מעל *yimmelū maal*, had prevaricated a prevarication. The sin of an individual is imputed to the whole people. This is on the ground of the constituted oneness of social and ecclesiastical bodies. A people, properly speaking, is but one moral person. See note on ch. 1. 12. In like manner, Mat. 26. 8, it is said, that 'the disciples had indignation, saying, To what purpose is this waste?' Whereas from John, 12. 4, 5, it appears that it was Judas only who made this remark.—No man, in sinning, can be sure that the consequences will stop with himself. For aught he knows, they may affect the whole extent of his relations; and this ought to make us watchful both over ourselves and others, that we neither commit nor countenance deeds that may spread desolation over the bosom of a whole community. Ch. 22. 20, 'Did not Achan, the son of Zerah, commit a trespass on the accursed thing, and wrath fell on all the congregation of Israel?' 'So venomous is sin, especially when it lights among God's people, that one drachm of it is able to infect the whole mass of Israel.' *Bp. Hall.*——¶ *In the accursed thing.* In respect to the accursed, or devoted, thing; in taking a portion of the spoils of the city, the whole of which God had commanded to be either destroyed or dedicated to the sanctuary. Gr. καὶ ἐνοσφίσαντο ἀπὸ τοῦ ἀναθέματος, *and have set apart for themselves some of the anathema*. ——¶ *Achan, the son of Carmi.* This Achan is elsewhere called *Achar*, *trouble* or *the troubler*, undoubtedly in allusion to the effect of his conduct on this occasion. See on v. 25 and ch. 6. 18. In like manner Bethel, *house of God*, is called Bethaven, *house of vanity*, Hos. 4. 15, on account

CHAPTER VII.

2. And Joshua sent men from Jericho to Ai, which *is* beside Beth-aven, on the east side of Beth-el, and spake unto them, saying, Go up and view the country. And the men went up and viewed Ai.

3 And they returned to Joshua, and said unto him, Let not all the people go up; but let about two or three thousand men go up and smite Ai: *and* make not all the people to labor thither; for they *are but* few.

---

of the idolatry practised there. Nothing is more common in the Scriptures, than for the names of persons and places to be changed in consequence of, and in allusion to, certain remarkable events by which they may have been distinguished.—— ¶ *Son of Zabdi.* Called also Zimri, 1 Chron. 2. 6. The line of his parentage is thus recited, among other reasons, that the discredit of such a foul deed might be reflected back upon those of his ancestors who, by being remiss in their duties as parents, had been, in one sense, the procuring cause of his sin. This is not an uncommon occurrence in the sacred writings. It seems to have been with a similar design, that the genealogy of Zimri is given, Num. 25. 14. In like manner the praise of the excellence of a son redounds to the honor of the line from which he springs. A warning is hereby administered to parents, to give the most diligent heed in training their offspring in the fear of God, lest they be a reproach to their memories when they themselves are no more.

2. *Sent men from Jericho to Ai.* Called also Hai, Gen. 12. 8, and Aija, Neh. 11. 31, a city near the northern limit of the tribe of Benjamin, about ten miles north of Jerusalem, and nearly two east of Bethel. After its destruction by Joshua, it was again rebuilt by the Benjamites and inhabited by them till the captivity. Sen-

nacherib at length destroyed it, but though it was rebuilt after the Babylonish captivity, there is no vestige of it to be found at the present time. Even in the fourth century, the ruins of this city were scarcely visible. The spies sent on this occasion were not to go *into* the city, but merely into its vicinity, for the purpose of reconnoitering.—— ¶ *Beside Beth-aven* This was a city of Benjamin, about three miles north of Ai, and nearly six miles east of Bethel, which gave name to the wilderness adjoining, ch. 18. 12. It was not the place called Beth-aven, Hos. 10. 5. See on v. 1. —— ¶ *Go up and view the country.* Heb. עלו ורגלו *alu veraggelu, go up and foot the country.* So afterwards 'and viewed,' Heb. וירגלו *yeraggelu, and footed.*

3. *Let not all the people go up,* &c. The easy conquest of Jericho had probably rendered the people presumptuous. They concluded that God would of course interpose for them just as he had done before. The counsel here given was based, as it would seem, upon a culpable assurance of success in the neglect of the proper means. To confide in God was right; but to expect his aid while they neglected to use their own endeavors, was nothing short of downright presumption. So prone is human nature to extremes. The first spies that were sent out by Moses brought back the most disheartening

76   JOSHUA.   [B. C. 1451.

4 So there went up thither of the people about three thousand men: ᵇ and they fled before the men of Ai.

5 And the men of Ai smote

ᵇ Lev. 26. 17.   Deut. 28. 25.

of them about thirty and six men: for they chased them *from* before the gate *even* unto Shebarim, and smote them in the going down: wherefore ᶜ the

ᶜ ch. 2. 9, 11.   Lev. 26. 36.   Ps. 22. 14.

report. The Canaanites were invincible, and they would surely fall before them. Those sent to Ai were as much on the other extreme. Their enemies are contemptible, and they can easily carry all before them. Even Joshua himself seems to have formed his measures without taking the usual precaution of consulting God as to his duty. The result showed that they should at least have had some intimation from heaven, that a part of the force was to be dispensed with in this instance. But the truth is, they were now under the Divine displeasure; sin unrepented had interrupted the communications of God's will, and where that is the case with a people or an individual, *all goes wrong*. No one can have security that he is planning or acting right, while the light of the Lord's countenance is hidden by sin. The pledge of the Divine blessing is wanting, and he is not to be surprised if all his counsels are carried headlong. ——¶ *Make not all the people to labor thither*. That is, to labor and fatigue themselves by going thither, probably implying the ascent of a mountainous region; an advice by which they obviously consulted the ease rather than the safety or glory of the people. It is perhaps in allusion to this incident, that Solomon says, Eccles. 10. 15, 'The labor of the foolish *wearieth* every one of them, because he knoweth not how to go to the city.'—— ¶ *For they are but few*. On which

Henry well remarks, that 'few as they were, they were too many for them.' It appears from ch. 8. 25, that Joshua slew in one day, twelve thousand of the citizens of Ai, and yet the spies reported the place meanly garrisoned, and proposed to send against it only a detachment of two or three thousand!

5. *Chased them—even unto Shebarim*. Heb. השברים *hash-shebârim*, *to the breaches, breakings*, or *shiverings*; so called probably from the event, because the ranks of the Israelites were *utterly broken* and the people, panic-struck, fled in the utmost confusion.——¶ *Smote them in the going down*. That is, in the descent or declivity of the hill on which the town stood. The effect of this defeat would naturally be (1) to serve as an evidence of God's displeasure, and a solemn call upon them to humble themselves under his mighty hand, and institute a rigid self-examination to discover if possible the cause of so sad a reverse. (2) To harden the Canaanites and make them more secure than ever in their sins, prompting them to say of Israel, as the enemies of David said of him, Ps. 71. 11, 'God hath forsaken him; persecute and take him, for there is none to deliver him.' Thus their ruin, when it came, would be the more dreadful. The Christian may derive some profitable hints from this narrative as to the conduct of the warfare in which he is engaged. Notwith-

B. C. 1451.] CHAPTER VII. 77

hearts of the people melted, and became as water.

6 ¶ And Joshua ^drent his clothes, and fell to the earth upon his face before the ark of the LORD until the even-tide, he

d Gen. 37. 29, 34.

and the elders of Israel, and ^e put dust upon their heads.

7 And Joshua said, Alas! O Lord GOD, ^fwherefore hast thou at all brought this people over

e 1 Sam. 4. 12. 2 Sam. 1. 2, and 13. 19. Neh. 9. 1. Job 2. 12. f Exod. 5. 22. 2 Kings 3. 10.

standing the Canaan which he seeks is the gift of God, yet it must be obtained by a manly and continued conflict with our spiritual enemies. He must not despise any as too weak, nor fear any as too strong. As to the weak especially, he should remember that there is none so weak but he will be able to overcome us if we indulge a careless habit, or confide in an arm of flesh.——¶ *The hearts of the people melted and became as water.* That is, were utterly discouraged. Thus the very effect which was threatened to be produced on the devoted nations by the approach of the Israelites, was now in the righteous judgment of God wrought in the hearts of his own sinning people. See on Ex. 15. 15; Josh. 2. 9, 11.

6. *Joshua rent his clothes.* A usual mode, among the ancients, of expressing the highest degree of sorrow or grief. See my Illustrations of the Scriptures, p. 156. It was not so much the defeat itself as the undoubted though unknown guilty cause of it that distressed Joshua. It showed evidently that, for some reason or other, the Lord's hand was turned against them, as otherwise it would not have been possible for the enemy to have prevailed.——¶ *Until even tide.* Thus spending the whole day in fasting and prayer. We cannot but highly applaud the conduct of Joshua on this occasion. The

7*

concern he expressed for the loss of so many lives evinced a heart full of tender and generous sympathies. Common generals would have accounted the loss of thirty-six men as nothing; but the blood of Israel was precious in the sight of Joshua. We might have expected, too, that he would have blamed the spies for deceiving him in relation to the strength of the city; and have punished the soldiers for cowardice; but he viewed the hand of God, rather than of man in this disaster; and this led to what all must admire, his deep humiliation before God. But his tender regard for the honor of the Divine name was that which eminently distinguished him on this occasion; 'O Lord, what wilt thou do unto thy great name?' This was the plea which Moses had often used, and to which God had paid especial regard; and the man that feels it in his soul, and urges it in sincerity and truth, can never be ultimately foiled. ——¶ *Put dust upon their heads.* Rending the clothes, beating the breast, tearing the hair, putting dust on the head, and falling down prostrate, have always been among Eastern nations the usual marks of deep affliction and distress.

7. *Wherefore hast thou brought this people,* &c. Heb. העברת העביר *hëabartâ haabir, passing, caused to pass,* i. e. by a most stupendous miracle. This prayer of Joshua ap-

Jordan, to deliver us into the hand of the Amorites, to destroy us? would to God we had been content, and dwelt on the other side Jordan!

8 O Lord, what shall I say, when Israel turneth their backs before their enemies!

9 For the Canaanites, and all the inhabitants of the land shall

---

pears at first view to have been prompted by a murmuring, complaining spirit very much akin to that manifested by the children of Israel on several occasions, in the wilderness. Ex. 14. 11, 12; 16. 3; Num. 14. 3. Taken according to the letter it has an air of bold and rather irreverent remonstrance, which would not have been expected from the pious Captain of Israel, especially in a season of fasting and prayer, when he appears to have been most profoundly humbled. But much of this, undoubtedly, arises from the difficulty of transfusing the precise import of the original into English. The expressions 'to deliver,' 'to destroy,' according to a very common idiom, imply not the *design*, but simply the *event*. Joshua would not intimate that God had led the people into Canaan with the *express intention* of delivering them into the hands of their enemies, but he humbly inquires why he had permitted an occurrence that seemed likely to *issue in such an event*, one entirely foreign to the original purpose. Before the phrase 'would to God,' &c., the word 'and' occurs in the Hebrew, which is totally disregarded by our translators, requiring the sentence to be filled out by some such addition as this:—' to destroy us, and (to cause us to say) would to God we had been content,' &c. It is as if he should say;—' Should thy promises, O Lord God, now fail of accomplishment on account of our sin, the great miracle thou hast wrought in bringing us over Jordan would seem to be unavailing, and all thy past mercies abortive. To all human view it would have been better for us to have remained on the other side of Jordan, and *we shall be strongly prompted to wish* that that had been the case, for it will be inferred from the event, that thy sole purpose in bringing us hither, was to deliver us into the hands of the Amorites for our destruction, rather than to deliver *them* into our hands.' This we have no doubt is the real drift of Joshua's expostulation, and as nothing in the answer which God makes to him carries the air of reprehension or rebuke, we see no reason to think that any thing of the kind was merited. His words were evidently prompted by the most commendable feelings. He felt for the thousands of Israel whom he considered as abandoned to destruction. He felt, too, for the glory of God, for he knew that should Israel be destroyed, God's great name would be blasphemed among the heathen. He therefore uses an argument based perhaps on the very words of God himself, Deut. 32. 27, 'Were it not that I feared the wrath of the enemy, lest their adversaries should behave themselves strangely, and lest they should say,' &c.

8. *What shall I say*, &c. Heb. 'what shall I say after (i. e. since, or seeing that) Israel hath turned the neck before his enemies.' What construction shall I put upon it, or

B. C. 1451.] CHAPTER VII. 79

hear *of it*, and shall environ us round, and ᵍcut off our name from the earth: and ʰwhat wilt thou do unto thy great name?

10 ¶ And the LORD said unto Joshua, Get thee up; wherefore liest thou thus upon thy face?

11 ⁱIsrael hath sinned, and they have also transgressed my covenant which I commanded them: ᵏfor they have even taken of the accursed thing, and have also stolen, and ˡdissembled also, and

g Ps. 83. 4. h See Ex. 32. 12. Num. 14. 13.   i ver. 1. k ch. 6..17, 18. l See Acts 5. 1, 2.

how shall I answer the reproaches and taunts of thine enemies, when Israel, thine own people, for whom thou hast done such great things, and to whom thou hast made such glorious promises, when *they* turn their backs in ignoble flight before their enemies! He speaks as one at a loss what to think of the unhappy event that had just occurred; as if nothing more strange or marvellous *could* have happened than the defeat of the chosen people.

9. *What wilt thou do to thy great name?* i. e., What wilt thou do *in respect to* thy great name? How wilt thou preserve its glory unstained when such a flood of obloquy shall be poured upon it by the scoffing heathen? The cutting off of our name, though that would vastly disparage thy power and faithfulness, yet that is a matter of less consequence; but, O Lord, how wilt thou consult the honor of thine own blessed and glorious name, were such an advantage to be given to the adversary? Comp. Ex. 32. 12; Num. 14. 13; Joel 2. 27.

10. *Get thee up.* Heb. לך קם *kūm lak, rise, or stand up for thyself.*—— ¶ *Wherefore liest thou thus upon thy face?* Heb. 'wherefore this, (that) thou art falling down upon thy face?' i. e. continuing to fall, doing it again and again. Not the language of rebuke, as though God were displeased with Joshua for prostrating himself

in this humble posture, and bemoaning in bitterness of soul the disaster that had befallen Israel; but merely implying that it was now enough; that God would not have him any longer continue that mournful posture; that he had other work to do than to spend time in grieving and afflicting himself in view of what was past; that he must arise and set about discovering the accursed thing, and casting it out; in a word that he must lay aside his mourning weeds, and enter upon that which was especially and pre-eminently at present incumbent upon him. 'For every thing there is a season, and it behoves us to see that the time is not spent in empty lamentation which God would have devoted to vigorous action in reforming what is amiss.' *Henry.*

11. *Israel hath sinned.* For a view of the reason why this is spoken of as the act of the whole body of Israel, see Note on v. 1.——¶ *Have also transgressed my covenant.* That is, have broken the conditions of the covenant or agreement of *general* obedience into which they had before entered, Ex. 19. 8; 24. 7; or, have transgressed the *particular* precept relative to the accursed thing, ch. 6. 19. Covenant, in the Scriptures, often has the sense of command, precept, ordinance.——¶ *Have also stolen.* Have sacrilegiously taken and appropriated to their own use the por-

80   JOSHUA.   [B. C. 1451.

they have put *it* even among their own stuff.

12 ᵐTherefore the children of Israel could not stand before their enemies, *but* turned *their* backs before their enemies, because ⁿthey were accursed: neither will I be with you any more, except ye destroy the accursed from among you.

13 Up, °sanctify the people,

ᵐ See Num. 14. 45. Judg. 2. 14. ⁿ Deut. 7. 26. ch. 6. 18. ° Exod. 19. 10.

and say, ᵖSanctify yourselves against to-morrow: for thus saith the Lord God of Israel, *There is* an accursed thing in the midst of thee, O Israel: thou canst not stand before thine enemies, until ye take away the accursed thing from among you.

14 In the morning therefore ye shall be brought according to your tribes: and it shall be, *that* the tribe which ᑫthe Lord

ᵖ ch. 3. 5. ᑫ Prov. 16. 33.

---

tion which I had reserved to myself, and ordered to be brought into the treasury.——¶ *And dissembled also.* Have covered the deed with deep dissimulation; instead of ingenuously confessing the sin and imploring pardon, have studiously endeavored to hide it, as if by concealing it from their brethren they had concealed it from me also. The crime is recited with the utmost particularity, in order that its various aggravations may he more impressively set forth. ——¶ *Have put it even among their own stuff.* Among their own goods.

12. *Because they were accursed.* In exact accordance with the threatening before denounced against them, ch. 6. 18. Joshua was thus informed that this, and nothing else, was the ground of the controversy which God now had with his people. They had, by their iniquity, put themselves out of the range of his protection and blessing, and unless summary punishment was executed upon the offender, they would transfer upon themselves the very curse denounced against their adversaries.——¶ *Except ye destroy the accursed.* The accursed person with all that pertains to him, v. 24.

13. *Up, sanctify the people.* That is, command and see that they sanctify themselves. Cause them to purify their persons by legal washings, but more especially to put themselves into a suitable frame of mind to appear before God, and submit to the Divine scrutiny. Although the act of Achan had been perpetrated with so much caution that it was unperceived by any human being, yet the eye of God had been upon it, and he declared to Joshua the true reason of his displeasure, and of Israel's defeat. But, though he revealed *the fact*, he did not name *the person* that had committed it, but left that to be discovered in a way more impressive to the nation, and more merciful to the offender, inasmuch as it gave him time for repentance and voluntary acknowledgment.——¶ *There is an accursed thing,* &c. The crime of sacrilege has been committed in the midst of thee, O Israel.

14. *Ye shall be brought.* Heb. נקרבתם *nikrabtem, ye shall come near.* i. e. to the tabernacle, or to the ark, wherever that might now be deposited. Persons deputed from each tribe, to represent it, shall successively come to appear before me, and re-

B. C. 1451.] CHAPTER VII. 81

taketh shall come according to the families *thereof;* and the family which the LORD shall take shall come by households; and the household which the LORD shall take shall come man by man.

15 ʳAnd it shall be, *that* he that is taken with the accursed thing shall be burnt with fire,

ʳ See 1 Sam. 14. 38, 39.

he and all that he hath: because he hath ˢtransgressed the covenant of the LORD, and because he ᵗhath wrought folly in Israel.

16 ¶ So Joshua rose up early in the morning, and brought Israel by their tribes; and the tribe of Judah was taken:

17 And he brought the family

ˢ ver. 11. ᵗ Gen. 34. 7. Judg. 20. 6.

---

ceive my orders.——¶ *The tribe which the Lord taketh.* That is, the tribe which shall be discovered or declared guilty by the lot. The tribe thus indicated is said to be 'taken by the Lord,' because the lot was disposed of by him, according to Prov. 16. 33; the transaction was specially overruled by him in his mysterious providence for the detection of the guilty. Of the sacred use of lots, see 1 Sam. 10. 20, 21; 14. 41, 42; Acts 1. 24, 26. The original for 'take' has the import of *arresting, seizing*, being the appropriate term for the *apprehension* of criminals.

15. *He that is taken with the accursed thing.* Heb. בחרם *ba'herem, in the accursed thing.* That is, he that is divinely pointed out as being involved in the guilt of the accursed thing.——¶ *Shall be burnt with fire.* The doom expressly appointed for persons or things accursed, Deut. 13. 15, 16. In addition to this, and previously to it, the culprit, as appears from v. 25, was to be stoned to death at the hands of the congregation. This was the punishment ordained for blasphemers and presumptuous offenders, Num. 15. 30, 35. We do read that Achan *verbally* blasphemed, but all high-handed, deliberate transgression is *virtual* blasphemy, and is

so regarded in the judgment of heaven.——¶ *He and all that he hath.* His sons, daughters, cattle and goods, &c., all being in the Divine estimation, in consequence of their connexion with him, considered as infected with the taint of his guilt, and therefore exposed to share with him in his condemnation. This may appear to human view a severe, if not an unjust sentence, but we can only say it is in strict accordance with the general analogy of God's providence in this world, and as such is to be unhesitatingly acknowledged as bearing the impress of perfect equity and justice.——¶ *Hath wrought folly in Israel.* That is, a base, foolish and sinful deed, such as every wise and well principled man would utterly condemn. In this sense the term 'folly' frequently occurs. See Gen. 34. 7; Deut. 32. 21; 2 Sam. 13. 12. It was a conduct that brought shame and disgrace upon a nation, sustaining the reputation of a wise and understanding people.

17. *And he brought the family of Judah.* That is, the several families, the collection of families, collect. sing. for plur.——¶ *He brought the family of the Zarhites, man by man.* It was ordered, v. 14, that all Israel should come near by tribes, and one

of Judah; and he took the family of the Zarhites; and he brought the family of the Zarhites man by man; and Zabdi was taken:

18 And he brought his household man by man; and Achan the son of Carmi, the son of Zabdi, the son of Zerah, of the tribe of Judah, ᵘwas taken.

19 And Joshua said unto Achan, My son, ˣgive, I pray

u 1 Sam. 14. 42. x See 1 Sam. 6. 5. Jer. 13. 16. John 9. 24.

---

tribe was to be fixed on; then that tribe came by its families, and one family was fixed on; then came that family by its households; and one household was fixed on; and finally that household coming man by man, one man was fixed on. In the present passage there appears to be some confusion in this prescribed order of selection. In speaking of Zarhi the phrase 'by households' is left out, and 'man by man' expressed twice. The probability is that a slight error has crept into the original text; instead of לגברים *laggebârim, man by man*, v. 17, the true word is undoubtedly לבתים *lebottim, by households*, and this reading, according to Kennicott, is preserved in six Hebrew copies, and in the Syriac version.— The Israelites are summoned before the Lord, and the hour of recompense is at hand. The lots are gone forth. At first Achan might stand enwrapped in security, and little fearful that among the mighty multitude assembled around him, he alone should be detected; but this groundless confidence could not long abide. The tribe of Judah, to which he belonged, is taken; and the probabilities of discovery are vastly increased. Some rising fear begins to struggle with his self-possession, and now his heart throbs with a quicker and louder alarm; for the family of the Zarhites, of which he was a member, is selected, as containing the guilty man.

That family comes now by its households, and lo, the household of Zabdi is taken. Whither now shall Achan flee, and where is the hope of concealment with which he lulled his soul to sleep in its guilt and crime? The family of Zabdi advances, and the last lots are given forth; and behold, Achan, the son of Carmi, is found and stands among the many thousands of Israel, pointed out by the unerring finger of God, as the man who had taken the accursed thing, and made himself a curse by this presumptuous act of sacrilege.— 'We may well imagine how Achan's countenance changed, and what horror and confusion seized him, when he was singled out as the delinquent, when the eyes of all Israel were fastened upon him, and every one was ready to say, Have we found thee, O our enemy!' *Henry.*

19. *And Joshua said unto Achan, My son.* Adopting this affectionate style of address to show that the present severe proceedings against him were not prompted by any personal ill will, or an angry spirit of revenge. Though he was obliged to *act* as a magistrate, yet he was willing Achan should know that he *felt* as a father, and in so doing proposed a noble example to all who have the administration of justice, 'not to insult over those who are in misery, though they may have brought themselves into it by their own wickedness, but to treat

CHAPTER VII.

thee, glory to the LORD God of Israel, [y] and make confession unto him; and [z] tell me now what thou hast done, hide *it* not from me.

[y] Numb. 5. 6, 7. 2 Chron. 30. 22. Ps. 51. 3. Dan. 9. 4. [z] 1 Sam. 14 43

20 And Achan answered Joshua, and said, Indeed I have sinned against the LORD God of Israel, and thus and thus have I done.

21 When I saw among the

---

even offenders with the spirit of meekness, not knowing what we ourselves should have done, if God had put us into the hand of our own counsels. *Henry.*——¶ *Give glory to the Lord God of Israel.* Heb. שים כבוד *sim kâbod, put, appoint, ordain, glory* to the Lord God. That is, by confessing the truth, by honestly pleading guilty to the charge, by ingenuously acknowledging the sin and the justice of the punishment which it incurred. By so doing he would not only ascribe to God the glory of his omniscience, from which no secrets are hid, in detecting and exposing the crime, but also of his justice in punishing it. He would in fact thereby most effectually give him the praise of all his perfections, and consult the best interests of his soul in the world to come. It appears from a similar usage in several other instances, that God regards the *confession of the truth* as very intimately connected with *giving him glory*. 2 Chron. 30. 8. Thus, Luke 23. 47, ' Now when the centurion saw what was done, he *glorified* God (i. e. gave him glory), saying, certainly this was a righteous man.' John 9. 24, ' Then again called they the man that was blind, and said unto him, *Give God the praise;* we know that this man is a sinner;' on which passage Mr. Barnes remarks, ' The meaning here is not, " give God the praise for *healing* you," but *confess* that you have declared to us a falsehood; and that you have endeavored to impose on us; and by thus confessing your sin give praise and honor to God, who condemns all imposture and falsehood; and whom you will thus acknowledge to be *right* in your condemnation.' Nothing should be more deeply impressed upon the mind of the sinner, than that the humble and penitent confession of guilt tends directly to the glory of God, and that withholding confession is robbing him of his right, as well as incurring his displeasure.——¶ *Tell me now what thou hast done.* The testimony of God would have been sufficient, who could neither deceive nor be deceived. Joshua also, who was now knowing to his crime, might have *declared* it, but he could not *prove* it; and as it was intended that the offender should be made a public monument of justice, and be held up as a warning to the whole nation, it was desirable that the most indisputable evidence of his guilt should be adduced. He is made therefore himself to supply a testimony which none could controvert or doubt; even to bear witness against himself. Joshua requires this confession to be made to him, because he stood, both to Achan and to the people, in God's stead. It was in effect the same, therefore, as making it to God himself.

20. *Indeed I have sinned,* &c. The confession, though not made till it was extorted, was finally made with great frankness and ingenuousness.

spoils a goodly Babylonish garment, and two hundred shekels of silver, and a wedge of gold of fifty shekels weight, then I coveted them, and took them, and behold, they *are* hid in the earth in the midst of my tent, and the silver under it.

He recites the circumstances of the act in all their particulars, and with all their aggravations; attempts no excuse or extenuation; complains not of the severity of the sentence, nor seeks to prevent or delay its execution; from which we may indulge the *hope*, however feeble, that the poor culprit found mercy for his soul.

21. *A goodly Babylonish garment.* Heb. אדרת שנער *addereth Shinar, a splendid or costly robe of Shinar*, rendered 'Babylonish garment,' because Babylon or Babel was situated in the plain of Shinar. Bochart and Calmet have shown at large that Babylonish robes were very splendid and in high repute. Ezek. 23. 15. Josephus calls it 'a royal garment woven entirely of gold.' The word signifies such a robe or mantle as princes wore when they appeared in state, Jon. 3. 6, and this probably belonged to the king of Jericho.——¶ *Two hundred shekels of silver.* In weight, not in coin. Its value in our currency was a little upwards of one hundred dollars.——¶ *A wedge of gold.* Heb. לשון זהב *leshōn zahab, a tongue of gold*, i. e. what we understand by an *ingot of gold*, a corruption, according to A. Clarke, of the word *lingot*, from the Lat. *lingula*, signifying a *little tongue*.——¶ *I coveted them and took them.* The three words occurring in this narrative, 'I saw—I coveted—I took,' strikingly express the rise, progress, and consummation of crime. The whole process is here laid open. The inward corruption of the heart is first drawn forth by some enticing object. The desire of gratification is then formed, and the determination to attain it fixed. Then comes the act itself, followed by its bitter and fearful consequences. In this instance the temptation entered by the eye; he *saw* those fine things as Eve saw the forbidden fruit; and he allowed his eyes to gaze and feast upon the interdicted objects. The sight inflamed his desire; and he *coveted* them. The next step was to carry out the feeling into act; the desire prompted him to *take* them, as he actually did, and thus accomplished the fearful deed. So naturally does lust, when it hath conceived, bring forth sin, and sin when finished bringeth forth death. The only way to avoid sin in action is to quench its incipient workings in the heart, to mortify sinful desires, especially the desire of worldly wealth, the source of such untold evils in the world. We are ever in this world surrounded by incitements to sin, but we are to pass in the midst of them, like the Israelites among the spoils of Jericho, under the abiding impression that the interdict of Heaven is upon the least forbidden indulgence. And as the eye is the great inlet to that mischief which works upon the heart, our only safety is in making, with Job, a covenant with our eyes, and continually uttering the prayer of David, 'Turn away mine eyes from beholding vanity, and quicken me in thy way.'—— ¶ *And the silver under it.* That is, under the Babylonish garment; cov-

22 ¶ So Joshua sent messengers, and they ran unto the tent, and behold, it *was* hid in his tent, and the silver under it.

23 And they took them out of the midst of the tent, and brought them unto Joshua, and unto all the children of Israel, and laid them out before the LORD.

24 And Joshua, and all Israel with him, took Achan the son of Zerah, and the silver, and the garment, and the wedge of gold, and his sons, and his daughters,

---

ered with it, concealed by it, or wrapped up in it.

22. *So Joshua sent messengers.* To put to the test the truth of his confession.——¶ *And they ran unto the tent.* Ran, not only to show their alacrity in obeying Joshua's orders, but to show also how uneasy they were till the camp was cleared of the accursed thing, and the Divine favor regained. ——¶ *It was hid.* That is, the parcel of things mentioned v. 21, 24.

23. *Laid them out before the Lord.* Heb. רצקום לפני יהוה *yatzikūm liphnë Yehovah, poured them out before the Lord.* That is, before the ark of the covenant, the hallowed sign of the Lord's presence, where Joshua and the elders were awaiting the issue of the transaction.

24. *And his sons and his daughters.* As no intimation is given that Achan's sons or any of his family were accessary to his crime, we are not warranted, perhaps, in supposing that they were now condemned to suffer on that account; although it may be admitted that he could not very easily have concealed the articles in the midst of the tent without some of its inmates being privy to it. But the supposition of their guilt we do not deem necessary to vindicate the equity and justice of the sentence. As all lives are really forfeited by sin; as the ungodly deserve worse punishment than temporal death, and as God, the supreme arbiter of life and death, may exact the debt which all owe in any way or time that seemeth to him good, we know not who can question the righteousness of his judgment on this occasion. If evil, no injustice would be done them, and if good, they would the sooner be taken to their reward; and we can easily conceive that the death of a few persons at this particular juncture, and under the solemn circumstances in which they now stood, might be attended with the happiest results. They were now in the commencement of their national existence in Canaan. It was necessary that the people should know, by a fresh demonstration, what a God they had to do with. Whilst they learned from his mercies how greatly he was to be loved, they needed also to learn from his judgments how greatly he was to be feared. This lesson would be effectually taught them by the present act of severity, and the death of a single individual might, by its admonitory influence, be the means of afterwards preventing the death of many thousands.——¶ *His oxen, and his asses, and his sheep.* Brute beasts are of course incapable of sin and so of punishment, properly so called, but as they are made for man's use, and are daily killed for food, there seems no impropriety in taking away their lives for *moral* purposes, to show us more impressively the destructive

and his oxen, and his asses, and his sheep, and his tent, and all that he had: and they brought them unto ᵃ the valley of Achor. 25 And Joshua said ᵇ Why hast thou troubled us? the LORD shall trouble thee this day. ᶜ And all Israel stoned him with stones, and burned them with fire, after they had stoned them with stones.

ᵃ ver. 26. ch. 15. 7. ᵇ ch. 6. 18. 1 Chron. 2. 7. Gal. 5. 12.
ᶜ Deut. 17. 5.

and detestable nature of sin. The truth is, the animal world being originally formed for the service of man, is to be considered as a kind of *appendage* to him and so is made to share in his lot, whether of weal or wo. On this principle the earth with its various tribes felt the effects of the curse when Adam sinned, and the whole creation has groaned in bondage ever since. Occurrences like that mentioned in the text are merely illustrations of this general law.——
¶ *And they brought them unto the valley of Achor.* Heb. ויעלו *vayaalū*, *brought them up*, *made them go up or ascend.* Persons are generally said to *descend* to a valley, but the phraseology here is probably founded on the relative situation of the valley and the camp. In going to it they may have been obliged to travel some distance over the hilly country, towards the interior. This would be *ascending* from the Jordan, and that such was the fact is to be inferred from ch. 15. 7. The valley is called Achor by anticipation. It was so named from the event.

25. *Why hast thou troubled us? the Lord shall trouble thee this day.* This is said in allusion to the words of the warning, ch. 4. 18, 'Lest ye make the camp of Israel a curse and *trouble* it.' From this circumstance his name *Achan* seems to have been changed to *Achar*, *trouble*, i. e. *troubler*.

1 Chron. 2. 7. See on ch. 6. 18. How strikingly did Achan's conduct verify the saying of Solomon, Prov. 15. 27, 'He that is greedy of gain *troubleth* his own house;' and how clear from this instance, is it that sin is a very *troublesome*, as well as a very wicked thing, and that not only to the sinner himself, but to all around him. When Ahab met Elijah, he cried, in the consciousness of his own offences, 'Art thou he that *troubleth* Israel?' 'I have not *troubled* Israel,' answered the indignant prophet, 'but thou and thy father's house, in that ye have forsaken the commandments of the Lord.' Such was virtually the language of Joshua to Achan on this occasion.—— ¶ *And all Israel stoned him with stones.* The burning therefore commanded, v. 15, must have reference to the dead body. He was first stoned, and his carcase then consigned to the flames, himself and all his sharing the same fate. 'He perished not alone in his iniquity.' The punishment is said to have been executed by 'all Israel,' not because every individual without exception had a hand in it, but because all were present as spectators, all were consenting to the act, and as many as could be were active agents in it in the name of the rest. This showed the universal detestation of the deed, and their anxiety to avert from them the Divine displeasure.

26 And they ^d raised over him a great heap of stones unto this day. So ^e the LORD turned from the fierceness of his anger: wherefore the name of that place was called, ^f The valley of Achor, unto this day.

^d ch. 8. 29.   2 Sam. 18. 17.   Lam. 3. 53.
^e Deut. 13. 17.   2 Sam. 21, 14.

^f ver. 24.   Isai. 65. 10.   Hos. 2. 15.

26. *Raised over him a great heap of stones.* As a monument to perpetuate the memory of this transaction, and to serve as a warning to all future generations to beware of presumptuous sin. The burying place of Absalom was distinguished by a similar erection, as a monument of his disgrace to future ages. 2 Sam. 18. 17.——¶ *Unto this day.* That is, that remaineth unto this day. In a parallel passage, ch. 8. 29, the supplementary words 'that remaineth' are inserted in the text.——¶ *Was called the valley of Achor.* Or, Heb. עמק עכור *ēmak akōr, the valley of trouble,* from the event. In Hos. 2. 15, the valley of Achor is said to be given to Israel as a 'door of hope,' in allusion to the transaction that now occurred here, and implying, perhaps, that when they had repented and put away the accursed thing, then there would begin to be a door of hope concerning them, and that the very places, which had before been the scenes of *troublesome* judgments and the memorials of wrath, should henceforth become only the mementos of the most signal mercies. Compare Ezra 10. 2. Where sin is seen and lamented, and decisive steps taken towards reformation, there are tokens for good, and even gross offenders may receive encouragement. God is always pleased to have the monuments of his displeasure converted, by the conversion of sinners, into the remembrancers of kindness.—From the foregoing narrative we may deduce the following reflections.

(1) The deceitfulness of sin. Achan, at first, had in mind only the satisfaction he should feel in possessing the Babylonish garment and the wedge and shekels of gold and silver. The ideas of shame and remorse and misery were hid from him. But ah! with what different thoughts did he contemplate his gains, when inquisition was made to discover the offender! How would he begin to tremble when he saw that his own *tribe* was selected as containing the guilty person! How would his terror be increased when he saw his own *family* pointed out! and what dread would seize upon him when the lot fell upon his *household!* What a paleness would spread over his cheeks, and what a trembling would take hold of his limbs! What now becomes of all his expected enjoyments? What beauty does he now see in the splendid garment, or what value in the shining metals? Ah! could he but recall the act, which has thus brought him to shame and ruin! But it is too late! The deed is done, and the sense of guilt, as with the fangs of a serpent, has fastened itself upon his inmost spirit! Thus too with the transgressor of every name. The thief, the adulterer, the seducer, in the commission of crime, thinks only of the pleasure the gratification of his lusts will afford. But he has no sooner attained his object than his before blinded eyes are opened, and

CHAPTER VIII.

AND the Lord said unto Joshua,ª Fear not, neither be thou dismayed: take all the people of war with thee, and arise, go up to Ai: see, ᵇI have

a Deut. 1. 21, and 7. 18, and 31. 8. ch. 1. 9.   b ch. 6, 2.

the enormity of his sin stares him full in the face. Then he finds that it stings like a serpent and bites like an adder.

(2) *The certainty of its exposure.* Achan took great precautions to conceal his iniquity, but it was unavailing. Men may hide their wickedness from their fellow men, but not from God. His providence will sooner or later bring the hidden iniquity to the light, and for the most part in this world. But certainly in the great day of the revelation of all things. To every sinner therefore may the solemn warning be addressed, 'Be sure your sin will find you out.'

(3) *The awfulness of its reward.* Who does not shudder at the thought of that vengeance which was executed on Achan and his family? Who does not see how fierce the indignation of God against sin was, when the sin of one single person prevailed more to provoke him against the whole nation, than the innocence of the whole did to pacify his wrath against the individual; when in fact nothing but the most signal punishment of the individual could reconcile him to the nation to which he belonged? Yet was all this but a faint shadow of the indignation which he will manifest in a future world. We should profit from such a history as this. We should learn to dread the displeasure of the Almighty, and to glorify him now by an ingenuous confession, that he may not be glorified hereafter in our eternal condemnation.

CHAPTER VIII.

1. *Fear not, neither be thou dismayed.* The sin of Achan and its consequences had probably weighed deeply on the spirits of Joshua, grieving and discouraging him, so as to render this renewed exhortation peculiarly seasonable at this time. When we have faithfully put away the sin that separated between God and us, we may confidently expect the light of his countenance to be restored to us, and that he will animate us with such encouragements as shall banish the fear of our most formidable enemies.──¶ *Take all the people of war with thee.* This can hardly be understood of the whole number of men of war in the congregation, which amounted to upwards of six hundred thousand. It is more probable that by 'all the people of war' is to be understood the thirty thousand men mentioned v. 3, the choicest part, the flower of the host, those who were most experienced in warlike affairs. The main body of the soldiery remained in the camp at Gilgal.──¶ *I have given.* I have purposed to give. The event is certain, that they shall be delivered into your power.──¶ *And his land.* That is, the territory immediately adjoining the city, and under the jurisdiction of the king.

2. *Thou shalt do to Ai and her king as thou didst unto Jericho and her king.* That is, in general, in the main, not in every particular. Ai was to be overcome and destroyed, and in this respect its fate was to re-

[B. C. 1451.] CHAPTER VIII. 89

given into thy hand the king of Ai, and his people, and his city, and his land.

2 And thou shalt do to Ai and her king, as thou didst unto ^cJericho and her king; only ^dthe spoil thereof, and the cattle thereof, shall ye take for a prey unto yourselves: lay thee an ambush for the city behind it.

3 ¶ So Joshua arose, and all the people of war, to go up against Ai: and Joshua chose out thirty thousand mighty men of valor, and sent them away by night.

c ch. 6. 21. d Deut. 20. 14.

semble that of Jericho. But the precise manner of its destruction was not the same; the king of Ai was not to be put to death by the sword, as the king of Jericho had been, nor was a curse denounced against him that should rebuild Ai, as was the case in regard to Jericho.——¶ *Only the spoil thereof—shall ye take to yourselves.* This was the grand point of difference in the prescribed manner of treating the two cities. In the one case, the spoil was granted to the people; in the other not. There was, therefore, no danger of their committing the same trespass here that they had there. 'Observe how Achan, who catched at forbidden spoil, lost that, and life, and all; but the rest of the people, who had conscientiously refrained from the accursed thing, were quickly recompensed for their obedience with the spoil of Ai. The way to have the comfort of what God allows, is, to forbear what he forbids us. No man shall lose by his self-denial.' *Henry.*——¶*Lay thee an ambush for the city behind it.* That is, on the west side of the city, as the Israelites, at the time of receiving this command, were on the east side of it, and the orientals, in designating the relative position of places, were always supposed to face the east. This stratagem is to be justified on the ground that God commanded it, and it is obvious that if it was right for them to overpower their enemies, it was equally right to out-wit them, if they could do it. 'No treaties were violated, no oaths broken, no falsehoods uttered; and it cannot be requisite to inform our enemies of our intentions and purposes, however they may be deceived by appearances. But perjuries, lies, and infractions of treaties cannot, in any war or in any case, be allowable or excusable.' *Scott.*

3. *So Joshua arose to go up against Ai.* That is, set about the business of going up, took measures preparatory to it, consulted and laid the plan of operations. It does not express the fact of their actually marching towards Ai, for this is inconsistent with what follows, but according to a familiar idiom of the Hebrew, on which we have remarked before, ch. 6. 25, merely implies their *entering upon the preliminary measures.* 'To arise,' in innumerable instances in the scriptures, means nothing more than *to address one's self to a particular business, to set about it, to engage in it.*——¶ *Chose out thirty thousand mighty men.* The whole number of men to be employed on this occasion. ——¶ *And sent them away by night.* That is, as we suppose, not the whole of the thirty thousand, but the party of five thousand expressly mentioned

8*

90   JOSHUA.   [B. C. 1451.

4 And he commanded them, saying, Behold ye shall lie in wait against the city, *even* behind the city: go not very far from the city, but be ye all ready:

5 And I, and all the people that *are* with me, will approach unto the city: and it shall come to pass when they come out against us, as at the first, that ᶠwe will flee before them,

6 (For they will come out after us) till we have drawn them from the city; for they will say, They flee before us, as at the first: therefore we will flee before them.

7 Then ye shall rise up from the ambush, and seize upon the city: for the Lord your God will deliver it into your hand.

8 And it shall be when ye have taken the city, *that* ye shall set the city on fire: according to the commandment of the Lord shall ye do. ᵍSee, I have commanded you.

9 ¶ Joshua therefore sent them forth; and they went to lie in ambush, and abode between

e Judg. 20. 29.   f Judg. 20. 32.   g 2 Sam. 13 28.

---

v. 12. The next verse, as well as v. 9, seems to limit it to those who were 'to lie in wait,' and these were unquestionably the five thousand, and not the whole detachment specified above, who could not well have executed such a design without being discovered. It is true that, according to this interpretation, we must suppose the pronoun 'them' to be put before its antecedent, which is left to be inferred from the tenor of the ensuing narrative, but this is no unusual thing with the sacred writers. See Ex. 14. 19; Ps. 87 1; 105. 19; Prov. 7. 8. On any other mode of construction it is extremely difficult to make out a consistent narration of the facts, unless it be supposed that the verbs here should be rendered 'had chosen,' and 'had sent,' and the entire portion, from this place to the end of v. 9, be taken as a parenthesis, which is not improbable. The reasons for sending an ambuscade *by night* are too obvious to require remark.

4. *And he commanded them.* That is, the party of 5,000 just spoken of as sent away by night.

5. *All the people that are with me.* That is, the 25,000 remaining after the 5,000 were sent away, and whom he kept for a lure to draw out the inhabitants of Ai from the city.——
¶ *As at the first.* As on the former expedition, when Israel was so sadly worsted.

6. *Till we have drawn them.* Heb. הֲתִיקֵנוּ *hattikēnū, till we have pulled, or plucked them.*

7. *Then shall ye rise up from the ambush.* Upon the signal given, v. 18.

8. *Ye shall set the city on fire.* Probably this means no more than that they should kindle a fire in the city, the smoke of which should be an indication that they had taken it. Had they set fire to the whole city, the spoils which were to be divided among the people, would have been all consumed. It appears, moreover, from v. 28, that the city was not burnt till afterwards.

9. *Joshua therefore sent them forth.* That is, the detachment of five thou-

CHAPTER VIII.

Beth-el and Ai, on the west side of Ai: but Joshua lodged that night among the people.

10 And Joshua rose up early in the morning, and numbered the people, and went up, he and the elders of Israel, before the people to Ai.

11 ʰ And all the people, *even the people* of war that *were* with him, went up, and drew nigh, and came before the city, and pitched on the north side of Ai: now *there was* a valley between them and Ai.

12 And he took about five thousand men, and set them to lie in ambush between Beth-el and Ai, on the west side of the city.

13 And when they had set the people, *even* all the host that *was* on the north of the city, and their liers in wait on the west of the city, Joshua went that night into the midst of the valley.

h ver. 5.

---

sand spoken of above, and designated by the pronoun 'them,' v. 3.—— ¶ *Joshua lodged that night among the people.* That is, the people of war, as they are called, v. 11, or in other words the 25,000. Others suppose the night was spent at the camp at Gilgal, with the main body of the people. But this is less likely.

10. *Numbered the people.* Or, Heb. ויפקד *va-yiphkōd, visited, inspected, mustered, set in order.* This again probably means the band of 25,000, whom he carefully reviewed to see that they were in perfect readiness, and that none had withdrawn themselves during the darkness of the night preceding. It would thus also appear more clearly when the work was done, that it was effected without any loss of men, whereby a new ground of encouragement and confidence in God would be afforded. ——¶ *He and the elders of Israel.* As a kind of council of war, to give more weight and solemnity to the proceeding, and to see to the just and equal distribution of the spoil. The elders were usually associated with the leader in every important measure that concerned the interests of the people.

12. *And he took about five thousand men.* Rather, 'he had taken.' The verse is apparently thrown in as a parenthesis, with a view to give a more particular explanation of what is said, in a general way, v. 3, 9. Incidents omitted in their proper place are often brought in, in this manner, in order to prevent the interruption of the previous narrative.

13. *Their liers in wait.* Heb. 'their lying in wait, their ambuscade,' abst. for concrete. Or it may be rendered 'their heel,' i. e. the hinder part of the army, referring to the party that lay in ambush.—— ¶ *Went that night into the midst of the valley.* That is, as is most likely, very early in· the morning, when it was yet dark, as John 20. 1. It seems hardly probable, that when every thing was ready they should have remained inactive during a whole day. We prefer the opinion that Joshua, having sent away the five thousand in the evening of the previous day, and having taken a few hours' sleep with the 25,000, rose

14 ¶ And it came to pass when the king of Ai saw *it*, that they hasted and rose up early, and the men of the city went out against Israel to battle, he and all his people, at a time appointed, before the plain: but he ⁱwist not that *there were* liers in ambush against him behind the city.

15 And Joshua and all Israel

ᵏmade as if they were beaten before them, and fled by the way of the wilderness.

16 And all the people that *were* in Ai were called together to pursue after them: and they pursued after Joshua, and were drawn away from the city.

17 And there was not a man left in Ai, or Beth-el, that went not out after Israel: and they

---

i Judg. 20. 34. Eccles. 9. 12.

k Judg. 20. 36, &c.

---

at a very early hour, perhaps a little after midnight, and had them inspected, which might be speedily done by the aid of the officers, and then went, at so early an hour that it might still be called night, into the valley, perhaps alone, to supplicate God for a blessing on the enterprise in which he was now engaged, and which had come so near to its crisis; or, it may imply that at this time he led the army *through the valley*, and when the day dawned appeared in full view of the city, from whence the king and people immediately sallied out in pursuit.

14. *When the king of Ai saw it, they hasted and rose up early.* That is, when the king *was informed* of it, by the city guards, an alarm was immediately given, and the citizens who had not yet risen hurried from their beds, and soon commenced the pursuit. 'To see,' in scripture usage, often has the sense of *to know, to learn, to understand.*——¶ *He and all his people.* That is, all the men of war; for the rest, the old men, the women, and children, remained in the city, as appears, v. 24.——¶ *At a time appointed.* Heb. מוֹעֵד *moëd,* either an *appointed time,* or a *concerted signal,* as the same word is

rendered where it occurs in Judg. 20. 38.

15. *Made as if they were beaten.* Turned their backs. Heb. וַיִּנָּגְעוּ *yinnâgeû, were beaten or smitten;* but rightly understood, as here rendered, of *apparently* suffering themselves to be beaten, to make a show or pretence of being beaten. See a like phraseology, Gen. 42. 7; 2 Sam. 13. 5.——¶ *Fled by the way of the wilderness.* Lying between Ai and Jericho or Gilgal.

16. *And all the people that were in Ai.* That is, all who had not sallied out before, all the men able to bear arms who remained behind when the first body of pursuers issued forth from the city. Some portion of the population, however, was still left, who were afterwards slain, v. 24. The original word for 'were called together' is יִזָּעֲקוּ *yizzâekû,* which properly signifies *were cried together,* that is, were summoned by mutual shouts and vociferations.——¶ *Were drawn away.* Heb. יִנָּתְקוּ *yinnâthekû, were plucked or pulled.*

17. *Was not a man left in Ai.* Not a man that was able to bear arms, not one fit for military service.——¶ *Or Bethel.* This city, situated at three miles distance from Ai, was

left the city open, and pursued after Israel.

18 And the LORD said unto Joshua, Stretch out the spear that *is* in thine hand toward Ai; for I will give it into thine hand. And Joshua stretched out the spear that *he had* in his hand toward the city.

19 And the ambush arose quickly out of their place, and they ran as soon as he had stretched out his hand, and they entered into the city, and took it, and hasted, and set the city on fire.

20 And when the men of Ai looked behind them, they saw, and behold, the smoke of the city ascended up to heaven, and they had no power to flee this way or that way: and the people that fled to the wilderness turned back upon the pursuers.

21 And when Joshua and all Israel saw that the ambush had taken the city, and that the smoke of the city ascended, then they turned again, and slew the men of Ai.

22 And the other issued out of the city against them; so they were in the midst of Israel, some on this side, and some on that side: and they smote them, so that they ¹let none of them remain or escape.

¹ Deut. 7. 2.

---

probably confederate with it, and aiding it with forces on the present occasion.

18. *Stretch out the spear that is in thine hand.* That is, hold extended or stretched out, continue it in that position. Comp. v. 26. This was probably agreed upon as the signal to be given by Joshua to the men in ambush, to notify them of the precise moment when to issue forth from their retreat and rush into the city. If, as some commentators suppose, a flag or a burnished shield were fixed to the end of a long spear, pike, or lance, making it conspicuous from a distance, it would still better answer the purpose intended. Conjoined with this there might have been, as far as we can see, another object in thus elevating the spear on this occasion; viz. that it should serve like the lifting up of Moses' hands in the battle with Amalek, as a token of the Divine presence and assistance, a pledge of the secret efficacy of the Almighty arm in securing them the victory. This seems highly probable from v. 26.——¶ *Set the city on fire.* See on v. 8.

20. *Had no power to flee.* Heb. לֹא יָדַיִם *lō yâdayim*, no hand, i. e. no place, no quarter, no direction to which to flee, being hemmed in on every side. Most of the ancient versions, however, render with ours, 'power, ability, strength,' in which sense it is certain that 'hand' is sometimes used.——¶ *Pursuers.* Heb. רוֹדֵף *rodëph, pursuer*, collect. sing.

21. *When all Israel saw.* That is, all the Israelites then present, all that were employed in this service. Such general expressions are often to be limited by the tenor of the narrative.

22. *And the other.* Heb. וְאֵלֶּה *ve-ëlleh, and these,* i. e. those who had formed the ambush.——¶ *So that they let none of them remain or escape*

23 And the king of Ai they took alive, and brought him to Joshua.

24 And it came to pass when Israel had made an end of slaying all the inhabitants of Ai in the field, in the wilderness wherein they chased them, and when they were all fallen on the edge of the sword, until they were consumed, that all the Israelites returned unto Ai, and smote it with the edge of the sword.

25 And *so it was, that* all that fell that day, both of men and women, *were* twelve thousand, *even* all the men of Ai.

26 For Joshua drew not his hand back wherewith he stretched out the spear, until he had

---

Heb. 'so that there remained not to them a survivor (i. e. one taken alive) or one that escaped.' They were all indiscriminately put to the sword. with the single exception mentioned in the next verse.

23. *The king of Ai they took alive.* He was reserved for a more exemplary and ignominious death as a warning to other kings who, like him, might be disposed to defy the power of Israel.

24. *Smote it with the edge of the sword.* Heb. לפי חרב *lephi 'hereb, with the mouth of the sword.* That is, the old men, women, and children who remained in the city, who had not joined in the pursuit, v. 16. 17.

25. *Both of men and women.* Heb. מאיש ועד אשה *mëish ve-ad ishah, from the man to the woman.*—— ¶ *Twelve thousand, even all the men of Ai.* It seems scarcely credible that this number should have included *all* that were slain on this occasion, as it would leave the fighting men not more than two or three thousand, and yet this mere handful daring to go forth against a force of between twenty and thirty thousand! Can we believe them so infatuated, doomed though they were to destruction? We are constrained therefore to understand the twelve thousand of the effective men of arms, the sense in which the phrase 'men of Ai' occurs in v. 20. 21, as also the sing. 'man,' v. 17. The assertion of the verse we suppose to be, that the number of the men of war who perished, together with their whole families, old men, women, and children, was twelve thousand. The latter are not expressly but implicitly included in the enumeration, and the proportion which they bore to the fighting men is a mere matter of inference. They were probably at least thrice as many.

26. *For Joshua drew not his hand back,* &c. The object of these words seems to be to assign the reason of the utter and unsparing destruction of the people of Ai. The movements of Israel were directed by the uplifted spear of Joshua. As long as that continued stretched out they were to persist in the work of slaughter. When it was let down they were to cease. This shows that the stretching out of the spear was not designed *merely* as a signal to the men in ambush, for in this case the continuance of the act would have been unnecessary. It was doubtless intended to answer the same end as the uplifted hands of Moses on the occasion before referred to, that is, as a visible sign of the presence and agency of Omnipotence in behalf of his people as long as it continued to be extend-

CHAPTER VIII.

utterly destroyed all the inhabitants of Ai.

27 ᵐOnly the cattle and the spoil of that city Israel took for a prey unto themselves, according unto the word of the LORD which he ⁿcommanded Joshua.

28 And Joshua burnt Ai, and made it °an heap for ever, *even* a desolation unto this day.

29 ᵖAnd the king of Ai he hanged on a tree until even-tide, ᵠand as soon as the sun was down, Joshua commanded that

m Numb. 31. 22, 26. n ver. 2. o Deut. 13. 16. p ch. 10. 26. Ps. 107. 40. and 110. 5. q Deut. 21. 23. ch. 10. 27.

---

ed. To the judgment of sense there was perhaps little connexion between Joshua's holding forth his spear and the success of the combatants at a distance, and it might have appeared that he would have been better employed at the head of the army, animating and directing them. But *he* knew who alone could give the victory, and that a compliance with God's commands was the surest means of obtaining help from Him. Hence without any apprehensions as to the issue, he maintained his stand before God, and held forth his spear till all his enemies were destroyed. Such is the confidence and perseverance which the Christian is to evince in his conflicts with sin and Satan, notwithstanding the apparently little connexion between his poor efforts and the destruction of such mighty foes. It is perhaps in allusion to this circumstance that the phrase 'stretching out the hand against' is employed by the prophets as equivalent *to contending with, or fighting against.* Thus Is. 5. 25, 'Therefore is the anger of the Lord kindled against his people, and *he hath stretched forth his hand against them,* and hath smitten them: and the hills did tremble and their carcasses are torn in the midst of the streets. For all this his anger is not turned away, but *his hand is stretched out still,*' i. e. his judgments still continue as did the slaughter of the Aiites while Joshua's outstretched spear was not withdrawn.——¶ *Until he had utterly destroyed.* Heb. החרים *he'herim,* had devoted to *a curse.*

28. *Made it an heap for ever.* Heb. תל עולם *tël ōlăm, an heap of eternity,* i. e. an everlasting heap, a perpetual pile of ruins. The meaning is, it was made such *for a long time,* through a long tract of ages; a frequent sense of the phrase 'for ever.' It seems to have been rebuilt about a thousand years afterwards, by the Benjamites, Neh. 11. 31, under the name of Aija or Aiya.——¶ *Unto this day.* Near the close of Joshua's life.

29. *The king of Ai he hanged.* The kings of the devoted nations were dealt with with more exemplary severity than the common people, because they were more deeply criminal, both in having formerly by their connivance encouraged the abominations of their subjects, and in now instigating them to resistance, when they might and should have known that resistance was vain. In the present case, though the king of Ai was taken alive and brought to Joshua, yet it is not certain that he was not first put to death in some other way, and his body hung upon a tree *after* his execution as a mark of the utmost disgrace and detestation. Upon consulting the following passages,

they should take his carcass down from the tree, and cast it at the entering of the gate of the city, and ʳraise thereon a great heap of stones, *that remaineth* unto this day.

30 ¶ Then Joshua built an altar unto the Lord God of Israel ˢin mount Ebal,

ʳ ch. 7. 26, and 10. 27.   ˢ Deut. 27. 4, 5.

---

this opinion will appear far more plausible than the one which maintains that he was first hung, a mode of capital punishment that does not appear to have been customary in those early days, ch. 10. 26; 2 Sam. 4. 12; 1 Sam. 31. 8-10.——¶*As soon as the sun was down.* This was according to the law, Deut. 21. 22, 23, 'If a man have committed a sin worthy of death, and he be to be put to death, and thou hang him on a tree; his body shall not remain upon the tree, but thou shalt in any wise bury him that day.'——¶*Cast it at the entering of the gate.* The gates of cities were usually the places of judgment, of the transaction of the most important public business, and of general resort and rendezvous. We know of no other reason for casting the dead body of the king of Ai in this place, than that it was the most public place that could be chosen, one that would stamp the act with the utmost possible notoriety.

30. *Joshua built an altar—in mount Ebal.* This was in obedience to the command given Deut. 27. 42-48, on which see Notes. Mount Ebal, as well as mount Gerizim, was situated near Shechem in what was afterwards the tribe of Ephraim, and not far from the ancient Samaria. It was at a considerable distance from the camp at Gilgal, yet as it was a ceremony that had been expressly commanded, and the performance of which was not to be delayed any longer than was absolutely necessary after they had entered Canaan, Deut. 27, 2, they seem to have penetrated in a body through the mountainous regions that intervened till they came to the appointed place, although no details of the journey thither are given. Viewed in connexion with their then present circumstances the incident was a remarkable one. While engaged in the mid career of conquest, the business of the war is suddenly suspended, and instead of pushing their victories on every side, after mastering the frontier towns, they commence a peaceful march into the heart of the country to attend upon a religious solemnity ! But God had ordered it, and they cheerfully obeyed. Whatsoever else stands still, the service of God must go forward. Whatever other interests may suffer, our spiritual concerns must receive attention. But in truth there is no danger that our worldly interests *will* suffer in consequence of a paramount regard to the one thing needful. God will take them into his own hand, and see that we are no losers by any thing done for him. In the present instance, we see that his providential care was wonderfully exercised towards his faithful servants. Though in the midst of an enemy's country, as yet unconquered, yet they passed on unharmed, the terror of God having fallen upon the cities round about, as when Jacob some ages before had passed through this very region on his way to Bethel, Gen. 35. 5. The way of duty is the way of safety.—

31 As Moses the servant of the LORD commanded the children of Israel, as it is written in the ᵗ'book of the law of Moses, an altar of whole stones, over which no man hath lifted up *any* iron : and ᵘ they offered thereon burnt-offerings unto the LORD, and sacrificed peace-offerings.

32 ¶ And ˣ he wrote there upon the stones a copy of the law of Moses, which he wrote in the presence of the children of Israel.

33 And all Israel and their elders, and officers, and their judges, stood on this side the ark and on that side before the priests the Levites, ʸ which bare the ark of the covenant of the LORD, as well ᶻ the stranger, as he that was born among them ; half of them over against mount Gerizim, and half of them over against mount Ebal ; ᵃ as Moses

ᵗ Ex. 20. 25.   Deut. 27. 5, 6.   ᵘ Ex. 20. 24.
ˣ Deut. 27. 2, 8.

ʸ Deut. 31. 9, 25.   ᶻ Deut. 31. 12.   ᵃ Deut. 11. 29, and 27. 12.

The object of erecting the altar was to offer the sacrifices spoken of in the next verse. It was a federal transaction in which they were now engaged. The covenant was now to be renewed upon their taking possession of the land of promise, and a formal profession made of their subjection to the law, and of their dependence for success in all their enterprises upon the blessing of the Most High. All this it was proper should be ratified by sacrificial offerings.

31. *Over which no man hath lifted up any iron.* Rather 'had lift up.' The writer does not intend to quote the precise words of the law, but merely to say that Joshua constructed an altar in accordance with the precept of Moses, Ex. 20. 25 ; Deut. 27. 5 ; viz., one over which no man *had* lifted up an iron tool.

32. *Wrote there upon the stones.* Upon comparing this with the injunction, Deut. 27. 2-7, it appears quite obvious that in addition to the altar they were required also to erect a number of stone pillars, and that the writing was to be done upon the pillars, instead of upon the altar, for which purpose they were previously to be plastered over.——¶ *A copy of the law.* Heb. משנה תורה *mishnëh torâh, a repetition, a duplicate of the law.* That is, a copy of the blessings and curses commanded by Moses; not a copy of the decalogue, as some imagine; nor of the book of Deuteronomy, as others think ; much less of the whole Pentateuch ; but simply that part of the law which contained the blessings and curses, and which was to be read on this solemn occasion. See Note on Deut. 27. 8.

33. *Before the priests, the Levites.* That is, in view of the priests, the Levites; not that the elders, officers, and judges stood nearer the ark than the priests, but that they so surrounded the ark that the priests who were carrying it had a full view of them. In like manner it might be said that a great crowd in a funeral were *before* the bearers and pall-bearers, if they stood full in their view.——¶ *Over against mount Gerizim and over against mount Ebal.* For an account of these mountains see on Deut. 11. 29. The two divisions

the servant of the Lord had commanded before, that they should bless the people of Israel.

34 And afterward [b] he read all the words of the law, [c] the blessings and cursings, according to all that is written in the book of the law.

35 There was not a word of all that Moses commanded, which Joshua read not before all the congregation of Israel, [d] with the women, and the little ones, and [e] the strangers that were conversant among them.

CHAPTER IX.

AND it came to pass, when all the kings which *were* on this side Jordan, in the hills, and in the valleys, and in all the coasts of [a] the great sea over against Lebanon, [b] the Hittite, and the Amorite, the Canaanite, the Perizzite, the Hivite, and the Jebusite heard *thereof;*

2 That they [c] gathered them

---

b Deut. 31. 11.   Neh. 8. 3.   c Deut. 28. 2, 15, 45, and 29. 20, 21, and 30. 19.   d Deut. 31. 12.   e ver. 33.

a Numb. 34. 6.   b Exod. 3. 17, and 23. 23.   c Ps. 83. 3, 5.

---

seem not to have stood upon the summit of the mountains, but were ranged along their base and some way up their sides, that they might be nearer the ark, which occupied the valley between, and more conveniently hear the reading of the law.——¶ *That they should bless the people.* And curse also, though the last is not expressly mentioned; it is however plainly to be inferred, both from the original command of Moses, Deut. 27. 13, and from the phraseology of the next verse.

34. *And afterward he read.* That is, he commanded the priests or Levites to read, as is evident from Deut. 27. 14. In innumerable instances in the Scriptures, a person is said to do that which he orders or procures to be done.——¶ *The words of the law, the blessings and cursings.* All the sanctions of the law; from which and from v. 35, it would seem that much more was read on this occasion than was written on the stones.

35. *With the women and little ones.* It was a word that concerned *all*, and all of all sexes and ages were present, giving a solemn and heedful attention to what was read. Children would be deeply impressed by the solemnities of the scene, and a salutary fear of offending God would sink into their tender hearts.——¶ *The strangers that were conversant among them.* Heb. הגר ההלך בקרבם *haggēr hahōlek bekirbâm, the stranger that walked among them.* Proselytes. No other strangers can well be supposed to have been present at this time.

CHAPTER IX.

1. *On this side Jordan.* The west side; where the children of Israel now were, and where the writer was at the time of penning this narrative. ——¶ *Heard thereof.* That is, of the remarkable events which had transpired since the Israelites had entered Canaan; of the sacking of Jericho and Ai, and of their being now assembled together at Mount Ebal.

2. *They gathered themselves together to fight.* Entered into a league, agreed to form a confederacy. It does not appear that they *actually*

CHAPTER IX.

selves together, to fight with Joshua and with Israel, with one accord.

3 ¶ And when the inhabitants of ᵈGibeon ᵉheard what Joshua had done unto Jericho and to Ai,

d ch. 10. 2.   2 Sam. 21. 1, 2.   e ch. 6. 27.

united their forces at this time, but they now consulted together and agreed to do it. Subsequent events, however, seem to have deranged their plans, and prevented a combined attack till some time afterwards.— In this conduct we see, as in a glass, the strange infatuation of the wicked! Though seeing and feeling that the hand of God is unquestionably against them, yet, instead of repenting and humbling themselves before him, these devoted kings, who, like Ahaz, 'in their distress trespassed yet more against the Lord,' madly seek by power and policy to counteract and defeat his designs! 'Thou hast stricken them, but they have not grieved ; thou hast consumed them, but they have refused to receive correction; they have made their faces harder than a rock.'——¶ *With one accord.* Heb. פה אחד *pëh ehâd, with one mouth;* expressive of their entire unanimity in the measure. Though of different clans, having different interests, and doubtless heretofore often at variance with one another, yet they are ready to make common cause against the people of God, showing that the hatred of the righteous is one of the strongest bonds of union between wicked men. 'And the same day Pilate and Herod were made friends together ; for before they were at enmity between themselves.' What an admonition to Christians to cease from dissension, to give up their petty feuds and animosities, to sacrifice party interests to the public welfare, and cordially unite against the common enemies of God's kingdom among men.

3. *The inhabitants of Gibeon.* Gibeon was a city of the Hivites, probably its capital. In the division of the land it fell to the tribe of Benjamin, and was situated on a hill about six miles north of Jerusalem. At the present time, a small village called *Geeb,* occupies the site of the ancient city. The inhabitants of this place declined entering into the alliance offensive and defensive above mentioned. This might have been owing to their form of government, which left more scope for the good sense of the people. Had they had a king, of which we nowhere read, he would probably have been induced, in the pride of his heart, to join the confederacy; but this city, with the three others mentioned v. 17, seem to have been governed by elders or senators, v. 11, who consulted the common safety more than their own personal dignity. In this case of the Gibeonites, we may see a striking instance of the different effects produced by the same tidings upon different minds. The news of the victorious progress of Israel excites the several kings to resistance, but moves the Gibeonites to think of making peace with their invaders. In the same manner the Gospel message is a savor of life to some, and of death to others. Some it irritates and provokes to deadly and self-destructive opposition, others it softens, melts, persuades to surrender, and brings to saving repentance. In such a difference Divine sover-

4 They did work wilily, and went and made as if they had been ambassadors, and took old sacks upon their asses, and wine-bottles, old, and rent, and bound up;

---

eignty must be acknowledged, though the obstinately impenitent are left without excuse.

4. *They did work wilily.* Heb. 'they also did work wilily,' i. e. cunningly, shrewdly, craftily. The term 'also,' which is omitted in our translation, but occurs in the original, carries in it a reference to the course adopted by the Canaanitish kings. They adopted the measures which seemed to them the wisest and most politic, under the circumstances. In like manner the Gibeonites *also* determined to exercise *their* ingenuity in the present emergency, but they had recourse to a subtle stratagem, entirely different from the more open, straightforward, but ruinous course pursued by their neighbors. As to the moral character of this device of the Gibeonites, we can only say of it, as our Saviour said of the unjust steward, 'they acted wisely in their generation;' they did what the common maxims of mere worldly prudence dictated under the circumstances, and yet their fraud and prevarication cannot be justified, nor have we any reason to think they fared so well by employing it, as they would have done without it. A more simple and upright course would undoubtedly have secured to them far greater advantages. Some correct notions of the God of Israel they had certainly formed, v. 9, 10, and these should have prompted some other expedient than that of lying and deceit. They should have followed up the little light they had, and inquired into the procuring causes of God's severity against them. They should have acknowledged that it was their heinous sins which were at the bottom of all their troubles; and having humbled themselves in deep repentance, and trusting to Providence for the issue, should have come to the Israelites, and simply submitted themselves without opposition or fraud, and there is every reason to believe they would have been spared, as Rahab and her relations had been. Lying and hypocrisy always defeat themselves in the long run; their success is only temporary, while truth and honesty will always ultimately redound to the safety, prosperity, and happiness of those who adhere to them.——¶ *As if they had been ambassadors.* The root of צִיר *tzir, ambassador,* properly denotes *a hinge;* because an ambassador is a person upon whom the business of his embassy *turns as upon a hinge.* So the Latin *cardinalis, cardinal,* from *cardo, a hinge,* was the title of the prime minister of the emperor Theodosius; but it is now applied only to the Pope's electors and counsellors, though the original reason probably holds with equal force here too. They are the *hinges* upon which the vast and complicated interests of the Papacy turn. See Note on the 'lords' and 'princes' (Heb. *axles*) of the Philistines, ch. 13. 3. ——¶ *Took old sacks.* 'Of course they profess to do what they would actually have done had they really come from a distant place. Hence we learn that at this time little accommodation except that of lodging, if that, was expected upon a journey, and that

5 And old shoes and clouted upon their feet, and old gar-

every one carried provisions and drink with him, as at present. This rendered necessary their sacks, doubtless for containing their provisions and baggage. All travellers now carry sacks with them for such purposes. If they can afford it, these sacks are large, containing a strange assortment of articles—of dress, bedding, food, and even of pots and pans for cooking the necessary meals. These are usually carried on animals hired for the purpose, or on the animal which the servant, if any, rides. A poorer traveller reduces his baggage to narrower limits, so that he wants but small bags, which, being thrown over the back of his ass or mule, he rides upon himself. Those who have but one ass to carry themselves and baggage, frequently dismount and walk a considerable part of the way to relieve their beasts. This may account for the manner in which the clothes *and shoes* of the Gibeonites were supposed to have been worn out by long travel, although they had asses on which to ride. The bags which travellers use are commonly of stout woollen cloth or carpeting, sometimes strengthened with leather to keep out the wet. Bags of hair cloth are also sometimes used for this purpose, and almost always for carrying the corn and chopped straw for the cattle.' *Pict. Bib.*——¶ *And wine bottles, old*, &c. Pretending to have come from a very distant country, and that their sacks and the skins that served them for carrying their wine and water were worn out by the length of the journey. Sir John Chardin informs us that the Arabs, and all those who lead a wandering life, keep their water, milk, and other liquors in leathern bottles. They keep more fresh in them than in any other way. These leathern bottles are made of goat skins. When the animal is killed they cut off its feet and its head, and then draw it out of the skin, which is thus left nearly whole. They afterwards sew up the places where the legs and the tail were cut off, and when it is filled they tie it about the neck. These nations and the country people of Persia never go a journey without a small leathern bottle of water hanging by their side like a scrip. These bottles are frequently rent, when old and much used; but they are capable of being repaired. This they do sometimes by putting in a piece, sometimes by gathering up the wounded place in the manner of a purse; sometimes they put in a round flat piece of wood, and by these means stop the hole. Similar bottles are still used in Spain, and are called *borrachas.* See *Burder's Orient. Cust.*, vol. i., p. 54.

5. *Old shoes and clouted.* This latter epithet, in the time of Shakspeare, when applied to shoes, meant such as had nails driven into the soles to strengthen them. (Cymb., Act IV., Sc. 2.) In this sense it may be derived from the French word *clou, a nail.* But this does not seem to correspond well with the original, which is a derivative from a root signifying *to spot, to patch, to spot with patches.* For this reason it is supposed by Adam Clarke, with much plausibility, to come from the old Saxon *clut, a clout, a rag, or small piece of cloth,* used for piecing

102 JOSHUA. [B. C. 1451.

ments upon them; and all the bread of their provision was dry *and* mouldy.

6 And they went to Joshua ͞unto the camp at Gilgal, and said unto him, and to the men of Israel, We be come from a far country: now therefore make ye a league with us.

f ch. 5. 10.

or patching. This makes our present version to express very precisely the spirit of the original. As their shoes or sandals were made of skins in those early ages, it means that those they now wore were in a miserable tattered condition, having been often *patched, pieced,* or *mended.*——
¶ *The bread of their provision was dry and mouldy.* Heb. נקדים *nikkūdim, pricked,* i. e. *spotted, speckled;* bread marked with spots of mould, to which the original term is here applied. 'The bread commonly used in the East is calculated to last only for the day on which it is baked; in a day or two more it becomes exceedingly hard and unfit for use. This common bread could not therefore be that usually employed for daily food, for then its dry condition would not serve as an indication of the length of the journey they had taken. It must rather have been a sort of bread which will keep a considerable time, though it does ultimately become hard and mouldy. They have such bread in the East, the use of which is almost exclusively confined to travellers. It is a kind of biscuit, usually made in the shape of large rings, nearly an inch thick, and four or five inches in diameter. The bread is, when new, very firm, and rather crisp when broken; but, not being so well prepared as our biscuits, it becomes gradually harder, and at last mouldy from the moisture which the baking had left in it. In general it is seldom used till previously soaked in water. The bread of the Gibeonites may have been something of this sort. There is another kind of bread, which will keep as well, or better. This is the thin broad sheet of crisp wafer-bread, as thin as wrapping-paper, the preparation of which has been described in the note to Lev. 2. 4. But this is seldom used for a journey, being speedily reduced to powder by the action in travelling.' *Pict. Bib.*

6. *And to the men of Israel.* Heb. איש ישראל *ish Yisraël, the man or manhood of Israel;* collect. sing. for plur. Not to the whole body of the people, but to the heads, elders, or princes of the congregation, v. 15–21, who in all important matters acted in the name of the rest. In this sense, as a term of eminence or dignity, the original איש *ish, man,* is often used. ——¶ *Make ye a league with us.* Heb. כרתו ברית *kirtho berith, cut a covenant with us;* on which see Notes on Gen. 15. 10. The assertion that they came from a far country, is made as a reason for the Israelites complying with their request. From v. 24 it appears that they were well acquainted with the Divine mandate in regard to the destruction of the devoted nations, and they may have heard of the exception mentioned Deut. 20. 15 in favor of the cities which were very far off, and which were not of the cities of these nations. Of this exception they intended to take advantage.

7 And the men of Israel said unto the ᵍHivites, Peradventure ye dwell among us; and ʰhow shall we make a league with you?

8 And they said unto Joshua, ⁱWe *are* thy servants. And Joshua said unto them, Who *are* ye? and from whence come ye?

9 And they said unto him,

ᵍ ch. 11. 19. ʰ Exod. 23. 32. Deut. 7. 2, and 20. 16. Judg. 2. 2.

ⁱ Deut. 20. 11. 2 Kings 10. 5.

---

7. *And the men of Israel.* Heb. ואיש ישראל *ve-ish Yisraël, and the man of Israel;* i. e. the elders or princes, as above.——¶ *Said unto the Hivites.* Heb. 'the Hivite.' This is the first intimation of the particular nation to which the Gibeonites belonged. In Josh. 11. 19 it is stated still more expressly.——¶ *Peradventure ye dwell among us.* Heb. בקרבי *be-kirbi,* '*dwell in my midst.*' They speak, in the confidence of faith, as if they were already actual possessors and occupants, old settled inhabitants, of the region which God had covenanted to give them.—— ¶ *And how shall we make a league with you?* Seeing God has expressly forbidden our forming any such alliance, Ex. 23. 31; 31.; 34. 12. Deut. 7. 2. They speak as acting entirely according to orders, and as having no discretion in the case; and by putting their answer into the form of a question do virtually appeal to the consciences, the innate sense of right, of these heathen people, for the propriety of their conduct in refusing. A contrary course even the Gibeonites themselves knew was not even to be thought of. Some duties are so obvious that we may unhesitatingly take it for granted that the consciences of the worst of men do really side with us in regard to them.

8. *We are thy servants.* We are willing to make any concessions; do but grant our request, and we will submit to any terms you may see fit to propose. Fix your own conditions, even should they require us to become your tributaries and bondmen for life. They clogged their purpose with no reservations. They surrendered themselves unconditionally to the mercy of Joshua and the princes of Israel. Liberty, property, military renown, were all merged in the paramount desire for preservation from the edge of the sword. They did not appeal to the avarice of Israel, as the Shechamites and Samaritans, in after days, appealed to that of Ishmael, the son of Nehemiah, Jer. 41. 8, 'Slay us not, for we have treasures in the field, of wheat, and of barley, and of oil, and of honey;' but they made an unlimited offering of themselves, and of their possessions, to be dealt with as Joshua might choose. 'All that a man hath will he give for his life.' How worthless then should any sacrifice appear, compared with the life of the soul! One thing is needful; that secured, the rest is of but little value.——¶ *Who are ye? and from whence come ye?* Probably this very intimation of such unconditional submission tended to excite the suspicions of Joshua, especially as they were so backward to name the country from whence they came.

9. *Because of the name of the Lord thy God.* Because of what we have heard of that name; because of the

JOSHUA.

ᵏFrom a very far country thy servants are come, because of the name of the Lord thy God: for we have ¹heard the fame of him, and all that he did in Egypt,

10 And ᵐall that he did to the two kings of the Amorites, that *were* beyond Jordan, to Sihon king of Heshbon, and to Og king of Bashan, which *was* at Ashtaroth.

11 Wherefore our elders, and all the inhabitants of our country spake to us, saying, Take victuals with you for the journey, and go to meet them, and say unto them, We *are* your servants: therefore now make ye a league with us:

12 This our bread we took hot *for* our provision out of our houses on the day we came forth to go unto you; but now, behold, it is dry, and it is mouldy:

13 And these bottles of wine which we filled, *were* new, and

ᵏ Deut. 20. 15. ¹ Ex. 15. 14. Josh. 2. 10. ᵐ Num. 21. 24, 33.

---

reverence with which it has inspired us; and because we are convinced that it is above every name. They pretend to have been moved mainly by religious motives in taking this journey, which was in part doubtless true, but it was truth mixed with both falsehood and hypocrisy. This pretence, however, was one well calculated to prevail with the Israelites, for those who are guileless themselves are least suspicious of guile in others, and nothing wins more upon the simple-heartedness of good men than the appearance of piety and devotion where it was little or not at all expected.——¶ *All that he did in Egypt.* They artfully confine themselves to the mention of events that happened a long time ago, avoiding any allusion to those of more recent occurrence, such as the dividing of Jordan and the destruction of Jericho and Ai, as if willing to have it believed that they lived so far off that the tidings of them had not yet reached their ears.

11. *Wherefore our elders,—spake to us.* Another evidence that they did not live under a kingly but a popular form of government.——¶ *Go to meet them.* Had they deferred till the Israelites came to the gates of their cities, it would have been too late; their yielding themselves up would have been of no avail. So the way to avoid a judgment is to meet it by repentance. Sinners should imitate the example of these Gibeonites, and while God, who is coming to make war against them, 'is yet a great way off, should send an ambassage and desire conditions of peace.' We have as clear evidence of God's determination to destroy all the ungodly, as the Gibeonites had of his purpose to root out the Canaanites. Let us learn then of these heathens; learn to come to Jesus ere it be too late. Let us not stay till besieged by sickness and death. Nor let us come covering our design with falsehoods, but confessing the whole truth. In the old and tattered garments of our native vileness we *may* come. Christ, the true Joshua, will receive us and make with us a league of life and peace; but let us come saying at first as they did after their imposture was

B. C. 1451.]   CHAPTER IX.   105

behold they be rent : and these our garments and our shoes are become old by reason of the very long journey.

14 And the men took of their victuals, [n] and asked not *counsel at the mouth of the* LORD.

15 And Joshua °made peace

[n] Numb. 27. 21. Isai. 30. 1, 2. See Judg. 1. 1. 1 Sam. 22. 10, and 23. 10, 11, and 30. 8. 2 Sam. 2. 1, and 5. 19. ° ch. 11. 19. 2 Sam. 21. 2.

---

discovered, 'Behold, we are in thine hand: as it seemeth good and right unto thee to do unto us, do.'

14. *And the men took of their victuals.* Chal. 'And the men assented to their words, and consulted not the oracle of God.' By the 'men' are meant those who are elsewhere termed *the princes* of the congregation, v. 18. 19. They took the victuals into their hands not to eat of them, but to satisfy themselves of the truth of their statement. Some suppose the meaning to be that they ate together with the Gibeonites in token of friendship, as is still common in the East, but this is less likely, especially as the words may be rendered, 'they received the men by reason of their victuals.'——¶ *And asked not counsel at the mouth of the Lord.* That is, *instead* of asking as they ought to have done at the lips of the high priest, whose duty it was to inquire through the medium of the Urim and Thummim, Ex. 28. 30; Num. 27. 21; 1 Sam. 30. 7, 8. It is by no means certain, if they *had* sought the Divine direction, that they would have been commanded to reject the suit of the Gibeonites and show them no mercy. The probability is, that upon *any* of the devoted nations voluntarily coming forward, professing repentance, renouncing idolatry, and embracing the true religion, the Israelites would have been authorized by God to spare their lives. See on ch. 11. 19. But

the circumstance is mentioned here as a severe reflection upon the princes of Israel for neglect of duty, for rashness, credulity, and impolicy. They rushed precipitately into an alliance which they had no right to form without the express sanction of Jehovah, and their 'lips became a snare to their souls.' In like manner how often do men now involve themselves in dangers and difficulties, and hedge up their own way with troubles, because they ask not counsel at the mouth of the Lord. They listen with a yielding ear to plausible representations, hurry forward in their chosen schemes, and enter heedlessly into doubtful connexions without weighing the consequences. But sooner or later we shall find that no business or interest truly prospers in which we engage without the counsel and approbation of Heaven, and with shame and sorrow shall seek to him to retrieve the evils which our rashness has procured. Let it then be engraven upon the tablets of our hearts, that *no proposed course of conduct can be so clear to a Christian as to excuse him from the duty of seeking direction from above.*

15. *Joshua made peace with them,* &c. Agreed to receive them into a friendly connexion with the Israelites, and to respect their lives and property. It has been doubted by some whether the Israelites were bound by an oath that had been obtained from them by means of a gross

with them, and made a league with them, to let them live : and the princes of the congregation sware unto them.

16 ¶ And it came to pass at the end of three days after they had made a league with them, that they heard that they *were* their neighbors, and *that* they dwelt among them.

17 And the children of Israel journeyed, and came unto their cities on the third day. Now their cities *were* ᵖGibeon, and Chephirah, and Beeroth, and Kirjath-jearim.

18 And the children of Israel smote them not, ᑫbecause the princes of the congregation had sworn unto them by the Lord God of Israel. And all the congregation murmured against the princes.

p ch. 18. 25, 26, 28. Ezra 2. 25. q Eccles. 5. 2. Ps. 15. 4.

---

imposition. But it is plain that they thought themselves solemnly bound by it, and were apprehensive that the wrath of God would fall upon them if they broke it. That they were right in this, and that their adherence to their oath was acceptable to God, is to be inferred, (1) From his expressing no displeasure at the time, and from the subsequent tenor of his dealings towards them, which was kind, and favorable, not implying rebuke, nor savoring of disapprobation. (2) From the fact that he long afterwards severely avenged the wrong done by Saul to the Gibeonites in violation of this treaty. Let us learn from this the binding nature of an oath. It lays a bond upon the soul from which we cannot be released. Even when an oath has been taken which it is unlawful to keep, still we are not to consider that it is a *light matter* to dispense with it, or that we stand in the sight of God just where we did before it was taken. We have in fact laid upon ourselves a load of obligation which he only can take off. It is he only who, in view of our unfeigned repentance for having taken it, can relieve the conscience of the awful burden which rests upon it. How much more then ought we to feel the force of those compacts and promises which are wholly lawful and right! How religiously and scrupulously should every promise be performed!

16. *That they dwelt among them.* Heb. בקרבו *bekirbo, dwelt in his midst,* collect. sing., the very thing which Joshua feared, and of which he hinted his suspicion, v. 7. 'They that suffer themselves to be deceived by the wiles of Satan, will soon be undeceived to their confusion, and will find that to be near; even at the door, which they imagined was very far off.' *Henry.*

17. *And the children of Israel journeyed and came unto their cities,* &c. This might better be rendered, 'For when the children of Israel journeyed, they came unto their cities.' According to the present translation they learnt the fraud practised upon them some days before they arrived at their cities. The contrary supposition seems the most probable, and we presume the 17th verse is intended to inform us how they became possessed of the information mentioned in the 16th.

18. *The congregation murmured.* Principally, no doubt, because they were deprived of the *spoils* of the

19 But all the princes said unto all the congregation, We have sworn unto them by the LORD God of Israel: now therefore we may not touch them.

20 This we will do to them; we will even let them live, lest ʳ wrath be upon us, because of the oath which we sware unto them.

21 And the princes said unto them, Let them live; but let them be ˢ hewers of wood, and

ʳ See 2 Sam 21. 1, 2, 6. Ezek. 17. 13, 15, 18, 19. Zech. 5. 3, 4. Mal. 3. 5. ˢ Deut. 29. 11.

Gibeonites. Though they did submit to the restraints laid upon them by this league, yet it was with an ill grace; they were vexed to have their hands thus tied by their rulers, and vented their disaffection in the most unequivocal manner. Some of them, however, might have honestly resented what they deemed a flagrant breach of the Divine commandment. There is often, nay generally, more conscience and principle among the common class of the people, than among those placed in authority over them, although this remark is not to be construed to the disparagement of Joshua.

19. *We have sworn unto them.* Chal. 'We have sworn to them by the Word of the Lord.' They plead neither the lawfulness nor the prudence of the oath, but only its obligation when taken. Although they had been *deceived* in the business, and the covenant had been made on a supposition which was afterwards proved to be false, yet having *sworn* *by Jehovah*, they did not feel at liberty to break their compact. It has been suggested that Joshua might have taken advantage of their own words to annul the treaty, and said to them, ' *Ye* are come, according to your own statement, from a far country; but *these* cities are near at hand; *their* inhabitants therefore are not the people with whom we have covenanted, and ye have nothing to do to interfere with or prevent their destruction.' But he would not resort to any shifts or quibbles to elude the oath. Like the good man of the Psalmist, though he had sworn to his own hurt, he would not change. Having made a solemn compact, he would abide by it at all events. If he had now broken his covenant the whole people of Canaan would have represented him as a violator of his engagements; it was therefore better to fulfil his agreement, however hasty and ill-advised, than by departing from it to give occasion to the enemies of God to blaspheme. His answer takes it for granted that the sentiments of the people accorded with his own as to the solemn obligations now resting upon them.—— ¶ *May not touch them.* May not hurt or injure them. For this sense of the word see Gen. 26. 11; Ruth 2. 9; Job 1. 11; Ps. 105. 15; Zech. 2. 8. Chal. 'May not give them damage.' ——¶ *We will even let them live.* Chal. 'We will make them to survive.'

21. *And the princes said unto them.* Rather 'said *concerning* them,' as the original for 'unto' often signifies. See on Gen. 20. 2.——¶ *Let them be hewers of wood and drawers of water.* Let them be taken at their word, v. 8, and made public servants, to be employed in the most menial offices and drudgeries which the service of the sanctuary might require. The ex

108 JOSHUA. [B. C. 1451.

drawers of water unto all the congregation; as the princes had 'promised them.

22 ¶ And Joshua called for them, and he spake unto them,

t ver. 15.

saying, Wherefore have ye beguiled us, saying, "We *are* very far from you; when ˣ ye dwell among us?

23 Now therefore ye *are*

u ver. 6. 9. x ver. 16.

---

pression is proverbial for the lowest and most servile employments of whatever kind, as appears from Deut. 29. 10, 11, where Moses thus recites the order of the different classes of the people, 'Ye stand this day all of you before the Lord your God; your captains of your tribes, your elders, and your officers, with all the men of Israel, your little ones, your wives, and thy stranger that is in thy camp, from the hewer of thy wood, unto the drawer of thy water.'——
¶ *Unto all the congregation.* To all the congregation considered as one great worshipping body, whose religious rites were concentrated at one place, and not to all the several families in their private capacity, as residing in their tents. They were to be made public and not private servants.——¶ *According as the princes had promised them.* Rather, Heb. 'had purposed, ordained, fixed upon concerning them;' that is, in a previous consultation. The whole verse, however, as it stands in the original, is exceedingly intricate, and commentators are very much divided as to its true construction. It would seem from the next verse that nothing had as yet been said directly *to* the Gibeonites.

22. *Wherefore have ye beguiled us?* The mode of their treatment having been previously resolved upon in a council of the elders or princes of the nation, Joshua now summons them into his presence and acquaints them with the result. 'He does not load them with ill names, does not give them any harsh, provoking language, does not call them, as they deserved to be called, *base liars*, but only asks them, "Why have ye beguiled us?" Under the greatest provocations it is our wisdom and duty to keep our temper and to bridle our passion; a just cause needs not anger to defend it, and a bad one is made never the better by it.' *Henry.*

23. *Now therefore ye are cursed.* Ye shall be subjected to a severe calamity. Ye shall pay a bitter penalty for your deception. Ye shall subject yourselves and your children to the curse of a degrading bondage, and thereby shall the ancient denunciation against your ancestor be fulfilled;—'Cursed be Canaan, a servant of servants shall he be.' Had they dealt fairly and ingenuously with Israel, their lives would no doubt have been spared on more favorable and honorable terms. As it was, however, it cannot be doubted that their punishment was overruled and turned to a signal blessing to them. They were hereby brought into a situation where they would naturally acquire the knowledge of the true God and of his revealed will, were made to dwell in the courts of the Lord's house, were honored with near access to him in the services of the sanctuary, and thus placed in circumstances eminently favorable to their spiritual and eternal interests.

CHAPTER IX.

ʸ cursed, and there shall none of you be freed from being bondmen, and ᶻ hewers of wood and drawers of water for the house of my God.

24 And they answered Joshua, and said, Because it was certainly told thy servants, how that the LORD thy God ᵃ commanded his servant Moses to give you all the land, and to destroy all the inhabitants of the land from before you, therefore ᵇ we were sore afraid of our lives because of you, and have done this thing

25 And now, behold, we are ᶜ in thine hand: as it seemeth

y Gen. 9. 25. z ver. 21. 27. a Exod. 23. 32. Deut. 7. 1, 2.
b Exod. 15. 14. c Gen. 16. 6.

If David could say, 'I had rather be a door-keeper in the house of my God, than to dwell in the tents of wickedness,' surely these poor benighted heathen may well have esteemed their lot a blessing, hard and toilsome and humble as it was. They are supposed to have been afterwards called *Nethinim*, i. e. persons *given, dedicated, consecrated* to the service of the sanctuary and the assistance of the Levites. See v. 27; 1 Chron. 9. 2.——¶ *There shall none of you be freed from being bondmen.* Heb. לֹא יִכָּרֵת מִכֶּם עֶבֶד *lō yikkârëth mikkem öbëd, there shall not be cut off from you a servant;* i. e. the line of servitude shall be kept up; a sentence by which the bondage imposed upon them should be entailed upon their posterity. Mr. Harmer undertakes to show from Shaw and other travellers, that these were the employments of females in the East, and that consequently the bitterness of their doom consisted not so much in being subjected to a laborious service, as in being degraded from the characteristic employments of men to those of women. There may be some force in this remark as applied to domestic *civil* life, but here the case is different; it is certain that these menial services, if they had not been performed by the Gibeonites, would have devolved upon the Israelites, and that too upon the *men*, and not the *women* of the congregation, for only males were employed about the sanctuary.——¶ *For the house of my God.* Chal. 'For the sanctuary of my God,' spoken primarily of the tabernacle, which was at that time the seat of worship, but with an ulterior reference to the temple which should be afterwards erected.

24. *And they answered,* &c. The words in which they make reply are well weighed. It is a delicate and very cogent appeal to the humanity and piety of Israel. They offer the best excuse for themselves which their conduct would admit. They attempt not to justify their prevarication, but in effect beg pardon for it; pleading that it was purely to save their lives that they had recourse to it. No one who feels the force of the law of self-preservation but must make great allowances for them, especially as they were not prompted by the fear of man, but of God himself, whom nothing can resist.

25. *We are in thine hand.* Chal. 'We are delivered into thine hand.' In thy power, at thy disposal, having nothing more to say for ourselves. ——¶ *As it seemeth good and right*

110 JOSHUA. [B. C. 1451.

good and right unto thee to do unto us, do.

26 And so did he unto them, and delivered them out of the hand of the children of Israel, that they slew them not.

27 And Joshua made them that day ᵈhewers of wood and drawers of water for the con-

ᵈ ver. 21, 23.

gregation and for the altar of the Lord, even unto this day, ᵉin the place which he should choose.

CHAPTER X.

NOW it came to pass, when Adoni-zedek king of Jerusalem had heard how Joshua

ᵉ Deut. 12. 5.

---

unto thee—do. Whatever justice and mercy dictate to thee to do unto us, that perform. They expect *justice* because they deceived the Israelites; yet they hope for *mercy* because they were driven to this expedient for fear of losing their lives. This willing submission of the Gibeonites may be improved by us. They accounted it no great matter to cede their cities, and to spend their days in servitude, seeing God had spared their lives. And shall we think much of sacrificing any temporal interests, or of performing any self-denying duties, when we have reason to think that God has spared the life of our souls? If we look for mercy at the hands of Jesus, all that we have and are must be the Lord's. We must be willing to *be* anything and *do* anything that he appoints for us.

26. *And so did he unto them.* That is, he dealt with them according to justice and mercy; he delivered them out of the hands of the people, who would fain have slain them, and yet he doomed them to servitude as a just retribution for their offence.

26. *And Joshua made them*, &c. Heb. יתנם *yittenâm*, gave them, whence the epithet נתינים *nethinim*, given, Lat. *dediti* or *deodati*, applied to them Ezra 2. 43, 58; 8. 20; Neh. 3. 26. See on v. 21.—¶ *In the place*

which he should choose. That is, the place which he should choose for his sanctuary, whether it were the tabernacle or temple; for here were their services more especially, though not exclusively, to be bestowed. They were not to keep possession of their cities, for we afterwards find that three of them fell to the lot of Benjamin, and one to that of Judah; nor were they to be at their own disposal, but were most of them probably dispersed through the cities of the priests and Levites, and came up with them in their courses to serve at the altar, out of the revenues of which they were doubtless maintained.

CHAPTER X.

1. *Adoni-zedek.* This name, signifying *lord of righteousness*, is very nearly akin to that of Melchizedek, *king of righteousness*, who reigned at the same place upwards of 400 years before. He might have been a descendant as well as successor of this distinguished personage, or the name, in one form or the other, may have been common, like Pharaoh in Egypt, or Abimelech in Gerar, to the royal line. How the epithet *righteous* came to be connected with the title of the kings of this remarkable city it is not possible now to determine. Viewed in connexion with

had taken Ai, and had utterly destroyed it; ᵃas he had done to Jericho and her king, so he had done to ᵇAi and her king;

and ᶜhow the inhabitants of Gibeon had made peace with Israel, and were among them; 2 That they ᵈfeared greatly,

ᵃ ch. 6. 21. ᵇ ch. 8. 22, 26, 28.

ᶜ ch. 9. 15. ᵈ Exod. 15. 14, 15, 16. Deut. 11. 25.

its subsequent history, it must be regarded as not a little remarkable, though from the case of this individual it does not appear to have been always a true index of the character of him who bore it.——¶ *King of Jerusalem.* The name *Jerusalem* here occurs for the first time in the scriptures. The original designation of the city seems to have been *Salem*, Gen. 14. 18; Ps. 76. 2, as it was called in the time of Melchizedek, though whether he were its founder is altogether uncertain. It was afterwards called ירושלים *Yerushalayim*, *Jerusalem*, a name supposed to. be compounded of יראו *yiru* (from ראה *raah, to see*), and שלם *shâlam, peace*, and. signifying *vision of peace*, or more literally, *they shall see peace*, in prophetic allusion to the *gospel of peace*, which was afterwards to issue from thence. Reland, Schultens and others, it is true, derive it from ירוש *yerûsh* and שלם *shâlam, possession of peace*, but we prefer the former, and are not unwilling to believe, with Masius, that the name carries in it a latent reference to the incident mentioned, and the words employed Gen. 22. 14, 'And Abraham called the name of that place Jehovah-jireh: as it is said to this day, In the mount of the Lord it shall be seen.' The Hebrew ראה *yireh* or *jireh*, seems to have been affixed to the ancient denomination *Salem*, and thus to have formed the word *Jerusalem*, mystically pointing to the *vision of peace* which Abraham saw in the future sacrifice that was to be offered up in the latter day on that same memorable mount or in its immediate vicinity. *Moriah*, one of the mountains of Jerusalem, signifying *vision of God*, is derived from the same root, and was probably so called for the same reason. After coming into the possession of the Jebusites, it was occasionally called *Jebus*, Josh. 18. 28; Judg. 19. 10, 11, from the inhabitants, but it seems never to have been familiarly known by that appellation among the Israelites. It is probable that the city retained in the main the name of *Salem*, which it had in the days of Abraham, till the Israelites came into the land of Canaan, and that it was called *Jerusalem* by them when they first took possession of it. Consequently it is so called by anticipation in this place. It was doubtless overruled in providence that a name should be bestowed on the place pre-intimating the nature of the glorious events by which it was afterwards to be distinguished. ——¶ *Had utterly destroyed.* Heb. החרימה *ya'harimâh*, had made a *curse, had devoted.*——¶ *Were among them.* Had made alliance with them, had come over to their interest, had put themselves under their protection, and so were entitled henceforth to dwell together with them in the country without being exterminated or disturbed.

2. *That they feared greatly.* He

112 JOSHUA. [B. C. 1451.

because Gibeon *was* a great city, as one of the royal cities, and because it *was* greater than Ai, and all the men thereof *were* mighty.

3 Wherefore Adoni-zedek king of Jerusalem sent unto Hoham king of Hebron, and unto Piram king of Jarmuth, and unto Japhia king of Lachish, and unto Debir king of Eglon, saying,

4 Come up unto me, and help me, that we may smite Gibeon: ᵉfor it hath made peace with Joshua and with the children of Israel.

5 Therefore the five kings of

e ver. 1. ch. 9. 15.

---

and his people; from which it appears that under the term 'king' in the preceding verse we are to understand also the people whom he represented.——¶ *As one of the royal cities.* Heb. כאחת ערי הממלכה *kea'hath ârai hammamlâkâh, as one of the cities of the kingdom.* Not that it was actually a royal city, the seat of a king, but it was *like* one, being a capital city and having others subordinate to it, ch. 9. 7. Chal. 'As one of the cities of the kingdoms.' It was great, well inhabited, and well fortified, after the manner of those cities which served for royal residences. But they were undoubtedly a small but powerful republic, governed by elders, as we hear nothing here or elsewhere of their having a king. See on ch. 9. 3.

3. *Wherefore Adoni-zedek sent.* Because he was most exposed to danger, Jerusalem being only six miles from Gibeon, and midway between that and the camp at Gilgal, and because also he might have possessed some degree of precedency over the other kings mentioned.

4. *That we may smite Gibeon.* That is, the Gibeonites. It is very conceivable that Adoni-zedek and his associates may have been glad of a plausible pretext for attacking the Gibeonites, as *their* more liberal form of government was a standing rebuke of the despotism that prevailed among themselves. But their *avowed* motive undoubtedly was to punish the citizens of Gibeon for making peace with Joshua, as if they had thereby acted the part of traitors to the country and greatly strengthened the common enemy. In this incident we see what usually takes place when any of the enemies of Christ submit themselves to him. Their former friends and companions consider them as deserters from their standard, and are often bitterly exasperated against them. 'He that departeth from evil maketh himself a prey.' Or if their opposition does not amount to actual enmity, it will at least show itself in a way of contempt and ridicule. Satan too is indignant at losing one of his vassals; and not only stimulates his subjects to commence hostilities against them, but labors by all possible wiles and devices to bring them back again to their former bondage. There is the same enmity existing against the cause of Christ now as ever. Earth and hell will still combine against his Church, and every one that enters into covenant with him will, like the Gibeonites, have a powerful confederacy to contend with.

5. *The five kings of the Amorites.* The name of this people is often taken in a large sense for that of the

the Amorites, the king of Jerusalem, the king of Hebron, the king of Jarmuth, the king of Lachish, the king of Eglon, ᶠgathered themselves together, and went up, they and all their

ᶠ ch. 9. 2.

hosts, and encamped before Gibeon, and made war against it.

6 ¶ And the men of Gibeon sent unto Joshua ᵍ to the camp to Gilgal, saying, Slack not thy hand from thy servants; come up to us quickly, and save us,

ᵍ ch. 5. 10, and 9. 6.

Canaanites generally, or any one of them, doubtless from their being the most powerful of the distinct tribes that inhabited the country. Strictly speaking, the people of Hebron were Hittites, ch. 11. 19, and those of Jerusalem, Jebusites, ch. 15. 63; and in one place, 2 Sam. 21. 2, the Gibeonites themselves, though generally termed Hivites, are said to be 'of the remnant of the Amorites.' The probability is, that the Amorites, being a numerous and powerful people in the Moabitish territory, sent out colonies to these several places, which, having subdued the original inhabitants, communicated their own name very extensively over the country.——¶ *Made war against it.* Put themselves in a warlike attitude, made ready for an assault, were on the eve of attacking them.

6. *Sent unto Joshua.* They trusted to the compassion, the nobleness, the generosity, if not the justice of their new ally. They doubted not that he would consider himself bound in honor and conscience to succor and defend them, although it may not have been expressly stipulated for in the articles of the treaty. It was because of their confidence in Israel and their having thrown themselves entirely upon their protection that they were now marked out as objects of the vengeance of their enemies, and to whom should they go

in their extremity but to these their natural defenders? So when the powers of darkness, like mighty Amorites, assail the children of God, to whom shall they betake themselves but to Christ, their true Joshua? It is when we are encompassed with evils that we feel the value of that covenant into which we have entered with him. If we attempt to resist our enemies in our own strength, we shall infallibly be vanquished; but if we betake ourselves to the Captain of our salvation by fervent prayer, we cannot but succeed.——¶ *Slack not thy hand from thy servants.* Do not leave them to the fate which threatens them, put forth vigorous efforts for their deliverance, relax not the hold which thou hast by covenant taken of them. Happy the men of Gibeon, that in this awful moment, this very crisis of their fate, they had an interest in Joshua and the armies of Israel! Happy every trembling suppliant at the throne of mercy, if he be interested by faith in the Almighty Joshua, who hath the armies of the living God at his command! Could a heathen say, when a bird pursued by a hawk flew into his bosom, 'I will not surrender thee to thine enemy, as thou hast come to me for sanctuary?' Shall not the Saviour then be an unfailing refuge to those who fly to him in their extremity? See on ch. 1. 5.——¶ *That*

10*

114 . JOSHUA. [B. C. 1451.

and help us: for all the kings of the Amorites that dwell in the mountains are gathered together against us.

7 So Joshua ascended from Gilgal, he, and ʰall the people of war with him, and all the mighty men of valor.

ʰ ch. 8. 1.

8 ¶ And the LORD said unto Joshua, ⁱFear them not: for I have delivered them into thine hand; ᵏthere shall not a man of them stand before thee.

9 Joshua therefore came unto them suddenly, *and* went up from Gilgal all night.

ⁱ ch. 11. 6. Judg. 4. 14. ᵏ ch. 1. 5.

---

dwell in the mountains. Heb. הָהָר יֹשְׁבֵי *yōshebē hâhâr, dwellers or inhabitants of the mountain;* i. e. of the mountainous regions. The allusion is to the tract lying to the southwest of Jerusalem called 'the hill country,' Luke 1. 39, 65, in which were situated the four cities mentioned above, v. 3.

7. *And all the mighty men of valor.* Rather, '*even* all the mighty men of valor;' so the particle translated 'and' is used in hundreds of instances, and it is not easy to suppose that 'all the people of war,' and 'all the mighty men of valor,' constituted two separate portions of the host. The meaning is simply that he went up with an army of picked men, men of approved valor and tried skill, to defend the Gibeonites, their new allies, against their invaders. A sufficient force would of course be left to guard the camp at Gilgal. Instead of taking any advantage of the mere *letter* of their compact, and saying that they never promised to run the hazard of their own lives to save theirs, he nobly acts on its *spirit*, and resolves that they shall be no losers by the confidence they have reposed in him; that they shall not suffer by any calamity which he can avert. 'To a good mind the strongest obligation is another's trust; and even permission in those things we may remedy, makes us no less actors, than consent. We are guilty of all the evil we might have hindered.' *Bp. Hall.*

8. *And the Lord said unto Joshua.* More correctly 'for the Lord had said;' as we cannot suppose that Joshua undertook this expedition *before* he had sought counsel of God, and received the encouragement contained in the ensuing words. Without some such encouragement as this, Joshua might have thought that this formidable host was sent against him and his new allies as a judgment upon him for negotiating an unlawful treaty. The verse properly falls into a parenthesis.——¶ *I have delivered them into thy hand.* The usual form of speech to express the absolute certainty of a future event.

9. *Went up from Gilgal all night.* The distance from Gilgal to Gibeon was about twenty-six miles. By a forced march this distance might have been accomplished in one night; but the words do not necessarily restrict us to this period of time. They imply only that he travelled all night, to which, if we please, we may add, part of the preceding or of the following day. The clause quoted reads somewhat awkwardly as it now stands, from its seeming to put the march *after* the arrival. By omitting the word 'and,' which does not

B. C. 1451.]   CHAPTER X.   115

10 And the LORD ¹discomfited them before Israel, and slew them with a great slaughter at Gibeon, and chased them along the way that goeth up ᵐ to Beth-horon, and smote them to ⁿ Azekah, and unto Makkedah.

11 And it came to pass as they fled from before Israel, *and* were in the going down to Beth-horon, ᵒ that the LORD cast down great stones from heaven upon them unto Azekah, and they

¹ Judg. 4. 15. 1 Sam. 7. 10, 12. Ps. 18. 14. Isai. 28. 21.   ᵐ ch. 16. 3, 5.   ⁿ ch. 15 35.

ᵒ Ps. 18. 13, 14, and 77. 17. Isai. 30. 30. Rev. 16. 21.

occur in the original, and inclosing the remainder in a parenthesis ('he had gone up from Gilgal all night,') every thing is made plain. Though he had received the positive assurance of a victory, yet he neglects no prudent means of effecting it, and therefore adopting a military stratagem, comes upon them by surprise. 'God's promises are not intended to slacken or supersede, but to quicken and encourage our own endeavors.' *Henry.*

10. *The Lord discomfited them.* Or, Heb. יְהֻמֵּם *yehummēm, struck with dismay, confounded.* It is the word employed Ex. 23. 27, in describing the effect that should be produced by Divine power upon the enemies of Israel, though there rendered less accurately 'destroy.' It occurs also Ps. 144. 6; 2 Chron. 15. 6.——¶ *And slew them with a great slaughter.* Or, 'he slew them,' i. e. Israel slew them. In consequence of the panic into which the Lord had thrown them, his people were enabled to effect a great slaughter. The direct work of God on the occasion appears to be described, v. 11.——¶ *At Gibeon.* Heb. בְּגִבְעוֹן *begibōn, in Gibeon ;* not in the city, but in the adjoining territory or domain called by the same name, as Joshua is said, ch. 5. 13, to be *in* Jericho, when he was merely in the immediate vicinity.——¶ *Beth-*

horon. The tribe of Ephraim contained two places of this name, the upper and lower. The latter is here probably referred to, which lay twelve or fifteen miles to the north-west of Jerusalem, and where Dr. Clarke says there is now an Arab village called *Bethoor,* or as Prof. Robinson writes it *Beit 'Ur.*——¶ *Azekah.* A city of Judah, situated about twelve miles west from Jerusalem. Eusebius and Jerome inform us that there was a town in their time about this place named *Ezeca,* which was probably the same with the ancient Azekah here mentioned. On referring to the map it will be seen that the conquered kings fled to the north-west of Gibeon, while the residue of their army wheeled off more southerly, flying towards Azekah.—— ¶ *Makkedah.* This place was also in the tribe of Judah, about fourteen miles southwest of Jerusalem.

11. *The Lord cast down great stones from heaven upon them.* That is, hail-stones of an extraordinary size, and capable of doing dreadful execution in their fall from heaven. Some have indeed contended that stones, in the common acceptation of the word, or rather meteoric stones, are intended, and that such stones have actually fallen from the clouds or from a greater height is an incontestible fact. But there is no good

died: *they were* more which died with hailstones than *they* whom the children of Israel slew with the sword

reason to suppose that any such phenomenon is alluded to here, for it is immediately added, as if to preclude any ground of mistake, that 'they were more which died with *hailstones* than they whom the children of Israel slew with the sword.' The Sept. in both places translates it by λιθοι χαλαζης, *hailstones;* Josephus calls it 'a violent tempest of *hailstones* of prodigious size;' and the author of Ecclesiasticus, ch. 46. 6, thus speaks of the event:—'With *hailstones* of mighty power he made the battle to fall violently upon the nations, and in the descent of Beth-horon he destroyed them that resisted.' That God has, on other occasions, made use of hailstones to destroy both men and cattle, is clear from the instance of the plague of hail in Egypt, Ex. 9. 18, and in the predictions of Ezekiel against Gog, ch. 33. 22, the Most High is introduced as threatening that 'he would plead against him with pestilence, and with blood, with an overflowing rain, and *great hailstones*, fire and brimstone.' God himself, moreover, speaks to Job, ch. 38. 22, 23, of treasures or magazines of snow and hail, which he has reserved for the day of battle and war. But although we have no doubt that a shower of hailstones is here intended, yet we are equally convinced that this shower, though *natural* in itself, was *supernaturally* employed on this occasion. They probably far exceeded the usual size, and it certainly indicates a miraculous interposition of Providence that they should have fallen at the very crisis when God promised to assist his people against their enemies, and that while in falling they slew multitudes of the fugitive Canaanites, they should not have harmed one of their pursuers! The following account of a similar phenomenon happening in our own times is graphically described by one of our own countrymen, who was something more than an eye-witness of its effects. The letter is dated Constantinople, Aug., 1831. 'We had got perhaps a mile and a half on our way, when a cloud rising in the west, gave indications of an approaching rain. In a few minutes we discovered something falling from the heavens with a heavy splash, and of a whitish appearance. I could not conceive what it was, but observing some gulls near, I supposed it to be them darting for fish; but soon after discovered that they were large balls of ice falling. Immediately we heard a sound like rumbling thunder, or ten thousand carriages rolling furiously over the pavement. The whole Bosphorus was in a foam, as though heaven's artillery had been discharged upon us and our frail machine. Our fate seemed inevitable; our umbrellas were raised to protect us; the lumps of ice stripped them into ribands. We fortunately had a bullock's hide in the boat, under which we crawled and saved ourselves from farther injury. One man, of the three oarsmen, had his hand literally smashed; another much injured in the shoulder; Mr. H. received a severe blow in the leg; my right hand was somewhat disabled, and all more or less injured. A smaller kaick accom-

12 ¶ Then spake Joshua to the LORD in the day when the

panied with my two servants. They were both disabled, and are now in bed with their wounds; the kaick was terribly bruised. It was the most awful and terrific scene that I ever witnessed, and God forbid that I should be ever exposed to such another. Balls of ice as large as my two fists fell into the boat, and some of them came with such violence as certainly to have broken an arm or leg had they struck us in those parts. One of them struck the blade of an oar and split it. The scene lasted, perhaps, five minutes; but it was five minutes of the most awful feeling that I ever experienced. When it passed over, we found the surrounding hills covered with masses of ice, I cannot call it hail; the trees stripped of their leaves and limbs, and everything looking desolate. We proceeded on our course, however, and arrived at our destination, drenched and awe-struck. Up to this hour, late in the afternoon, I have not recovered my composure; my nerves are so affected as scarcely to be able to hold my pen, or communicate my ideas. The scene was awful beyond all description. I have witnessed repeated earthquakes; the lightning has played, as it were, about my head; the wind roared, and the waves have at one moment thrown me to the sky, and the next have sunk me into a deep abyss. I have been in action, and seen death and destruction around me in every shape of horror; but I never before had the feeling of awe which seized upon me on this occasion, and still haunts, and I feel will ever haunt me. I returned to the beautiful village of Buyuc-

dere. The sun was out in all its splendor, at a distance all looked smiling and charming, but a nearer approach discovered roofs covered with workmen repairing the broken tiles, desolated vineyards, and shattered windows. My porter, the boldest of my family, who had ventured an instant from the door, had been knocked down by a hailstone, and had they not dragged him in by the heels, would have been battered to death. Of a flock of geese in front of our house, six were killed, and the rest dreadfully mangled. Two boatmen were killed in the upper part of the village, and I have heard of broken bones in abundance. Many of the thick brick tiles, with which my roof is covered, are smashed to atoms, and my house was inundated by the rain that succeeded this visitation. It is impossible to convey an idea of what it was. Imagine to yourself, however, the heavens suddenly frozen over, and as suddenly broken to pieces in irregular masses, of from half a pound to a pound weight, and precipitated to the earth. My own servants weighed several pieces of three-quarters of a pound; and many were found by others of upwards of a pound. There were many which fell around the boat in which I was, that appeared to me to be as large as the swell of a large-sized water decanter. You may think this romance. I refer to the bearer of this letter, who was with me, and witnessed the scene, for the truth of every word it contains.' *Com. Porter's Letters from Constantinople and its Environs,* Vol. i. p. 44.

12. *Then spake Joshua to the Lord.*

118 JOSHUA. [B. C. 1451.

Lord delivered up the Amorites before the children of Israel, and he said in the sight of Israel, ᵖSun, stand thou still upon

p Isai. 28. 21. Hab. 3.,11.

That is, before, in the presence of, having a reference to. Chal. 'Then declared Joshua before the Lord.' There is nothing said of a direct address *to* Jehovah, though we cannot doubt that such an one was made on the occasion, but the address here mentioned was to the sun and moon. The phraseology in the original is not that which is usually employed to intimate a direct address whether in prayer or otherwise from one person to another. Instead of אל יהוה *to Jehovah*, it is ליהוה properly importing *before Jehovah*, or *in reference* to him. It is a similar mode of expression to that employed by Paul, 1 Cor. 14. 2, 'He that speaketh in an unknown tongue speaketh not unto men but *unto God;*' i. e. not directly to God, but so that God understands him, God takes cognizance of what he says. 2 Cor. 5. 13, 'For whether we be beside ourselves it is *to God*,' i. e. in reference to God, he is the ultimate object of it. So here Joshua's speaking was not directly *to* God, but there was a unison between his spirit and the spirit of God in his speaking, and he had all along a *believing reference* to God. See on v. 14. Seeing the day far spent, Joshua feared that he might not have time to complete the victory which he had so auspiciously begun, and being suddenly prompted from above, and inspired with Divine confidence, he commanded, in the name of Jehovah, the occurrence of a stupendous miracle in order to prolong the day till the destruction of his enemies was completely effected.——

¶ *He said in the sight of Israel, Sun, stand thou still*, &c. Or, Heb. 'he said, In the sight of Israel, Sun, be thou silent in Gibeon.' The verb in the original (דום *dōm*) generally rendered *cease, rest, be still, keep silence,* properly implies *cessation from action or noise,* rather than from motion, and is perhaps most frequently used metaphorically to signify a *silent, submissive frame of spirit, a subdued, patient, expectant attitude of soul,* like that of the Psalmist when he says, Ps. 62. 1, using this very word, 'Truly my soul *waiteth upon* (Heb. דומיה *dūmmiyâh, is silent to*) God.' See also Sam. 14. 9; Ps. 4. 4; 37. 7; Is. 23. 2. It is usually spoken of an intelligent agent, and as the import of the Heb. word for sun, is *servant,* or *minister,* it is used with great propriety here as expressive of the command of a master to a servant to *pause,* to *rest,* in his routine of service, and to assume a *still, quiet, patient* posture, indicative of the most entire subjection, and as if waiting for further orders. Such is the genuine force of the original, which cannot perhaps be fully expressed in any version.—The phrase 'in Gibeon,' means in this connexion *over* Gibeon, implying that Joshua looked off to a distance and saw the sun *apparently* standing over the city or cities of Gibeon.—As to the nature of the miracle itself, on which much has been written, it may be remarked, (1) That the scriptures generally speak in *popular*, and not in *scientific* language; that they describe the things of the natural world, not ac-

B. C. 1451.] CHAPTER X. 119

Gibeon, and thou Moon, in the valley of ᵠAjalon.

ᵠ Judg. 12, 12.

13 And the sun stood still, and the moon stayed, until the peo-

cording to strict philosophic truth, but according to appearance and common apprehension. Thus they speak of the sun's *rising* and *setting*, of the *ends* of the earth, of passing from one *end* of heaven to another, &c. Indeed, it was only in this way that Joshua could have conveyed any clear idea to the people of what he intended to express by the command. Had he uttered the words, 'Earth, stand thou still upon thine axis;' they would have thought him absolutely distracted. He spake therefore in the common popular style adopted by philosophers themselves in ordinary discourse, and every one can see that this was obviously the proper mode. Nor can any one object to this diction in the sacred writers without virtually entering his protest against the every-day language of all enlightened countries on the earth. Whether, therefore, the sun or the globe be supposed to have been arrested in its career on this occasion, is immaterial to the truth of the narrative, as the *appearance*, in each case, would be the same, and it is the *appearance*, and not the *reality*, which is described. (2) Of the precise mode in which the miracle took place, two solutions may be given, though it must necessarily ever be impossible to determine positively which of them is the true one. The effect *may* have been owing to the actual cessation of the earth's motion round its axis. This, however, without an equally miraculous interference of the Almighty, would have produced the most tremendous effects, not only upon the globe itself but perhaps upon the entire solar system, and the equilibrium of the whole material universe. But the more probable explanation in our opinion is, that the phenomenon related was merely *optical;* that the rotatory motion of the earth was not disturbed; but that instead of this the light of the sun and moon was supernaturally prolonged by the operation of the same laws of refraction and reflection that ordinarily cause the sun to appear *above* the horizon when he is in reality *below* it. He who created the heavenly luminaries, and established the laws which regulate the transmission of light, may at this time have so influenced the medium through which the sun's rays passed, as to render his disk still visible long after the time when in ordinary circumstances it would have disappeared. This would of course have had all the *visible effect* of actually bringing the earth to a pause in its revolution round its axis, and as this answers all the demands of the text, we are not solicitous to seek any more satisfactory solution of the difficulty. —— ¶ *Thou moon in the valley of Ajalon.* That is, *over* the valley of Ajalon. A city of Benjamin in the near neighborhood of Gibeon, so near, in fact, that what is here termed the valley of Ajalon, seems, in Is. 28. 24, in allusion to this event, to be called the valley of Gibeon. Junius and Tremellius, for the most part extremely judicious commentators, understand the import of the command to be, that the sun should stay itself

ple had avenged themselves upon their enemies. *Is not this written in the book of

r 2 Sam. 1. 18.

from *setting* over Gibeon, and the moon from *rising* or *advancing* over Ajalon, because the appearance of the moon is the signal for the coming on of night, which Joshua would now have to be delayed. Certain it is, that the light of the moon, even when seen, is of very little service while the sun is above the horizon, and as we suppose the sun itself to have been at this time near the horizon, we take this command to the moon to be introduced merely as a poetic ornament to make out the parallelism so common to the poetical style of the Hebrews. It is in fact doubtful whether the whole passage be not a quotation from the book of Jasher mentioned below, and whether that book were not a collection of national songs or lyric poems composed in praise of Joshua and other distinguished heroes and champions of Israel.

13. *Written in the book of Jasher.* Or, Heb. ספר הישר *sëpher hayâshâr, the book of the upright*; i. e., perhaps, of eminently good and upright men, men distinguished at once for moral worth and military prowess. As this book is generally supposed to have long since perished, though affirmed by some of the Jews to be still in existence, it is impossible to determine with certainty what it was. Mention of it occurs again 2 Sam. 1. 18,where David's lamentation over Saul is said to be extracted from it. It was probably a collection of poems, or national ballads, celebrating the chief events of the wars of Israel and the praises of their most distinguished heroes.——¶ *In the midst of heaven.* Heb. בחצי השמים *bahatzi hashshâmayim, in the division, or the half of the heavens*; i. e. above the horizon, where the upper is divided from the lower hemisphere of heaven. Some have supposed it to mean the same as 'in the meridian of heaven,' but at that hour of the day how could the moon be visible, or how did Joshua know but he should have ample time, before sunset, to complete the victory ? The other view is, therefore, we think, to be preferred.——¶ *Hasted not to go down about a whole day.* Heb. 'hasted not to go down כיום תמים *keyôm tâmim, as at the perfect day*; i. e. as it naturally does when the day is finished, when the ordinary space of a day has elapsed. This we conceive to be the true force of the original, though aware that it requires one to be acquainted with the Hebrew in order to feel the force of the evidence in favor of such a rendering. Such an one, however, upon turning to the original of Ex. 31. 18; Deut. 16. 6; 24. 13; Ps. 73. 19, will find, if we mistake not, ample proof of the correctness of this interpretation. The meaning, as we understand it, is not that the day was miraculously lengthened out to the extent of twelve hours, or another whole day, but simply that when the ordinary duration of a day was completed, the sun still delayed his setting, but for how long a time we are not informed: long enough, however, we may presume,

Jasher? So the sun stood still in the midst of heaven, and hasted not to go down about a whole day.

14 And there was ª no day like that before it or after it, that the LORD hearkened unto the voice of a man: for ᵗ the LORD fought for Israel.

15 ¶ ᵘ And Joshua returned, and all Israel with him, unto the camp to Gilgal.

ª See Isai. 38. 8. t Deut. 1. 30. ver. 42, and ch. 23. 3. ᵘ ver. 43.

---

for fully accomplishing the object for which the miracle was granted.

14. *That the Lord hearkened unto the voice of a man.* Chal. 'That the prayer of man should be heard before the Lord.' That is, for such a purpose. Not that this was the first time that the prayers of a mortal had power with God, for those of Moses had often prevailed with him, but he had never before hearkened to the voice of man to alter so signally the course of nature, or to grant such an illustrious display of his power in behalf of his people. At the voice of a man, the sun that rules the day was stopped, as he descended, and the moon that governs the night, as she arose in the east. These eyes of the lower world, which were probably the gods whom the Amorites worshipped, were compelled, as it were, to stand still and look down upon their mistaken idolaters, who might cry to them for life and deliverance. The passage imports that the command of Joshua was *in effect*, though not in form, a prayer to Jehovah for the performance of the miracle. In like manner that which seems to have been uttered by Elijah, 1 Kings 17. 1, as a *prophecy*, is spoken of by James, ch. 5. 17, as a *prayer*. Probably no miracles were wrought by the ancient prophets or servants of God but in connexion with the most fervent 'in-wrought' prayer. It is only by earnest prayer that we take hold of the strength of God.——¶ *For the Lord fought for Israel.* Chal. 'For the Lord fought by his Word.' This seems to be added as if in answer to the natural inquiry, 'Why was such a miracle wrought on this occasion? To what was it owing that Israel was so favored?' Because, says the writer, the Lord fought for them. He was engaged on their side; and it was in consequence of his purpose and his promise to befriend them, v. 8, 12, that he graciously heard the prayer of Joshua.

15. *And Joshua returned to Gilgal.* The occurrence of this verse in this place has occasioned great perplexity to commentators. As it is *verbatim* the same as the last verse of this chapter, and is wanting in some of the ancient versions, many have thought that it was inserted here by the error of some transcriber, and that the only way to obtain a correct view of the thread of the narrative is to neglect it altogether. It cannot, it is said, be supposed that Joshua should have broken off in the mid-career of his victory, and just after the above-mentioned miracle marched his army twenty or thirty miles to Gilgal, and then have immediately returned again to the scene of action to complete the work of conquest. What could be the object of such a strange diversion of his forces at such a crisis? But we are inclined to consider it as inserted here merely by anticipation. The writer's drift is apparently to close the general account of the engagement de-

16 But these five kings fled, and hid themselves in a cave at Makkedah.

17 And it was told Joshua, saying, The five kings are found hid in a cave at Makkedah.

18 And Joshua said, Roll great stones upon the mouth of the cave, and set men by it for to keep them:

19 And stay ye not, *but* pursue after your enemies, and smite the hindmost of them; suffer them not to enter into their cities: for the LORD your

---

scribed above by saying that when it was ended Joshua and the Israelites returned to the camp; not, however, that this took place immediately; there were some additional incidents that occurred prior to that return, which are too important to be overlooked in the history, and which he here takes occasion to relate. This he does in the ensuing verses, 16-42, after which he inserts again, in its proper place, the account of Joshua's return to the camp. The repetition of the words at the end of the chapter seems designed to correct the misapprehension that might arise, on reading them in their first connexion, as to the precise time to which they refer. This we regard as a safer solution of the difficulty than to suppose an error in the copyist, which in this instance seems to us improbable. It is not, however, to be disguised, that the entire context, v. 11-15, has very much the air of a supplementary insertion, as it evidently breaks the continuity of the narrative, which requires v. 16 to come in immediate connexion with v. 11, and is marked by a higher and somewhat poetical style of expression. If such a conjecture may be admitted, it will perhaps account for the occurrence of v. 15 in this connexion. The author may have seen fit to append to his inserted matter an intimation of what Joshua did after the miracle, and for this purpose have taken the 15th v. from the ensuing narrative.

16. *In a cave at Makkedah.* Heb. במקדה *bemakkĕdâh, in Makkedah;* that is, in the vicinity of Makkedah, in the region adjoining the city, not in the city itself. See what is said above of the phrase 'in Jericho,' ch. 5. 13, and 'in Gibeon,' ch. 10. 10. Compare too with this what is said Am. 9. 2-4, of the vain attempts of God's enemies to conceal themselves from his presence.

18. *Set men by it.* Heb. הפקידו עליה אנשים *haphkidu âlëhâ anâshim, give men charge over it.*

19. *Smite the hindmost of them.* Heb. וזנבתם *zinnabtem, cut off the tail,* as the rear-guard of an army is called. The Vulg. of Jerome renders it, 'cut off the last of the fugitives.' Arab., 'Clip off their hindmost.' The original term occurs only once elsewhere, Deut. 25. 18. 'Servants, dependants, or courtiers, in the East, always *follow* their superiors. Should one of them cease to serve or follow his master or patron, having gained his end, another on seeing this, asks, "Where is your tail?"—"The tail has been long in my way, I have cut it off."' *Roberts.*

—¶ *Suffer them not to enter into their cities.* Heb. 'Give them not to come to their cities.' Where they would recover strength and renew

God hath delivered them into your hand.

20 And it came to pass, when Joshua and the children of Israel had made an end of slaying them with a very great slaughter, till they were consumed, that the rest *which* remained of them entered into fenced cities.

21 And all the people returned to the camp to Joshua at Makkedah in peace : ˣ none moved his tongue against any of the children of Israel.

ˣ Exod. 11. 7.

---

the war. It seems, however, from the next verse, that a few stragglers succeeded in getting refuge in these defenced cities, but they were soon followed thither and destroyed.

20. *When Joshua and the children of Israel*, &c. That is, Joshua *by* the children of Israel, by their agency. It is evident from v. 21 that Joshua did not accompany them in person, but awaited their return at Makkedah. It is, however, entirely according to scripture analogy to speak of that as done by a commander, which was done by the soldiers under his authority and control. The phrase *may* also be rendered, ' Joshua, *even* the children of Israel.'

21. *All the people returned to the camp at Makkedah.* That is, the whole detachment which Joshua had sent out to scour the country and cut off the remaining straggling Canaanites. Probably a temporary encampment had been formed here for the accommodation of the army after the victory, in consequence of the kings being imprisoned in a cave near it. ——¶ *In peace.* Safe and sound. See Gen. 28. 21 ; Judg. 8. 9. Vulg. ' Unhurt and in the same number.'——
¶ *None moved his tongue.* That is, none of the Canaanites ; or, as the verb has no nominative, we may understand ' dog,' from Ex. 11. 7 ; implying that their victory was so complete, that not even a dog dared to bark against them. Comp. Judith 11. 13. They were struck dumb with astonishment ; they were so utterly confounded by the display of supernatural power put forth in behalf of Israel, that they presumed not to breathe a whisper of insult or reproach. As the Israelites marched in triumph through their towns and villages, so far from venturing to lift a hand against them, they did not even open their lips. It is a proverbial expression, intimating a freedom from any kind of insult or molestation. ' When a person speaks of the fear to which his enemy is reduced, he says, " Ah ! he dares not now to shake his tongue against me." " He hurt you ! the fellow will not shake his tongue against you." ' *Roberts.* See a similar mode of speech Ex. 11. 7. The Chal. renders it, ' There was no hurt or loss to Israel, for which any man should afflict his soul.' Whether or no this be the sense of the words, such was no doubt the fact. When the army came to be reviewed after the battle, there was none slain, none wounded, none missing, not one Israelite had occasion to lament the loss of a friend or the loss of a limb. The original is very express that *not one single Israelite* was harmed either by word or weapon. So complete, so superhuman, so glorious was the victory. Such a consummation fitly shadows forth the glorious end of that

22 Then said Joshua, Open the mouth of the cave, and bring out those five kings unto me out of the cave.

23 And they did so, and brought forth those five kings unto him out of the cave, the king of Jerusalem, the king of Hebron, the king of Jarmuth, the king of Lachish, *and* the king of Eglon.

24 And it came to pass, when they brought out those kings unto Joshua, that Joshua called for all the men of Israel, and said unto the captains of the men of war which went with him, Come near, ʸ put your feet upon the necks of these kings. And they came near, and put their feet upon the necks of them.

25 And Joshua said unto them,

ʸ Ps. 107. 40, and 110. 5, and 149. 8, 9. Isai. 26. 5, 6. Mal. 4. 3.

---

warfare in which, as soldiers of Jesus Christ, we profess to be engaged. When the last enemy shall be destroyed, the last alarm hushed, the last victory gained, and all the ransomed of the Most High shall come to the camp of their Almighty Leader, in final peace and rest, all the envy, the opposition, the hatred, the malice that was cherished against the Saviour and the saints, will have become extinguished for ever. 'The ransomed of the Lord shall return, and come to Zion with songs, and everlasting joy upon their heads; and sorrow and sighing shall flee away.'

22. *Then said Joshua, Open the mouth of the cave,* &c. Rosenmüller, after Usher, suggests that this was probably done the next day after the defeat of the confederated kings; but although it is clear that a vast amount of action was compressed into the space of a single day, yet we are not to forget that the day was miraculously lengthened by the special interposition of the Most High.

24. *All the men of Israel.* Heb. כל איש ישראל *kol ish Yisrael, all the man,* or *manhood of Israel,* i. e. all the men of war, the flower and prime of the army by whom the recent victory had been obtained. We have already remarked, in the notes on ch. 9. 6, that the term 'men' is often used in a peculiarly emphatic sense, to denote the *chief men,* or *the princes* of the congregation. A passage strikingly confirmative of this usage occurs Deut. 29. 10, 'Ye stand this day all of you before the Lord your God; your captains of your tribes, your elders and your officers, (*with*) all the men of Israel.' Here the 'with,' as indicated by the Italics, is not found in the original, and the sense undoubtedly is, '*even* all the men of Israel,' making the clause to stand simply in opposition with what goes before.——¶ *Put your feet upon the necks of these kings.* Not as a personal insult to the kings, but *symbolically,* in token not only of the present complete victory, but of the absolute subjection to which all their adversaries would finally be reduced, as Joshua himself explains it in the next verse. 'This in the East is a favorite way of triumphing over a fallen foe. When people are disputing, should one be a little pressed, and the other begin to triumph, the former will say, "I will tread upon

CHAPTER X.

ᶻFear not, nor be dismayed, be strong and of good courage: for ᵃthus shall the LORD do to all your enemies against whom ye fight.

26 And afterwards Joshua smote them, and slew them, and hanged them on five trees: and they ᵇwere hanging upon the trees until the evening.

27 And it came to pass at the time of the going down of the sun, *that* Joshua commanded, and they ᶜtook them down off the trees, and cast them into the cave wherein they had been hid, and laid great stones in the cave's mouth, *which remain* until this very day.

28 ¶ And that day Joshua took Makkedah, and smote it with the edge of the sword, and the

ᶻ Deut. 31. 6, 8. ch. 1. 9. ᵃ Deut. 3. 21, and 7. 19. ᵇ ch. 8. 29.

ᶜ Deut. 21. 23. ch. 8. 29.

---

thy neck, and after that beat thee." A low caste man insulting one who is high, is sure to hear some one say to the offended individual, "Put your feet on his neck."' *Roberts*. In like manner, *we* are also taught to regard our victories past as pledges of future and greater conquests.—The severity enjoined towards the vanquished kings, though abhorrent to our humane feelings, was right, because it was commanded, Deut. 20. 16, 17, and it was important that in doing the Lord's work the Israelites should be taught the lesson elsewhere inculcated by the prophet, Jer. 4. 8; 'Cursed be he that doeth the Lord's work deceitfully, and cursed be he that keepeth back his sword from blood.' The act here mentioned was in fulfilment of the prediction, Deut. 33. 29, 'Thou shalt tread upon their high places,' on which see Note.

26. *Hanged them on five trees*, &c. Chal. 'On five crosses.' See on ch. 8. 29.

27. *At the time of the going down of the sun*. Whether this was on the evening of the day so miraculously lengthened out, or of the following, has been doubted by commentators. But if the fact of the preternatural extension of the day be admitted, we can see no objection to this view.——¶ *Cast them into the cave.* 'That which they thought would have been their shelter, was made their prison first, and then their grave. So shall we be disappointed in that which we flee to from God; yet to good people the grave is still "a hiding-place," Job 14. 3.' *Henry.*—— *Laid great stones in the cave's mouth.* Mainly, we presume, for the same reason that a similar monument was raised over the place where Achan was stoned and burnt, ch. 7. 26, to perpetuate the memory of the event in connexion with the disgrace and ignominy of the culprits who suffered there. Masius remarks, without specifying his authority, that 'those who have visited this region say, that the cave is still shown in a hill near Makkedah, its mouth being closed by a wall, to preserve it as a monument.'

28. *That day Joshua took Makkedah.* The same day on which the kings were hung, and which we have already remarked was probably the day *subsequent* to that on which the sun stood still. Yet it is possible that the sense may be, that *about that time*

king thereof he utterly destroyed, them, and all the souls that *were* therein; he let none remain: and he did to the king of Makkedah ᵈ as he did unto the king of Jericho.

29 Then Joshua passed from Makkedah, and all Israel with him, unto Libnah, and fought against Libnah:

30 And the Lord delivered it also, and the king thereof, into the hand of Israel: and he smote it with the edge of the sword, and all the souls that *were* therein: he let none remain in it;

d ch. 6. 21.

but did unto the king thereof as he did unto the king of Jericho.

31 ¶ And Joshua passed from Libnah, and all Israel with him, unto Lachish, and encamped against it, and fought against it:

32 And the Lord delivered Lachish into the hand of Israel, which took it on the second day, and smote it with the edge of the sword, and all the souls that *were* therein, according to all that he had done to Libnah.

33 ¶ Then Horam king of Gezer came up to help Lachish; and Joshua smote him and his

---

—not on the identical day—he took the city of Makkedah. It might have been a day or two later.——¶ *The king thereof he utterly destroyed.* Heb. החרים *he'harim, devoted, made a curse.*——¶ *All the souls.* Heb. כל נפש *kōl nēphesh, all the soul.* That is, all the people, men, women, and children; for it would appear from ch. 11. 14, that the cattle and spoils were given to the conquerors.—— ¶ *As he did unto the king of Jericho.* How he had dealt with this king we are not expressly informed. Probably he had been first slain, and then hanged up, as was the king of Ai and the five kings here mentioned.

29. *And all Israel with him.* That is, all of Israel that had been engaged with him in this late expedition. ——¶ *Unto Libnah.* A city in the tribe of Judah near its western border, not far from Makkedah, about twelve miles west or south-west from Jerusalem. It was afterwards given to the priests, ch. 21. 13. Even its ruins have now disappeared.

31. *Unto Lachish.* Situated a few miles directly south of Libnah, near the western limits of Judah. It was probably a strongly fortified place, as Joshua could not take it till the second day, and Sennacherib afterwards was obliged to 'raise the siege.' 2 Kings, 19. 8; Is. 37. 8. Nothing is here said of the king of Lachish, as he was one of the five who had been executed before.

33. *Horam king of Gezer.* There was a city of this name in the tribe of Ephraim twenty miles southwest of Jerusalem, ch. 16. 3, 10; Judges 1. 19. But this seems too remote from the scene of action. The probability is, that it was some place in the tribe of Judah but little distant from Lachish, the king of which either as an ally of the king of Lachish, or for his own security, offered to aid in resisting the further progress of Joshua. 'Thus wicked men are often snared in their counsels, and, by opposing God in the way of his judgments, bring them sooner upon their own heads.' *Henry.*

34. *Unto Eglon.* Another city of

B. C. 1451.]. CHAPTER X. 127

people, until he had left him none remaining.

34 ¶ And from Lachish Joshua passed unto Eglon, and all Israel with him: and they encamped against it, and fought against it:

35 And they took it on that day, and smote it with the edge of the sword, and all the souls that *were* therein he utterly destroyed that day, according to all that he had done to Lachish.

36 And Joshua went up from Eglon, and all Israel with him, unto ᵉHebron; and they fought against it:

37 And they took it, and smote it with the edge of the sword, and the king thereof, and all the cities thereof, and all the souls that *were* therein; he left none remaining, according to all that he had done to Eglon, but destroyed it utterly, and all the souls that *were* therein.

38 ¶ And Joshua returned,

ᵉ See ch. 14. 13, and 15. 13. Judg. 1. 10.

Judah, near to Lachish, and fifteen miles from Jerusalem. See Map.

35. *Took it on that day.* The same day on which they encamped against it.

36, 37. *Unto Hebron—and the king thereof.* Probably a successor to him who had been slain and hanged before, v. 23, 26. The rank which this city evidently held among its sister cities doubtless made it important that, in such a crisis as the present, a new head should be immediately appointed.—Though now taken, the city of Hebron seems afterwards to have fallen back into the hands of the Canaanites, which made it necessary for Caleb to take it a second time as related, ch. 15. 14; Judges 1. 10. The case appears to have been the same in regard to some other of the places captured on this occasion. Judges 1. 11–13. The reason of it was, that Joshua, in his rapid conquests, contented himself with taking, demolishing, and burning those cities, but did not garrison any of them for fear of weakening his army. The scattered Canaanites in several instances no doubt took advantage of this, returned, repeopled, and put in a state of defence, the cities from which they had been expelled. Hence the Israelites were obliged to conquer them a second time. So the Christian in his spiritual warfare finds it as much as he can do to keep possession of the ground which he has once gained. His old enemies are incessantly returning upon him. His battles must be fought and his victories achieved anew. The lusts which appeared to be slain, are ever and anon giving signs that they still live; and are intent upon regaining their former ascendency. This makes it dangerous to remit our activity for a single hour. Constant vigilance is the grand condition of final triumph. ——¶*All the cities thereof.* The cities subject to its jurisdiction and dependant upon it; so that Hebron was properly speaking a *metropolis,* i. e. *a mother city.* Such too was Gibeon, spoken of above, v. 2; ch. 9. 17.

38. *And Joshua returned.* That is, turned his course, began to march in a new direction. It is not implied that he had been at Debir before; but that having now advanced to the southwest as far as he thought fit, even as far as Gaza, v. 41, he turned

JOSHUA. [B. C. 1451.

and all Israel with him, to ᶠDebir; and fought against it:

39 And he took it, and the king thereof, and all the cities thereof, and they smote them with the edge of the sword, and utterly destroyed all the souls that *were* therein : he left none remaining: as he had done to Hebron, so he did to Debir, and to the king thereof; as he had

ᶠ See ch. 16. 15. Judg. 1. 11.

done also to Libnah, and to her king.

40 ¶ So Joshua smote all the country of the hills, and of the south, and of the vale, and of the springs, and all their kings: he left none remaining, but utterly destroyed all that breathed, as the LORD God of Israel ᵍcommanded.

ᵍ Deut. 20. 16, 17

---

and directed his course towards Gilgal, lying to the northeast, and fell upon Debir on his way. This city was in the tribe of Judah, about thirty miles southwest of Jerusalem and ten miles west of Hebron. It was also called Kirjath-Sepher, ch. 15. 15, and Kirjath-Sannah, ch. 15. 19, perhaps from its being one of the seats of learning among the Canaanites; the name Kirjath-Sepher signifying the *city of books* or of *letters.* The Canaanites having subsequently retaken it, Caleb, to whom it fell by lot, gave his daughter Achsah in marriage to Othniel for his bravery in having carried it by storm, ch. 15. 16. It was afterwards given to the priests, ch. 21. 15, but no trace of it is to be found at the present time.

40. *Smote all the country of the hills.* Overrun as a conqueror, subdued and took possession of all the southern section of Canaan, familiarly known by the appellation of ההר *Hahar,* i. e. *the hill-country,* which subsequently fell to the lot of Judah. Of this mountainous region Burckhardt says, the whole country between Tekoa and Hebron is finer and better cultivated than in the neighborhood of Jerusalem; while the sides of the hills, instead of being

naked and dreary, are richly studded with the oak, the arbutus, the Scotch fir, and a variety of flowering shrubs. Of the hitherto unknown tract south of Hebron, Bankes, Leigh, Irby and Mangles inform us that three days to the south of Hebron, they passed towards the Dead Sea through a country well cultivated, but extremely uninteresting; eight or nine miles beyond Kerek they found themselves on the borders of an extensive desert, entirely abandoned to the wandering Bedouins. A tribe of Jellaheen Arabs here told them, that in years of scarcity they were accustomed to retire into Egypt. The same necessity compelled Jacob to the same expedient: and the custom seems handed down from the patriarchs. See *Russell's Palestine.*——¶ *Of the South.* That is, of Canaan. The southern part of the tribe of Judah and Idumea was designated by the general term, *the south.* Gen. 20. 1.——¶ *Of the vale.* Heb. השפלה *hashshephëlâh the low country,* i. e. the level champaign on the Mediterranean Sea, extending from Joppa to the borders of Egypt. Deut. 1. 7; Judg. 1. 9; Jer. 17. 26.——¶ *The springs.* Heb. האשדות *hâashdoth, the descents,* i. e. probably the slopes or declivities of

B. C. 1450.] CHAPTER XI. 129

41 And Joshua smote them from Kadesh-barnea even unto ʰGaza, ⁱand all the country of Goshen, even unto Gibeon.

42 And all these kings and their land did Joshua take at one time; ᵏbecause the LORD God of Israel fought for Israel.

43 And Joshua returned, and

ʰ Gen. 10. 19. ⁱ ch. 11. 16. ᵏ ver. 14.

all Israel with him, unto the camp to Gilgal.

CHAPTER XI.

AND it came to pass, when Jabin king of Hazor had heard *those things*, that he ᵃsent to Jobab king of Madon, and to the king ᵇof Shimron, and to the king of Achshaph,

ᵃ ch. 10. 3. ᵇ ch. 19. 15.

---

mountains, tracts formed by the washing down of the mountains, and so capable of cultivation. See Num. 21. 15; Deut. 3. 17.—¶ *Destroyed all that breathed.* That is, of mankind; for they kept the cattle for spoil.

41. *All the country of Goshen.* Not the country of that name in Egypt, the former residence of the Hebrews, but a place so called in Judah, fourteen miles south of Hebron, ch. 11. 16; 15. 51.

42. *At one time.* Heb. פעם אחת *paam ehâth, at one turn or one stroke,* i. e. in one uninterrupted course of vigorous action; or, as we should say, in one campaign. The leading idea is that from the time Joshua entered upon this career of victories, till it was closed, there was no pause, no intermission, no cessation.— ¶ *Because the Lord fought for Israel.* This clause is introduced in order to give credibility to the foregoing narrative. Viewed in any other light than as the result of omnipotence, such a tide of victories would naturally stagger all belief.

CHAPTER XI.

1. *Jabin king of Hazor.* After the very remarkable reduction of the southern parts of Canaan, related in

the foregoing chapter, the kings of the north becoming apprehensive for their safety, are here presented in the act of making a common interest, and uniting with Jabin to put a stop to the further progress of the Israelites. Jabin was probably the common name of all the kings of Hazor, as we find that the king by whom the Israelites were afterwards kept in bondage for twenty years, and who was defeated by Deborah and Barak, was so called. The name signifies *wise,* or *intelligent.* Hazor was a strong city on the west side of the waters of Merom, or lake Samechonitis, and the capital of northern Canaan. In the distribution of the land it fell to the tribe of Naphtali. It was in subsequent times frequently the seat of war, but not a ruin now remains to mark the place where it stood.—¶ *Madon.* The position of this city is unknown. It was doubtless in the neighborhood of the others here mentioned.——¶*Shimron.* Called also Shimron-Meron, ch. 12. 10. It fell afterwards to the lot of Zebulon, and was situated about eleven miles to the north-east of Nazareth.——¶ *Achshaph.* Situated in the tribe of Asher, near the confines of Zebulon. It was reduced to a small village, called *Chasalus,* in

2 And to the kings that *were* on the north of the mountains, and of the plains south of ᶜCinneroth, and in the valley, and in the borders ᵈof Dor on the west,

3 *And to* the Canaanite on the east and on the west, and *to* the Amorite, and the Hittite, and the Perizzite, and the Jebusite in the mountains, ᵉand *to* the Hivite under ᶠHermon ᵍin the land of Mizpeh.

4 And they went out, they and all their hosts with them, much people, ʰeven as the sand that is upon the sea-shore in multi-

ᶜ Num. 34. 11. ᵈ ch. 17. 11. Judg. 1. 27. 1 Kings 4. 11.
ᵉ Judg. 3. 3. ᶠ ch. 13. 11. ᵍ Gen. 31. 49. ʰ Gen. 22. 17, and 31. 12. Judg. 7. 12. 1 Sam. 13. 5.

---

the time of Jerome, at the close of the fourth century, but is now entirely swept away.

2. *That were on the north of the mountains.* Heb. מצבון בהר *mitz-zephōn bāhār, from the north in the mountain,* i. e. residing in the mountainous region of the north, the tract of Anti-Libanus.—¶ *The plains south of Cinneroth.* Heb. בערבה *bāarabāh, plain.* An ancient city, belonging afterwards to the tribe of Naphtali, and supposed to have occupied the same site with the more modern Tiberias. From this city or village, the sea of Chinneroth, or Gennesareth, probably had its name. From the original it is not perfectly clear whether the plain spoken of lay to the south of Chinneroth, or Chinneroth to the south of that. In the former case, it would seem to have been the plain of the Jordan, which we think less likely.—¶ *In the valley.* In the low or valley tracts generally, in contradistinction from the mountainous points which were inhabited.—¶ *The borders of Dor.* This was a place on the coast of the Mediterranean, about nine miles north of Cesarea Palestine, and at a little distance from mount Carmel. A small village, called *Tortura,* is in the vicinity of the ruins of the an-

cient town, containing forty or fifty houses.

3. *The Canaanite on the east,* &c. The Canaanites, properly so called, dwelt part of them in the east near Jordan, and part on the west near the sea; both are here united.—— ¶ *The Hivite under Hermon.* At the foot of mount Hermon; of which mountain see on Deut. 3. 9. They are designated in this way to distinguish them from another portion of the same race dwelling at Gibeon, of whom we have already spoken. ——¶ *In the land of Mizpeh.* That is, *the land of watching or espial,* so called from its commanding an extensive prospect of the surrounding country, from which the approach or movements of an enemy might be discovered. There were several places of this name, but reference is here undoubtedly had to that lying in the northern quarter of Gilead, where Laban and Jacob made their covenant, as related Gen. 31. 48, 49.

4. *And they went out.* Took the field; a phrase frequently employed by the sacred writers for *going forth upon a military expedition.* Thus 2 Sam. 11. 1, 'And it came to pass —at the time when kings *go forth,*' i. e. to battle, as our version rightly understands it. Comp. Num. 21. 23

tude, with horses and chariots very many.

5 And when all these kings were met together, they came and pitched together at the waters of Merom, to fight against Israel.

6 ¶ And the LORD said unto Joshua, ⁱBe not afraid because of them: for to-morrow about this time will I deliver them up all slain before Israel: thou shalt ᵏhough their horses, and burn their chariots with fire.

i ch. 10. 8. k 2 Sam. 8. 4.

Job 39. 21.——¶ *As the sand that is upon the sea-shore.* A proverbial expression used to denote a vast but indefinite number—a number of which no accurate estimate could be formed. Josephus, upon what authority we know not, is more particular. He states the number at 300,000 foot, 10,000 horse, and 20,000 chariots of war. Whether this be correct or not, the words of the text lead us to infer that a vast population now occupied the land of promise, and that the soil must have been of exuberant fertility to sustain it. The immense multitude, moreover, of the enemy went to heighten the glory of Joshua's victory.——¶ *With horses and chariots very many.* Heb. סוּס ורכב רב מאד *sûs vâ-rëkeb rab meōd, horse and chariot very much.* The horses were probably brought out of Egypt or Armenia, and not bred in Canaan, which was not a country favorable to their production or use. Deut. 17. 16; 1 Kings 10. 28, 29. The war chariots of the Canaanites are supposed to have been armed with iron scythes fastened to the poles and to the ends of the axletrees. When furiously driven they would make fearful havoc in the ranks of infantry—of which only were the forces of Israel composed—mowing them down like grass. In view therefore of such a formidable armament mustered against him,

Joshua receives from the Lord a special encouragement and promise of success.

5. *Were met together.* Heb. רועדו *yivvâedû, were assembled by appointment.* In pursuance of previous arrangements. Chal. 'Met at a time agreed upon.'——¶ *At the waters of Merom.* Generally understood of the lake Semechon or Samechonitis, lying between the head of the river Jordan and the lake of Gennesaret. The name imports ' highness,' and is supposed to be so called because its waters were higher than those of the sea of Galilee. The Arabic *Samaka,* from which Semechon is derived, has the same import. It is situated in a valley, and is now called *Bahhrat el-Hhule,* i. e. *the lake of the valley,* a valley formed by the two branches of mount Hermon. In summer the lake is for the most part dry, and covered with shrubs and grass, in which lions, bears, and other wild beasts conceal themselves.

6. *Shall hough their horses.* That is, hamstring them, cut the sinews of their legs. On the effects of such a treatment of these animals, Michaelis remarks, that 'irom ignorance of military affairs, most expositors have understood this command, as if it meant, not that the horses should be killed, but merely lamed in their hind legs, and then let go. But a horse so treated, must, instead of run-

7 So Joshua came, and all the people of war with him, against them by the waters of Merom suddenly, and they fell upon them.

8 And the Lord delivered

---

ning off, fall instantly backwards, and writhe about miserably till he die, which generally happens from loss of blood, by the stroke of the sabre cutting the artery of the thigh. This is still, as military people have since informed me, the plan adopted to make those horses that are taken, but cannot be easily brought away, unserviceable to the enemy again. They hamstring them, which can be done in an instant; and they generally die of the wound by bleeding to death; but though they should not, the wound never heals; so that even if the enemy recover them alive, he is forced to dispatch them; and every compassionate friend of horses who has ever seen one in that situation, will do so in order to terminate his misery. There is no foundation for Kimchi's opinion, that mere laming was enjoined, because it would be wrong to put an animal unnecessarily to death. For thus to lame a horse that would still live, in my opinion, would rather have been extreme cruelty; because, being then useless, nobody would be likely to give him any food.' (*Comment. on Laws of Moses, Art.* LXIV.) The reasons for prescribing such a treatment probably were (1) Because God would have his people act upon the resolution expressed by the Psalmist, Ps. 20. 7, 'Some trust in chariots and some in horses; but we will remember the name of the Lord our God.' If horses had been in common use among them, they would have been apt to rely upon them instead of trusting to the aid of omnipotence in achieving their conquests. But God's design was to cut them off from human resources, and by enabling a company of raw and inexperienced footmen to rout bodies of cavalry, to secure the glory of the victory to his own right arm, to which only it was due. (2) Because horses were a kind of useless plunder to the Israelites. From the nature of the country they could not well be employed for purposes of agriculture. In that rough and mountainous land, oxen and asses could be employed to much greater advantage; and as to travelling, it was never designed that the Israelites should be a travelling people. They were to be an agricultural and not a commercial race. They were to live apart from other nations as a religious community. Their stated journeys to Jerusalem to attend upon the religious festivals would be about all the travelling that would be necessary, and this on their rough roads could be better performed on foot or on asses than on horses. Such of these animals therefore as they took in war could be of no use to them, unless they sold them, and this would not be wise, as they might finally have come round again into the hands of their enemies. The true policy accordingly was to diminish as far as possible this race of animals, which might give their enemies a signal advantage, and in this policy we suppose the present order to have originated.

7. *Suddenly.* The great feature of Joshua's military operations appears to have been *dispatch.* In the

B. C. 1450.] CHAPTER XI. 133

them into the hand of Israel, who smote them, and chased them unto great Zidon, and unto ¹Misrephoth-maim, and unto the valley of Mispeh eastward; and they smote them, until they left them none remaining.

9 And Joshua did unto them ᵐ as the LORD bade him: he houghed their horses, and burnt their chariots with fire.

l ch. 13. 6. m ver. 6.

10 ¶ And Joshua at that time turned back, and took Hazor, and smote the king thereof with the sword: for Hazor beforetime was the head of all those kingdoms.

11 And they smote all the souls that *were* therein with the edge of the sword, utterly destroying *them:* there was not any left to breathe: and he burnt Hazor with fire.

---

celerity of his movements he seems to have equalled the most renowned generals whether of ancient or modern times. Being now apprised of this grand combination of the northern kings, he loses no time, but by a forced march, and before they could have supposed him at hand, comes suddenly upon them and puts them to the rout.

8. *Unto great Zidon.* A well known city of Ancient Phenicia, situated on the east coast of the Mediterranean, about twenty-five miles north of Tyre, fifty south of Berytus (Beyroot), and sixty-six west of Damascus. Its modern name is *Said.* The epithet רבה *rabbâh, great,* here affixed to it, is expressive of *number* rather than of *size,* and implies not only its *populousness,* but the *extent and variety of its resources* of every kind.——¶ *Misrephoth-maim.* Or, Heb. משרפות מים *Misrepoth of the waters,* i. e. *the burning of the waters;* but whether so called from its being noted for *hot springs,* or the manufacture of *glass,* or of *salt,* each of which has been conjectured, or from some other cause, it is not possible to determine. It is supposed to have been a place on the sea coast, about three miles north of Sidon.——¶ *Valley of*

Mizpek. Under mount Hermon, as appears by comparing this with v. 5 and 17, in the latter of which it appears to be called *the valley of Lebanon.* This place lay on the east, as Sidon did on the west, so that the vanquished enemy fled in two different directions, in both of which they were pursued by the conquerors.——¶ *Until they left them none remaining.* From other portions of the history, it is plain that this language here and elsewhere, is not to be construed in its most literal import. Numbers of the Canaanites did undoubtedly escape the sword of the Israelites, and fled to Zidon, Tyre and other maritime cities; and even here it appears that Jabin escaped with his life from the battle. But the drift of the words is to intimate, that they left none alive who fell into their hands, whomsoever they encountered or overtook they slew.

10. *Hazor—was the head,* &c. Not of all Canaan, but of those northern principalities which were combined in this expedition against Israel. This city, however, afterwards recovered itself, and grievously oppressed the people of Israel, Judges 4. 2.

11. *Not any left to breathe.* Heb.

12

12 And all the cities of those kings, and all the kings of them, did Joshua take, and smote them with the edge of the sword, *and* he utterly destroyed them, ⁿ as Moses the servant of the LORD commanded.

13 But *as for* the cities that stood still in their strength,

ⁿ Num. 33. 52.   Deut. 7. 2, and 20. 16, 17.

נשמה *nishmâh, any breath,* i. e. not any human being.——¶ *He burnt Hazor with fire.* Comp. v. 13. It is not said expressly of the Israelites, in this part of the narrative, that *they* burnt any city whatever, as such a statement might give rise to the impression that, in the ardor of military zeal, they were guilty of excesses, and in the spirit of a licentious soldiery, were eager to apply the torch to the devoted cities. On the contrary, the act is attributed to Joshua, implying that it was done calmly and deliberately, and in all likelihood by Divine direction. The phraseology is so constructed as to give a striking testimony to the moderation and self-control of the armies of the Most High.

12. *Utterly destroyed them.* That is, the persons, the inhabitants; for many of the cities themselves, as well as the spoils which they contained, were preserved, as we learn in the ensuing verse.

13. *The cities that stood still in their strength.* Heb. עמדות על תלם *ōmeedeth al tillâm, standing upon, or by, their heaps.* It would be difficult to point out any single expression in the whole book of Joshua, perhaps in the whole Scriptures, more difficult of explanation than this. The exact literal version of the words we have given above; but our common translation has followed the Chaldee paraphrase in rendering the Heb. תל *tal,* by 'strength,' a sense which it has in no other instance, that we can discover, in the compass of the sacred writings. Its prevailing and legitimate import is a 'heap of ruins.' Thus Deut. 13. 16, in reference to the city which had become the seat of idolatry; 'Thou shalt gather all the spoil of it into the midst of the street thereof, and shalt burn with fire the city, and all the spoil thereof for the Lord thy God; and it shall be *an heap* (תל) for ever; it shall not be built again.' Josh. 8. 28, 'And Joshua burnt Ai, and made it *an heap* (תל) for ever, even a desolation unto this day.' Jer. 49. 2, 'I will cause an alarm of war to be heard in Rabbah of the Ammonites, and it shall be a *desolate heap* (תל שממה *tal shemâmâh*), and her daughters shall be burned with fire.' Jer. 30. 18, 'The city shall be builded upon her own *heap* (תלה *tillâh*);' i. e. upon its own ruins. These examples show the genuine force of the word. The mass of expositors, however, from the affinity of the ideas of a *heap of ruins* and an *eminence,* or *elevation* of any kind, and not knowing what to understand by cities 'standing upon their ruinous heaps,' have been led to interpret it of cities standing upon *hills,* or *rocky heights,* forming natural fortresses of great strength, and such as the Israelites chose to retain for their own use. To this solution we should have nothing to object were it warranted by the native import of the term; but we are persuaded it is not. The true rendering is unquestionably that which we have

B. C. 1450.] CHAPTER XI. 135

Israel burned none of them, save Hazor only; *that* did Joshua burn.

14 And all the spoil of these cities, and the cattle, the children of Israel took for a prey unto themselves: but every man they smote with the edge of the sword, until they had destroyed them, neither left they any to breathe.

15 ¶ ° As the LORD commanded Moses his servant, so ᵖ did Moses command Joshua, and ᵠ so did Joshua: he left nothing undone of all that the LORD commanded Moses.

16 So Joshua took all that land, ʳ the hills, and all the south country, ˢ and all the land of Goshen, and the valley and the plain, and the mountain of Israel, and the valley of the same:

° Exod. 34. 11, 12.   p Deut. 7. 2.   q ch. 1. 7.   r ch. 12.8.   s ch. 10. 41.

---

given, and a consistent sense is to be sought for the phrase. From an attentive comparison of the context, it appears that the kings and the inhabitants of these cities were all put to the sword, while the cattle and the spoil generally went into the hands of the captors. During the time, therefore, of the actual occurrence of these events, the cities in question must have presented a fearful scene of carnage and desolation. Heaps of lifeless bodies and of gathered spoil would be accumulated in the streets, and wherever such a complete conquest and pillage could be easily effected without demolishing the walls, buildings, or fortifications of the cities, those cities might be said to 'stand still, or continue to stand upon, over, or by their ruinous heaps,' i. e. heaps of the slain and heaps of spoil. This doubtless was the case in numerous instances. It was not absolutely *necessary* to raze and burn all the cities, and so many of them were spared; but Hazor being the head of the confederacy and more guilty than the rest, was properly made an exception and utterly destroyed.——¶ *Save Hazor only.* As this city had begun the war, and from its being a royal residence and strongly fortified might, if it should fall back into the hands of the Canaanites, possess peculiar facilities for renewing and carrying it on afresh, Joshua deemed it prudent to guard against all danger from that quarter by demolishing it altogether.—So the Christian, if he finds his spiritual enemies likely to entrench themselves in any particular corruption or infirmity of his nature, and thence to make violent inroads upon his peace, is bound at all hazards, by crucifying such a lust, to deprive them of this advantage. If they can be dislodged from their stronghold in no other way, let him destroy the stronghold itself.

14. *All the spoils of these cities—Israel took.* With the exception of such things as had been employed for idolatrous purposes, Deut. 7. 25.

15. *As the Lord commanded Moses*, &c. A virtual vindication of the Israelites from the charge of cruelty which might possibly be brought against them in view of the severities exercised towards these vanquished kings and people of Canaan. ——¶ *He left nothing undone.* Or, Heb. לא הסיר דבר *lō hēsir dâbâr, removed, rejected, diminished nothing.*

17 ᵗ*Even* from the mount Halak, that goeth up to Seir, even unto Baal-gad, in the valley of Lebanon under mount Hermon;

18 Joshua made war a long time with all those kings.

ᵗ ch. 12. 7. ᵘ Deut. 7. 24. ch. 12. 7.

and ᵘall their kings he took, and smote them, and slew them.

---

16. *The mountain of Israel and the valley of the same.* Not any particular mountain and valley, but the *mountains* and *valleys* generally included in the whole extent of the land of Israel.

17. *From the Mount Halak.* That is, Heb. הָהָר הֶחָלָק *hâhâr hëhâlâk, the bare, smooth,* or *bald mountain,* so called from its being destitute of trees. The writer's design seems to be to specify the extreme southern and northern limits of the promised land. Joshua's conquests extended from the borders of Seir or Edom, where Mount Halak was situated, northward to Baal-gad, which lies at the foot of Mount Lebanon.

18. *Joshua made war a long time.* Heb. ימים רבים *yàmim rabbim, many days.* As many at least as six or seven years; as appears from comparing ch. 14. 7-10; the first having been occupied in the conquest of the *southern* portion of the land, and the remaining five or six in that of the *northern.* It would seem that the writer by inserting this statement here designed to guard the reader against the impression that, as the record of these wars is very brief, so the space of time in which they were accomplished was also brief. This by no means follows, as the present account is intended as a mere rapid sketch or outline of Israel's victories over the nations of Canaan. In the sacred writings the compass of a few sentences often contains the events of many years.—We may not perhaps be able to state all the reasons that weighed in the Divine mind for thus prolonging the warfare of his people, but of *one* we are assured by God himself, Deut. 7. 22, 'The Lord thy God will put out those nations before thee by little and little; thou mayest not consume them at once, *lest the beasts of the field increase upon thee.*' In addition to this, it was no doubt the purpose of heaven to try the faith and patience of his people by a long series of arduous struggles. Although the *commencement* of the work was marked by a succession of wonderful interpositions in their behalf, yet in its *progress* they were to be left more to their personal exertions. God would not make his miraculous aid too cheap in their eyes by making it common. He would train them to a course of the most vigorous efforts on their part, while at the same time they were taught their continual dependence on Him for success in their conflicts. This is in beautiful analogy with the warfare of the Christian. In its commencement, at the outset of the Christian life, the power of God is no less wonderfully displayed than in the history before us. The transition of a soul from darkness to light is virtually a miracle. It is effected by the sovereign power of God as really, and to the sinner's consciousness in many instances as marvellously, as the passage of Israel through the cloven waters of Jordan. But in its progress, the work is carried forward

B. C. 1450.] CHAPTER XI. 137

19 There was not a city that made peace with the children of Israel, save ˣ the Hivites the inhabitants of Gibeon: all *other* they took in battle. 20 For ʸ it was of the LORD to

ˣ ch. 9. 3. 7. ʸ Deut. 2. 30. Judg. 14. 4. 1 Sam. 2. 25. 1 Kings 12. 15. Rom. 9. 18.

more appropriately by his own actings. He has the armor given him, but his own activity is called forth in the use of it. His whole life is to be a state of warfare, and it is by hard fighting that he is to obtain the victory. No one enemy will submit to him without an obstinate resistance, nor until violently smitten with the sword of the Spirit. There will be some seasons of more than ordinary conflict, when he will need peculiar succor from on high; and there will be other seasons of comparative rest; but there is no entire discharge in this war till mortality is swallowed up of life; and then he shall enjoy the fruit of his victories in everlasting rest.

19. *Not a city that made peace—save the Hivites*, &c. Although in the commands given to Moses respecting the extirpation of the Canaanites we have no *express* intimation that any of them were to be spared upon their voluntary surrender and submission, yet from the example of Rahab and the Gibeonites, and especially from these words, the presumption is, that this was the case. The Divine laws, wherever it can be done without compromising the interests of justice, always lean to the side of mercy. Besides, it has been justly remarked, that the *reason* of the law *is* the law. The evil designed to be prevented by the order for the universal destruction of the Canaanites, was the infecting of the Israelites with their idolatry, Deut. 7. 4. But if these devoted nations renounced their idolatry, and came heartily into the interest of Israel, the danger was effectually prevented, the reason of the law ceased, and consequently, we may suppose, the obligation ceased also. But the Canaanites in general were not in the least disposed to do this, nor did they so much as propose terms of accommodation. Of the cause, or occasion rather, of this utter infatuation, we are informed in the ensuing verse. —¶ *All* other *they took in battle.* That is, all whom they did take, they took in battle. They received none upon submission. It is certain from other parts of the sacred narrative, that the Canaanites were neither utterly exterminated, nor absolutely driven from their settlements, either by Joshua or his immediate successors. On the contrary, a large proportion of them fled, it is supposed, to Tyre and Zidon, and thence migrated into distant countries, particularly Africa, where they established numerous and flourishing colonies. Procopius relates that the Phœnicians fled before the Hebrews into Africa, and spread themselves abroad as far as the pillars of Hercules, and adds, ' In Numidia, where now stands the city Tigris (Tangiers) they have erected two columns, on which, in Phœnician characters, is the following inscription:—" We are the Phœnicians, who fled from the face of that notorious robber, Jesus (or Joshua) the son of Nave (Nun)." ' Numbers, however, yet remained to dispute, for ages, the possession of

12*

harden their hearts, that they should come against Israel in battle, that he might destroy them utterly, *and* that they might have no favor, but that he might destroy them ᶻ as the Lord commanded Moses.

21 ¶ And at that time came Joshua and cut off ᵃ the Ana-

ᶻ Deut. 20. 16, 17.

kims from the mountains, from Hebron, from Debir, from Anab, and from all the mountains of Judah, and from all the mountains of Israel: Joshua destroyed them utterly with their cities.

22 There was none of the Anakims left in the land of the

ᵃ Num. 13. 22. 33. Deut. 1. 28. ch. 15. 13, 14.

---

the land with their invaders, and to cause them infinite trouble.

20. *It was of the Lord to harden their hearts.* On the subject of God's hardening the hearts of men, see Note on Ex. ch. 4. 21. The meaning here is simply that having sinned for a long tract of ages against the light of conscience and providence, God was now pleased to leave them to a *judicial hardness of heart*, to give them up to vain confidence, pride, stubbornness, and malignity, that they might bring upon themselves his righteous vengeance and be utterly destroyed. This result is said to be 'of or from the Lord,' because he did not interpose to prevent it.——¶ *As the Lord commanded Moses.* This expression occurs here and elsewhere in this connexion, v. 15, 'to show that Joshua and Israel did not act out of cruelty, revenge, and avarice; but simply in obedience to God, *which alone* could induce pious men to make such undistinguishing slaughter of their fellow-creatures: and doubtless many of them did very great violence to their own feelings and inclinations, while engaged in that service.' *Scott.*

21. *At that time.* That is, during this war; in the course of these conquests. The words refer to no *special point* of time, as the work was gradually accomplished during the lapse of a considerable period. Some suppose this to be merely a recapitulation of the military operations detailed ch. 10. 36-41, adding here a memorable circumstance there omitted, viz. the destruction of the Anakims, with the rest of the inhabitants of those places. Of this gigantic race, see on Num. 13. 33. Their cutting off is particularly mentioned here, because they had been such a terror to the spies forty years before, to whom their bulk and strength made them appear as absolutely invincible. Even the opposition which they feared the most was overcome. 'Never let the sons of Anak be a terror to the Israel of God, for even *their* day will come to fall. Giants are dwarfs to Omnipotence.' *Henry.* Though these Anakims were now for the most part reduced, yet numbers of them escaped and took refuge in the country of the Philistines, and settled there, from whom Goliath, and other giants, descended. After a time some of them returned with followers, and rebuilt the cities from which they had been expelled; and Caleb and Othniel, to whom that region was assigned, vanquished and destroyed them after the division of the land. Ch. 14. 6-15; 15. 13-17.

22. *So Joshua took the whole land.*

children of Israel: only in Gaza, in ᵇGath, ᶜand in Ashdod, there remained.

23 So Joshua took the whole land, ᵈaccording to all that the LORD said unto Moses, and Joshua gave it for an inheritance unto Israel ᵉaccording to their divisions by their tribes. ᶠAnd the land rested from war.

ᵇ 1 Sam. 17. 4. ᶜ ch. 15. 46. ᵈ Num. 34. 2, &c. ᵉ Num. 26. 53. ch. 14. and 15. and

CHAPTER XII.

NOW these *are* the kings of the land, which the children of Israel smote, and possessed their land on the other side Jordan toward the rising of the sun, ᵃfrom the river Arnon, ᵇunto mount Hermon, and all the plain on the east:

16. and 17. and 18. and 19. ᶠ ch. 14. 15, and 21. 44, and 22. 4, and 23. 1. ver. 18. ᵃ Num. 21. 24. ᵇ Deut. 3. 8, 9.

Not absolutely the whole, for in ch. 13. 1, the Lord himself is represented as saying to Joshua, 'There remaineth yet very much land to be possessed,' but all the country described here and in the preceding chapter; the greatest and best part of it.

23. *Gave it for an inheritance unto Israel.* The *actual distribution* of the land is detailed afterwards.

CHAPTER XII.

We have in the present chapter a recapitulation of all the victories thus far achieved. As the writer is about to enter upon a particular account of the distribution of the land among the tribes, he here pauses to give previously a general view of the territory to be divided, including the tracts on both sides the Jordan. This he does by specifying the kings, rather than the countries over which they reigned; for the power of a state is concentrated in the person of its sovereign, and such an enumeration presents the subject more vividly to the mind of the reader.—The first six verses contain a list of the kings on the east side of Jordan, conquered by Moses, with their territories, and the remainder of the chapter is occupied with a catalogue of those that were reduced by Joshua. 'The enjoyment of present blessings under living benefactors, should not be suffered to efface the remembrance of former mercies procured by the instrumentality of God's honored servants who have entered into their rest. The services and achievements of Joshua should not eclipse those of Moses.' *Henry.* The passages referred to in the margin give all the useful information that can now be gleaned respecting those places, but recourse to a good map of ancient Canaan is indispensable to obtaining a clear idea of the subject.

1. *From the river Arnon unto Mount Hermon.* The small river Arnon was the boundary of all the southern coast of the land *occupied* by the Israelites beyond Jordan. The mountains of Hermon were the boundaries on the north. The Arnon takes its rise in the mountains of Gilead, and after running a considerable distance from north to south, turns to the north-west and falls into the Dead Sea not very far from the place where the Jordan discharges itself. See Num. 21. 13; Deut. 2. 24.——¶*And all the plain on the east.* Or, even all the plain; all

2 ᶜSihon king of the Amorites, who dwelt in Heshbon, *and* ruled from Aroer, which *is* upon the bank of the river Arnon, and from the middle of the river, and from half Gilead, even unto the river Jabbok, *which is* the border of the children of Ammon;

ᶜ Num. 21. 24. Deut. 2. 33, 36, and 3. 6, 16.

3 And ᵈfrom the plain to the sea of Cinneroth on the east, and unto the sea of the plain, *even* the salt sea on the east, ᵉthe way to Beth-jeshimoth; and from the south, under ᶠAshdoth-pisgah:

ᵈ Deut. 3. 17. ᵉ ch. 13. 20. ᶠ Deut. 3. 17, and 4. 49.

the arable champaign country on the east of the Jordan, and called, Deut. 34. 1, 'The plains of Moab.' On the physical features of this country, see Note on Num. 3. 2.

2. *Ruled from Aroer.* The kingdom of Sihon was bounded by the Arnon on the south, the Jabbok on the north, the Jordan on the west, and the mountains of Arabia on the east.——¶ *And from the middle of the river.* Heb. וְתוֹךְ הַנַּחַל *vethōk hannàhal, and that which lies between the streams.* A line passing along the middle of a stream, and that stream by no means a large one, is so remarkable a boundary to be adopted by ancient barbarous clans, that we are quite satisfied the translation is erroneous. The word 'from,' introduced by our translators, does not occur in the original, either here or in the ensuing clause, 'from half Gilead,' and the meaning undoubtedly is, that Sihon ruled from Aroer over the country *lying between the rivers* (collect. sing. for plur.) even the half of Gilead, as far north as to the river Jabbok. See on ch. 13. 9. All the region *lying intermediate* between the above-mentioned streams, and sometimes called 'half Gilead,' was subject to his authority. This interpretation is strikingly confirmed by the words of Josephus relative to the territory of Sihon, which, he says, 'is a country *situate between three rivers*, and naturally resembling an island; the river Arnon being its southern limit, the river Jabbok determining its northern side, while Jordan itself runs along by it on its western coast.' (Antiq. B. 41, ch. 5.) The other half of Gilead, as appears from v. 4, 5, lay beyond the Jabbok, and belonged to the kingdom of Og.

3. *And from the plain,* &c. Here again the word 'from' is gratuitously, and, as we conceive, erroneously inserted. The design of the writer is merely to give a more distinct view of the position of the tract called 'the plain,' which embraced, as we suppose, the plain of the Jordan on its eastern side, extending from the sea of Cinneroth or Gennesaret on the north to the salt or Dead Sea on the south. It is not implied that *he reigned to* the sea of Cinneroth, but that the *plain in question extended that far*, the largest part of which fell into his dominions.——¶ *Sea of the plain.* The Dead Sea is so called from its occupying what was once a fertile, luxuriant, and beautiful plain, in which were situated the cities of Sodom and Gomorrah, called also the 'cities of the plain.'——¶ *Beth-jeshimoth.* Situated about ten miles east of the Jordan, and about the same distance from its mouth.——¶ *From the south.* Or, Heb. מתימו

B. C. 1452.] CHAPTER XII. 141

4 ¶ And ᵍthe coast of Og king of Bashan, *which was* of ʰthe remnant of the giants, ⁱthat dwelt at Ashtaroth and at Edrei,

5 And reigned in ᵏ mount Hermon, ˡand in Salcah, and in all Bashan, ᵐunto the border of the Geshurites, and the Maachathites, and half Gilead, the border of Sihon king of Heshbon.

6 ⁿThem did Moses the servant of the LORD, and the children of Israel smite: and ᵒMoses the servant of the LORD gave it *for* a possession unto the Reubenites, and the Gadites, and the half-tribe of Manasseh.

7 ¶ And these *are* the kings of the country ᵖwhich Joshua and the children of Israel smote on this side Jordan on the west, from Baal-gad in the valley of Lebanon, even unto the mount Halak that goeth up to ᑫSeir; which Joshua ʳgave unto the tribes of Israel *for* a possession according to their divisions;

8 ˢIn the mountains, and in the valleys, and in the plains, and in the springs, and in the wilderness, and in the south country; ᵗthe Hittites, the Amorites, and the Canaanites, the Perizzites, the Hivites, and the Jebusites:

9 ¶ ᵘThe king of Jericho, one; ˣthe king of Ai, which *is* beside Beth-el, one;

ᵍ Numb. 21. 35. Deut. 3. 4, 10. ʰ Deut. 3. 11. ch. 13, 12. ⁱ Deut. 1. 4. ᵏ Deut. 3. 8. l Deut. 3. 10. ch. 13. 11. ᵐ Deut. 3. 14. n Numb. 21. 24, 33. ᵒ Numb. 32. 29, 33. Deut. 3. 11, 12. ch. 13. 8. p ch. 11. 17. ᑫ Gen. 14. 6. and 32. 3. Deut. 2. 1, 4. ʳ ch. 11. 23. ˢ ch. 10. 40, and 11. 16. ᵗ Ex. 3. 8. and 23. 23. ch. 9. 1. ᵘ ch. 6. 2. ˣ ch. 8. 29.

---

mittëmân, from Teman.——¶ *Under Ashdoth-pisgah.* Seated in the plains, or rather the slopes at the foot of mount Pisgah. The original word, אשדות *Ashdoth,* probably signifies the *low places* at the foot of a mountain. Comp. Deut. 3. 17; 4. 49.

4. *And the coast of Og, king of Bashan.* Supply here from v. 1, *And the children of Israel smote and possessed* the coast,' &c. Varying a little the phraseology with which he commenced, the writer here speaks first of the *country* of the king of Bashan, instead of enumerating *the king himself.*——¶ *Of the remnant of the giants.* See on Deut. 3. 11.——¶ *That dwell at Ashtaroth and at Edrei.* Refering to Og, and not to the giants. Probably both were royal cities, and he resided sometimes in one, and sometimes in the other. The reader will find their position on the map, as also that of the places mentioned in the ensuing verse.

6. *Gave it for a possesson.* The word 'it' has no antecedent expressed, but it is easily referred to the whole extent of country here spoken of, which was taken by Moses and given to the two tribes and a half as an inheritance.

7. *From Baal-gad.* A repetition of what is mentioned, ch. 11. 17.

8. *In the mountains, and in the valleys,* &c. The meaning probably is, that he smote the nations *dwelling in* the mountains, valleys, &c., even the Hittites, the Amorites, &c. The words convey at the same time a striking intimation of the general features of the country, its rich variety of soils, contributing at once to its fruitfulness and its pleasantness.

10 ʸThe king of Jerusalem, one; the king of Hebron, one;
11 The king of Jarmuth, one; the king of Lachish, one;
12 The king of Eglon, one; ᶻthe king of Gezer, one;
13 ᵃThe king of Debir, one; the king of Geder, one;
14 The king of Hormah, one; the king of Arad, one;
15 ᵇThe king of Libnah, one; the king of Adullam, one;
16 ᶜThe king of Makkedah, one; ᵈthe king of Beth-el, one;
17 The king of Tappuah, one; ᵉthe king of Hepher, one;
18 The king of Aphek, one; the king of ᶠLasharon, one;
19 The king of Madon, one; ᵍthe king of Hazor, one;
20 The king of ʰShimron-meron, one; the king of Achshaph, one;
21 The king of Taanach, one; the king of Megiddo, one;
22 ⁱThe king of Kedesh, one; the king of Jokneam of Carmel, one;
23 The king of Dor in the ᵏcoast of Dor, one; the king of ˡthe nations of Gilgal, one;
24 The king of Tirzah, one: all the kings, thirty and one.

CHAPTER XIII.

NOW Joshua ᵃwas old *and* stricken in years; and the LORD said unto him, Thou art old *and* stricken in years, and there remaineth yet very much land ᵇ to be possessed.

ʸ ch. 10. 23.   ᶻ ch. 10. 33.   ᵃ ch. 10. 38.
ᵇ ch. 10. 29.   ᶜ ch. 10. 28.   ᵈ ch. 8. 17. Judg. 1. 22   ᵉ 1 Kings 4. 10.   ᶠ Isai. 33. 9.   ᵍ ch. 11. 10.
ʰ ch. 11. 1, and 19. 15.   ⁱ ch. 19. 37.   ᵏ ch. 11. 2.   ˡ Gen. 14. 1, 2. Isai. 9. 1.   ᵃ ch. 14. 10, and 23. 1.   ᵇ Deut. 31. 3.

---

24. *All the kings, thirty and one.* From the number of these kings, we may learn how numerous and yet how small were the petty principalities into which the land of Canaan was divided. The extent of this country from north to south was not more than 150 miles, and not more than fifty from east to west. In like manner were nearly all the different nations of the world divided. The consequence was that civil wars and border feuds continually prevailed, making them an easy prey to foreign invaders. Thus history informs us that when Cæsar invaded Britain there were no less than four kings in the single county of Kent.

CHAPTER XIII.

1. *Joshua was old.* In all probability about a hundred, as he employed not far from seven years in the conquest of the land, and is supposed to have spent about one in dividing it, and he died about ten years after, aged one hundred and ten years. ch. 24. 29.——¶ *Stricken in years.* Heb. בא בימים *bâ bǎyâmim, coming or entering into days.* See Gen. 18. 11.
——¶ *There remaineth yet very much land to be possessed.* Heb. לרשתה *lerishtâh, to possess it.* This is mentioned to Joshua not as a reason for *his* continuing the war, but for suspending it, though to the Israelites the intimation would answer a different purpose. *They* were admonished by it that they were still to hold themselves in readiness for prosecuting the war in due time, and not to think of putting off the harness as long as there remained any land to be possessed. But as to Joshua, at

B. C. 1445.] CHAPTER XIII. 143

2 ᶜ This *is* the land that yet remaineth: ᵈ all the borders of the Philistines, and all ᵉ Geshuri,

ᶜ Judg. 3. 1. ᵈ Joel 3. 4. ᵉ ver. 13. 2 Sam. 3. 3, and 13. 37, 38.

3 ᶠFrom Sihor, which *is* before Egypt, even unto the borders of Ekron northward, *which*

ᶠ Jer. 2. 18.

his advanced age he could not expect to see an end of the war, and therefore it was expedient that he should lay aside other cares and make preparation at once for dividing the land among those tribes which had not yet received their inheritance. This work was to be done, and done speedily, and done, moreover, under the superintendence of Joshua. Consequently as he was now old, and not likely to continue long, he was to lose no time in setting about it. 'All people, but especially the aged, should set themselves to do that quickly which must be done before they die, lest death prevent them. Eccl. 9. 10.' *Henry*.

2. *The land that yet remaineth*. That yet remaineth to be conquered. ──¶ *All the borders of the Philistines*. Lying on the southern coast of the Mediterranean. The Philistines are no where else mentioned among the devoted nations of Canaan, and the reason of their being enumerated here probably is, that their territories formerly belonged to the Canaanites, who were driven away and supplanted by them, Deut. 2. 23. Viewed in this light, therefore, as being originally and legitimately the country of the Canaanites, the possessions of the Philistines were appointed to come into the hands of Israel.──¶ *And all Geshuri*. There were two places of this name. The one probably intended here was situated in the half tribe of Manasseh, on the east of Jordan, and in the north-eastern quarter of the promised land. As the Geshu-

rites were not extirpated by the Israelites they continued even in the time of Absalom to be governed by their own princes, one of whom, Talmai, had a daughter married to David, 2 Sam. 13. 37.

3. *Sihor*. In all probability a name of the river Nile. Heb. שיחור *Shihor*. The word in the original has the import of *black*, and is applied to the Nile from its color when it brings down the slime and mud by which Egypt is rendered fertile. Hence it implies the *black, muddy*, or *turbid* river. The Greeks give to the Nile the name of μέλας *black*, and the Latins occasionally called it *Melo* (Serv. ad Virg. Geor. 4. 291). It was called *Siris* by the Ethiopians, the affinity of which with *Sihor* is obvious. The version of Jerome renders the present passage, 'From the turbid river which irrigates Egypt,' and 'the seed of Sihor,' Is. 23. 3, it also renders 'the seed of Nilus.' It is not to be denied that there are peculiar difficulties in making the Nile the southern boundary of Canaan, as the promised possession of the Israelites, but the difficulties in any other view are in our opinion still greater.──
¶ *Unto the borders of Ekron*. One of the five lordships—*Gaza, Ashdod, Askalon, Gath*, and *Ekron*—belonging to the Philistines, and the most northern of all the districts they possessed, its territory being the border of the land of Judah. The city of Ekron was situated about thirty-four miles west of Jerusalem, ten miles north-east of Ashdod, nine miles

is counted to the Canaanite: ᵍfive lords of the Philistines; the Gazathites, and the Ashdothites, the Eshkalonites, the Gittites, and the Ekronites; also ʰthe Avites:

4 From the south all the land of the Canaanites, and Mearah that is beside the Sidonians, ⁱunto Aphek to the borders of ʲthe Amorites:

5 And the land of ᵏthe Giblites, and all Lebanon toward the sun-rising, ˡfrom Baal-Gad under mount Hermon unto the entering into Hamath.

g Judg. 3. 3. 1 Sam. 6. 4. 16. Zeph. 2. 5. h Deut. 2. 23.

i ch. 19. 30. j See Judg. 1. 34. k 1 Kings 5. 18. Ps. 83. 7. Ezek. 27. 9. l ch. 12. 7.

---

west by north of Gath, and ten miles east of the shore of the Mediterranean. It is particularly mentioned in Scripture as the seat of the idolatrous worship of Baalzebub, or the 'Lord of flies,' 2 Kings 1. 2, but the Divine prediction against it, that 'Ekron should be rooted up,' Zeph. 2. 4, has long since been accomplished, not even a single ruin of it remaining to mark the place where it stood. Am. 1. 8.——¶ *Which is counted to the Canaanites.* Because the original possessors of this country were the descendants of Canaan, the youngest son of Ham. The Philistines sprung from Misraim, the second son of Ham, and having dispossessed the Avites, or Avim, from the places they held in this land, dwelt in their stead. See Gen. 10. 13, 14.——¶ *Five lords.* Petty princes. The term is put for the *lordships* themselves, just as king is often used for kingdom. The original סרנים *sarnaim, princes,* literally signifies *axles;* and so the Arab. for chief magistrate is *Katbun, axis;* because public affairs and the people did, as it were, *revolve* round and depend upon him, as the parts of a wheel upon its axis. See Note on ch. 9. 4.——¶ *Also the Avites.* The remnant of the tribe or clan of the Avims said in Deut. 2. 23, to have been expelled by the Caphthorim. The scattered relics of this people remained mixed up with the five Philistine lordships above-mentioned.

4. *From the south,* &c. The whole maritime country from the southern limits here mentioned, as far north as to Sidon and some of the Amoritish possessions in that quarter, is hereby made over in promise to Israel. Joshua himself does not appear to have made any conquests on the sea-coast.——¶ *Mearah.* Or, Heb. 'the cave;' by which Le Clerc understands the mountainous tract of Upper Galilee, sometimes called the *cave-country* of the Sidonians, abounding in caves and fastnesses, which served as sheltering places in time of war, and as asylums also for roving bands of marauders. Josephus often speaks of such places in the bounds of the Holy Land; and the Maronite monks of Canobin assured M. de la Roque, that among the mountains between which the river Kadisha runs, there were not less than eight hundred caves or grottos. Others suppose it to have been a single large and remarkable cave between Sarepta and Sidon, described by William, Bishop of Tyre. This, however, is less likely.

5. *The land of the Giblites.* The name of a people dwelling in Gebal, near Sidon. 1 King 5. 18; Ezek. 27.

6 All the inhabitants of the hill-*country* from Lebanon unto ᵐ Misrephoth-maim, *and* all the Sidonians, them ⁿ will I drive

ᵐ ch. 11. 8. ⁿ See ch. 23. 13. Judg. 2. 21, 23.

out from before the children of Israel: only °divide thou it by lot unto the Israelites for an inheritance, as I have commanded thee

o ch. 14. 1, 2.

9. Their land was not given to the Israelites, because it lay *without* the precincts of Canaan. From among this people, Solomon employed a number of artists in the erection of the temple, 1 Kings 5. 18. They were also famed for ship-building, Ezek. 27. 9. It is supposed by many that the modern *Byblus* is the same as the ancient Gebal. They were certainly situated in the same region.

6. *Them will I drive out.* The original is emphatic; 'It is *I* that will do it; I who have all power, and am ever faithful; I who have promised, and can and will perform.' Chal. 'I will do it by my Word;' i. e. by my eternal Word, the Captain of the Lord's hosts. This, however, like other similar declarations, is to be understood *conditionally.* God never promised to put them in possession of the whole land, but upon condition of their *fidelity* to him. If they failed in obedience, they would fail in becoming masters of the country. Accordingly we find that they never did actually possess the *whole* land here assigned to them. The Sidonians were never expelled by the Israelites, and were only brought into a state of comparative subjection in the days of David and Solomon. Joshua, however, notwithstanding the cavils of infidels, actually *did* all that it was promised he *should do.* God never said that he should *conquer* all the land, but simply that he

should *bring* Israel *into* it, and divide it among them, both which he did, and procured them footing by his conquests sufficient to have enabled them to establish themselves in it for ever. Their failure to do so was owing wholly to themselves. So *we* must work out our salvation, depending upon God to work in us, and to work with us. We must resist our spiritual enemies, and look to God to trample them under our feet.——

¶ *Only divide thou it by lot.* Heb. הפילה *happilëyah, cast it, cause it to fall.* See Note on Gen. 25. 18. A phraseology derived from the *casting* of the lots by which its distribution was governed. Joshua, no doubt, supposed that the land was first to be *conquered,* before it was *divided,* but here his mistake is corrected. The great Proprietor would have his people consider the country as even now *theirs,* and as a pledge of his purpose to give it them, directs that without further delay it be forthwith apportioned out among the tribes. This order would not only strengthen their assurance of the final possession of the land, but serve also as an incentive to prosecute the work of conquest with fresh vigor, and to keep themselves from all leagues, and every kind of entangling connexion which might obstruct the attainment of their ultimate object. So the exercise of a lively faith puts the Christian even now in possession of the heavenly Canaan, the land of his

7 Now therefore divide this land for an inheritance unto the nine tribes, and the half-tribe of Manasseh,

8 With whom the Reubenites and the Gadites have received their inheritance, *p* which Moses gave them, beyond Jordan eastward, *even* as Moses the servant of the Lord gave them;

p Num. 32. 33. Deut. 3. 12, 13. ch. 22. 4.

9 From Aroer that *is* upon the bank of the river Arnon, and the city that *is* in the midst of the river, *q* and all the plain of Medeba unto Dibon;

10 And *r* all the cities of Sihon king of the Amorites, which reigned in Heshbon, unto the border of the children of Ammon;

q ver. 16. Num. 21. 30.   r Num. 21. 24, 25.

---

eternal inheritance. Of all such it may be truly said;—

'They view the triumph from afar,
And seize it with their eye.'

8. *With whom.* Heb. עִמּוֹ *immo, with him,* i. e. with the other half-tribe of Manasseh, who were to have no part in Canaan proper, as their inheritance had already fallen to them, on the other side of Jordan. The relative is put for an antecedent; which is to be supplied from the general tenor of the narrative, as in Num. 7. 89; Ps. 114. 2; Is. 8. 21; Jer. 1. 3. The speaker here and henceforward is not God, whose words terminate with v. 7, but the historian, who takes occasion to rehearse the allotment made by Moses to the two tribes and a half on the other side Jordan, in order that the reader might understand the reason why nothing is said of them in the distribution now to be made by Joshua, but the whole land on this side the river is ordered to be given to the nine tribes and a half. The other two and a half had been already provided for; and the restatement of the fact here, in the formal record of the division of the land, would serve to ratify, in the strongest manner, the grant formerly made by Moses. As he had settled the affair, so Joshua would leave it. He would not alter what Moses had done, and the reason why he would not, is intimated in the fact that Moses was 'the *servant* of the Lord,' faithful in all his house, and acting in this matter by a secret direction from him.

9. *The city that is in the midst of the river.* For the true meaning of the expression, 'in the midst of the river,' see Note on ch. 12. 2. Judging from the reports of travellers, we see no reason to believe that such an inconsiderable stream as Arnon, a mere rivulet, contained an island large enough for the site of a city. These verses, from v. 9 to 14, comprise a general description of the *whole country* given to the two tribes and a half. The remainder of the chapter is occupied with a detailed account of the *several districts allotted to each.* Here, in v. 9, taking 'city' and 'river,' according to the common Heb. idiom, as the collect. sing. for the plur., we conceive the writer's drift is to say, 'that beginning at Aroer, Moses gave to the two tribes and a half *all the cities lying between the several rivers* mentioned ch. 12. 1, 2, together with all the plain or champagne country of Medeba, even to Dibon. These, in the next verse, are called the cities

[B. C. 1445.] CHAPTER XIII. 147

11 ᵃAnd Gilead, and the border of the Geshurites and Maachathites, and all mount Hermon, and all Bashan unto Salcah;

12 All the kingdom of Og in Bashan, which reigned in Ashtaroth and in Edrei, who remained of ᵗthe remnant of the giants. ᵘFor these did Moses smite, and cast them out.

13 Nevertheless, the children of Israel expelled ˣnot the Geshurites, nor the Maachathites: but the Geshurites and the Maachathites dwell among the Israelites unto this day.

14 ʸOnly unto the tribe of Levi he gave none inheritance; the sacrifices of the LORD God of Israel made by fire *are* their inheritance, ᶻas he said unto them.

15 ¶ And Moses gave unto the

ₛ ch. 12. 5.   ᵗ Deut. 3. 11.   ch. 12. 4.
ᵘ Numb. 21. 24, 35.

ˣ ver. 11.   ʸ Numb. 18. 20, 23, 24.   ch. 14. 3, 4.   ᶻ ver. 33.

of Sihon, because they lay within his territories.

13. *The children of Israel expelled not the Geshurites,* &c. Spoken apparently by way of reflection upon the Israelites who succeeded Moses, for their remissness in driving out these nations. The failure of Moses to make a clean riddance of them at his first conquest, might be entirely excusable, as he was intent upon reaching Canaan, and could not well subject himself to the delay necessary for their complete extermination. But this plea would not hold after Canaan was entered. The tribes ought to have gone forward at once and finished the work which Moses had begun. Instead of this, it is related, to their disgrace, that they still suffered these people to dwell among them down to the time when this history was written. The spirit of inspiration discovers, if we may so speak, a wonderful tact, both in administering censure and bestowing praise. Instances of both, managed with the most consummate skill, abound in the compass of the sacred scriptures.

14. *Unto the tribe of Levi he gave* *no inheritance.* See on Num. 18, 20—24.——¶ *The sacrifices made by fire.* The term is to be understood in a large sense, including not only all the oblations of which any part was burnt, but also the first fruits and tithes assigned to the Levites for their support. This is repeated again v. 43, to intimate that the Levites had as good a title to their tithes and perquisites, as the rest of their brethren had to their estates, and also to enjoin upon the tribes a cheerful and conscientious compliance with the will of God in this respect. Withholding their dues from the Levites he considered as no less than actually robbing himself.

15. *Moses gave unto the tribe of the children of Reuben.* The writer now enters upon a minute specification of the portions assigned by lot to the tribes of Reuben, Gad, and the half tribe of Manasseh. This is very fully and exactly detailed. On this mode of assigning to the children their inheritances, and on this account of it, it may be remarked, (1) That it was the most equitable and satisfactory method that could be adopted. Had the distribution been

148 JOSHUA. [B. C. 1445.

tribe of the children of Reuben *inheritance* according to their families.

16 And their coast was ᵃfrom Aroer that *is* on the bank of the river Arnon, ᵇand the city that *is* in the midst of the river, ᶜand all the plain by Medeba:

17 Heshbon, and all her cities that *are* in the plain; Dibon, and ᵈBamoth-baal, and Beth-baal-meon,

18 ᵉAnd Jahaza, and Kedemoth, and Mephaath,

19 ᶠAnd Kirjathaim, and ᵍSibmah, and Zareth-shahar in the mount of the valley,

20 And Beth-peor, and ʰAshdoth-pisgah, and Beth-jeshimoth,

21 ⁱAnd all the cities of the plain, and all the kingdom of Sihon king of the Amorites which reigned in Heshbon, ʲwhom Moses smote ᵏwith the princes of Midian, Evi, and Rekem, and Zur, and Hur, and Reba, *which were* dukes of Sihon, dwelling in the country.

ᵃ ch. 12. 2. ᵇ Numb. 21. 28. ᶜ Numb. 21. 30. ver. 9. ᵈ Numb. 32. 38. ᵉ Numb. 21. 23.
ᶠ Numb. 32. 37. ᵍ Numb. 32. 38. ʰ Deut. 3. 17. ch. 12. 3. ⁱ Deut. 3. 10. ʲ Numb. 21. 24. ᵏ Numb. 31. 8.

made by arbitrary appointment, as all could not receive portions equally good, some would probably have complained that their brethren were better dealt by than themselves. Dividing the land by lot, therefore, by cutting off all pretence for the charge of favoritism on the part of Moses, was the readiest way of satisfying all parties, and preventing discontent and discord. (2) The several allotments are here very minutely detailed in order that litigation growing out of disputed boundaries might ever after be prevented. When the limits of each tribe were so clearly settled, there could be little room for contending claims, or if there were, an authentic register of the lot of each tribe would be at hand to be appealed to for a decision, and there is no doubt that it was often made use of in after ages for this purpose. We cannot but learn from this the great importance of devising every prudent method to prevent litigations about property. (3) The reading of this account by succeeding generations would tend to excite a very deep and lively impression of the goodness of God in bestowing upon their ancestors, for the benefit of their posterity, such a large and fertile country, an inheritance so replete with all the worldly blessings which heart could wish. 'God's grants look best, when we descend to the particulars.' *Henry*.——

¶ *According to their families.* As every tribe had its inheritance divided by lot; so it is probable, that afterwards the subdivisions to every family and each individual were regulated in the same manner. Thus their estates would descend to posterity, not so much as the inheritance of their fathers, as that which the Lord had immediately assigned them. They could thus say, with the Psalmist, Ps. 16. 5, 6, 'The Lord is the portion of mine inheritance and of my cup: thou maintainest my lot. The lines are fallen unto me in pleasant places; I have a goodly heritage.'

21. *Dukes of Sihon.* Probably so called because they had been his tributaries, subject to his jurisdiction.

22 ¶ ¹Balaam also the son of Beor, the soothsayer, did the children of Israel slay with the sword, among them that were slain by them.

23 And the border of the children of Reuben was Jordan, and the border *thereof*. This *was* the inheritance of the children of Reuben, after their families, the cities and the villages thereof.

24 And Moses gave *inheritance* unto the tribe of Gad, *even* unto the children of Gad according to their families.

25 ᵐAnd their coast was Jazer, and all the cities of Gilead, ⁿand half the land of the children of Ammon, unto Aroer that *is* before ᵒRabbah;

26 And from Heshbon unto Ramath-mizpeh, and Betonim; and from Mahanaim unto the border of Debir;

27 And in the valley, ᵖBeth-aram, and Beth-nimrah, ᑫand Succoth, and Zaphon, the rest of the kingdom of Sihon king of Heshbon, Jordan and *his* border, *even* unto the edge ʳof the sea of Cinnereth, on the other side Jordan eastward.

28 This *is* the inheritance of the children of Gad after their families, the cities, and their villages.

29 ¶ And Moses gave *inheritance* unto the half-tribe of Manasseh: and *this* was *the possession* of the half-tribe of the children of Manasseh by their families.

30 And their coast was from Mahanaim, all Bashan, all the kingdom of Og king of Bashan, and ˢall the towns of Jair, which *are* in Bashan, threescore cities:

31 And half Gilead, and ᵗAshtaroth, and Edrei, cities of the kingdom of Og in Bashan, *were pertaining* unto the children of Machir the son of Manasseh, *even* to the one half of the ᵘchildren of Machir by their families.

32 These *are the countries* which Moses did distribute for inheritance in the plains of Moab, on the other side Jordan by Jericho eastward.

33 ˣBut unto the tribe of Levi,

l Num. 22. 5, and 31. 8. m Num. 32. 25. n Compare Num. 21. 26, 28, 29, with Deut. 2. 19, and Judg. 11. 13, 15. &c. o 2 Sam. 11. 1, and 12. 26. p Num. 32. 36. q Gen. 33. 17. ः Kings 7. 46.
r Num. 34. 11. s Num. 32. 41. 1 Chron. 2. 23. t ch. 12. 4. u Num. 32. 39, 40. x ver. 14. ch. 18. 7.

They are indeed called 'kings of Midian' in Num. 31. 8, but by 'kings' in the sacred writings we are often to understand no more than mere petty chieftains, who might be at the same time subject to some more potent sovereign. See Gen. 14. 1, 2.

22. *Balaam also—did the children of Israel slay.* He fell with those who instigated him to his wickedness. 'This was recorded before, Num. 31. 8, but is repeated here, because the defeating of Balaam's purpose to curse Israel was the turning of that curse into a blessing, and was such an instance of the power and goodness of God as was fit to be had in everlasting remembrance.' *Henry.* Divine justice knows well how to put the brand of perpetual infamy upon those who sin, like Balaam, against light and knowledge.

Moses gave not *any* inheritance: the LORD God of Israel *was* their inheritance, ʸas he said unto them.

CHAPTER XIV.

AND these *are the countries* which the children of Israel inherited in the land of Canaan, ᵃwhich Eleazar the priest, and Joshua the son of Nun, and the heads of the fathers of the tribes of the children of Israel distributed for inheritance to them.

y Num 18. 20.   Deut. 10. 9, and 18. 1. 2.
a Num. 34. 16, 18.

2 ᵇBy lot *was* their inheritance, as the LORD commanded by the hand of Moses, for the nine tribes, and *for* the half-tribe.

3 ᶜFor Moses had given the inheritance of two tribes and an half-tribe on the other side Jordan: but unto the Levites he gave none inheritance among them.

4 For ᵈthe children of Joseph were two tribes, Manasseh and Ephraim: therefore they gave no part unto the Levites in the

b Num. 26. 35, and 33. 54, and 34. 13.   c ch. 13. 8, 32, 33.   d Gen. 48. 5.   1 Chron. 5. 1, 2.

CHAPTER XIV.

1. *These are the countries*, &c. The historian having, in the preceding chapter, given an account of the disposal of the countries on the other side of Jordan, comes now to state the allotments made to the remaining nine tribes and a half in the bounds of Canaan proper. The directions which Moses had formerly given, Num. 36. 53-56, respecting the mode of making this distribution, are now to be punctually observed. Previously to entering upon the account of this division, the writer premises two or three things which fall in here more properly than any where else, as that the Levites were not comprehended in the grant made to the tribes; that the tribe of Joseph was reckoned as two; and that Caleb had given to him at his request a certain tract of country which had been before promised by Moses.——¶ *The heads of the fathers of the tribes.* That is, heads or chief men among the fathers of the tribes. These were twelve in number, including Joshua and Eleazar. They had been before expressly appointed by Moses, Num. 34. 19. This was done that every tribe, having a representative of its own, might be satisfied that there was fair dealing, and might consequently abide more contentedly by its lot.

2. *By lot was their inheritance.* This distribution by lot was overruled by a special providence, so as to correspond with the inspired predictions of Jacob and Moses, respecting the allotment of each tribe. The fact is very remarkable, yet unquestionable, that the tribes found themselves placed *by lot* in the very sections of the country, which Jacob had foretold two hundred and fifty years before, and Moses shortly before his death. Comp. Gen. 49, and Deut. 33. To Judah fell a country abounding in *vineyards* and *pastures;* to Zebulon, *sea-coasts;* to Issachar, a *rich plain between ranges of mountains;* to Asher, one abounding in plenty of *oil, wheat,* and *metals;* and so of the others. See Masius and Calmet for more particular details.

4. *The children of Joseph were two*

B. C. 1444.] CHAPTER XIV. 151

land, save cities to dwell in, with their suburbs for their cattle, and for their substance.

5 ᵉ As the LORD commanded Moses, so the children of Israel did, and they divided the land.

6 ¶ Then the children of Judah came unto Joshua in Gilgal: and Caleb the son of Jephunneh the ᶠKenezite said unto him, Thou knowest ᵍthe thing that the LORD said unto Moses the man of God concerning me and thee ʰin Kadesh-barnea.

7 Forty years old was I when

ᵉ Num. 35. 2. ch. 21. 2.
ᶠ Num. 32. 12, and ch. 15. 17. ᵍ Num. 14. 24. 30. Deut. 1. 36, 38. ʰ Num. 13. 26.

---

tribes. That is, had a double portion or the portion of two tribes. By Joseph's being reckoned two tribes, the nation was made to consist of twelve tribes, though Levi was excluded.

5. *And they divided the land.* They entered upon the business of dividing it; they took the preliminary measures; they consulted together and settled the manner in which it should be done. The *actual* dividing took place afterwards. The Scriptures often speak of that as *done*, which is merely begun or resolved upon. It must have required a considerable time to make all the geographical arrangements necessary for this purpose.

6. *Then the children of Judah came.* 'Then'—while they were at Gilgal, preparing to make the division, which it seems was finished at Shilo, ch. 18. 1. The thread of the narrative is again interrupted to introduce the digression concerning the allotment of Caleb. The children of Judah, that is, probably, the heads and chief men, accompanied Caleb, who belonged to the same tribe, in order to testify their consent to the measure, and to aid and countenance him in obtaining the object of his request. As Caleb was one of the twelve whom God had chosen to superintend the partition of the land, Num. 34. 12, it might seem, if he came unattended, that he designed to take advantage of his authority as a commissioner to promote his private interest; he therefore takes his brethren along with him to preclude any such imputation. Some suppose that this transaction took place previous to the siege and capture of Hebron, related ch. 10. 36, 37, and that the expedition detailed in its minute particulars, in ch. 15. 13-15, is there barely touched upon, or described in the most general manner. The fact, however, that the application of Caleb was made to Joshua at Gilgal, and not while he was pursuing his conquests over the south of Canaan, seems decisive against this opinion.

——¶ *Thou knowest the thing,* &c. Caleb probably alludes to what is said Num. 14. 24, 'But my servant Caleb him will I bring into the land whereinto he went; and his seed shall possess it.' Deut. 1. 36, 'Caleb the son of Jephunneh, to him will I give the land that he hath trodden upon, and to his children, because he hath wholly followed the Lord.' This seems to be spoken, not of the land of promise in general, but of some particular district to which he had penetrated when sent out by Moses. This, undoubtedly, was Hebron, Num. 13. 22, and was so understood by all parties at the time. The promise then made by God to Moses he

Moses the servant of the Lord sent me from Kadesh-barnea to espy out the land; and I brought him word again as *it was* in mine heart.

8 Nevertheless, ᵏ my brethren that went up with me made the heart of the people melt: but I wholly ˡ followed the Lord my God.

ⁱ Num. 13. 6, and 14. 6. ᵏ Num. 13. 31, 32. Deut. 1. 28. ˡ Num. 14. 24. Deut. 1. 36.

9 And Moses sware on that day, saying, ᵐ Surely the land ⁿ whereon thy feet have trodden shall be thine inheritance, and thy children's for ever; because thou hast wholly followed the Lord my God.

10 And now, behold, the Lord hath kept me alive, ᵒ as he said, these forty and five years, even

ᵐ Num. 14. 23, 24. Deut. 1. 36. ch. 1. 3. ⁿ See Num. 13. 22. ᵒ Num. 14. 30.

now pleads; and what can be more confidently expected than the fulfilment of his gracious word? There is more presumption in declining and neglecting his promises, than in urging their performance.

. 7. *Brought him word again as it was in mine heart.* Made a true and honest statement; spake sincerely; uttered the real sentiments of my heart. His conscience bore him witness, and now enabled him to say, that neither *fear* nor *favor* influenced him on the occasion; he told what he believed to be the truth, the whole truth, and nothing but the truth. It has been remarked in this connexion, that Caleb's name signifies, *according to the heart.*

8. *I wholly followed the Lord.* Heb. מִלֵּאתִי אַחֲרֵי יְהוָה *millëthi ahari Yehovah, fulfilled after the Lord.* Arab. ' I perfected my obedience before the Lord my God.' On the import of this expression, see Note on Num. 14. 24. The energy of the expression is well preserved in our version. The words give the idea of a traveller, who, intent upon following his guide, so treads in his steps, as to leave hardly any void space between. As he had obtained this testimony from God himself, it was not vain-glory for him to speak of it, especially as this was the main ground on which he had become entitled to the object of his petition. It is not pride, but simply a tribute of due acknowledgment, to declare what a gracious God has done for us and by us. It was peculiarly to the honor of Caleb that he maintained such an unbending fidelity to God when his brethren and associates in that service, except Joshua, proved so faithless and faint-hearted. ' It adds much to the praise of following God, if we adhere to him when others desert and decline from him.' *Henry.*

9. *Moses sware on that day.* See Num. 14. 24; Deut. 1. 36. In these passages God himself is the speaker; and it is he that swears according to the words here recited. But as Moses was the organ through whom the assured promise was conveyed, the swearing is attributed to him.—— ¶ *The land whereon thy feet have trodden.* Not the land of Canaan in general, but this particular, this identical district. See on v. 6.

10. *Hath kept me alive.* Heb. הֶחֱיָה אוֹתִי *hehëyâh othi, hath vivified me.* See on ch. 6. 25. According to our previous interpretation, it implies that he was kept alive, when,

since the LORD spake this word unto Moses, while *the children of* Israel wandered in the wilderness: and now, lo, I *am* this day fourscore and five years old.

11 ᵖ As yet I *am as* strong this day, as *I was* in the day that

ᵖ See Deut. 34. 7.

Moses sent me: as my strength *was* then, even so *is* my strength now, for war, both ᵠto go out, and to come in.

12 Now therefore give me this mountain, wherefore the LORD spake in that day; for thou

ᵠ Deut. 31. 2.

in the ordinary course of things, he would have been dead; that it was *in despite* of the tendencies of nature to decay and dissolution that he now stood among the living in so much health and strength. His present existence was a kind of resurrection from the dead. The longer we live, the more sensible should we be of the *special* upholding hand of Providence in prolonging our frail and forfeited lives.——¶ *These forty and five years.* Of which thirty-eight were spent in the wilderness, and seven in the prosecution of the wars in Canaan.—— ¶ *Wandered in the wilderness.* Heb. הלך *hâlak, walked.* As a punishment for their unbelief and rebellion.—— ¶ *Lo, I am this day four score and five years old.* Heb. 'a son of fourscore and five years.' Caleb was now, with the exception of Joshua, not only the oldest man in all Israel, but was *twenty years* older than any of them; for all that were above twenty when he was forty, had died in the wilderness. ' It was fit, therefore, that this phœnix of his age should have some particular marks of honor put upon him in the dividing of the land.' *Henry.*

11. *As my strength was then, so is my strength now.* My ability not only for counsel, but for action, remains unimpaired; I am as competent as ever for the hard services and difficult exploits of war. He

mentions this, both to give glory to God who was the strength as well as the length of his days, and also to intimate to Joshua that it would not be throwing away a portion upon a weak old man, who was unequal to the task of either taking or retaining it. On the contrary, even if it were to be taken from the hands of giants, and should require the utmost prowess, energy and nerve of the youthful warrior, he was still able to put it forth. He was not afraid to cope at eighty with the same power which he would readily have encountered at forty.—If we would make sure of a 'green old age,' let us begin early to follow the Lord fully. It is usually the excesses of youth which bring on the premature decay of the bodily and mental powers. It is precisely that sobriety, temperance, and moderation which religion enjoins, that secures to us the longest continuance and the highest enjoyment of life, health, and strength; and these habits cannot begin to be practised too early.——¶*Both to go out and to come in.* A proverbial phrase, equivalent to performing all the duties belonging to an official station. See on Num. 27. 17.

12. *Give me this mountain.* Not any particular mountain, but this mountainous tract or region; for such was eminently the country about Hebron. He does not mention

heardest in that day how ʳthe Anakims *were* there, and *that* the cities *were* great *and* fenced:

ᵃif so be the Lord *will be* with me, then ᵗI shall be able to drive them out, as the Lord said.

ᵣ Num. 13. 28, 33.

ₛ Ps. 18. 32, 34, and 60. 12. Rom. 8. 31.
ₜ ch. 15. 14. Judg. 1. 20.

---

and cannot mean the city of Hebron alone, which had been before taken by Joshua, but he included in his request all the adjacent country, to the caves and strongholds of which the Anakim had retired, and where they were now abiding in considerable force. The city itself fell afterwards to the lot of the Levites, ch. 21. 13, and became a city of refuge, ch. 20. 7. 'When Caleb had it, he contented himself with the country about it, and cheerfully gave the city to the priests, the Lord's ministers; thinking it could not be better bestowed, no, not upon his own children, nor that it was the less his own for being thus devoted to God.' *Henry.* Hebron, at a still later period, became a royal city, being made in the beginning of David's reign the metropolis of the kingdom of Judah.──¶ *For thou heardest—how the Anakims were there.* This, it would seem, was the place from which more than any other the spies took their unfavorable report; for here they met with the sons of Anak, the sight of whom so much intimidated them. 'We may suppose that Caleb, observing what stress they laid upon the difficulty of conquering Hebron, a city garrisoned by the giants, and how from thence they inferred that the conquest of the whole land was utterly impracticable, bravely desired to have that city which they called *invincible* assigned to himself for his own portion; "I will undertake to deal with that, and if I cannot get it for my inheritance, I will do without." "Well," said Moses, "it shall be thine own then, win it and wear it." *Henry.* Such is the spirit of the true Christian hero. All indeed are not such, but some are; and he who is, is not only willing, but forward, in the strength of God, to encounter the most formidable enemies and the most apparently insuperable obstacles in working out the will of his heavenly Master. If there is any enterprise of peculiar difficulty to be undertaken, or any post of especial danger to be occupied, he is prompt to volunteer his services for the occasion. Not that he courts the perilous work, merely for the purpose of a vain-glorious display of courage or skill, but because he wishes to honor God by his faith; to give him an opportunity, through such an humble instrument, to glorify his great name and confound the infidelity of his enemies and his timorous friends. In one who feels the missionary impulse, this Caleb-like spirit will prompt to a fearless survey of the whole field, and if there be any spot which is at once promising and yet appalling, desirable and yet dreadful; a spot where the greatest force of heathen opposition is concentrated, that is the spot which will be really most attractive in his eye. Its difficulties and dangers will be among its highest recommendations. .This spirit shone conspicuously in Paul in the whole course of his life and labors, and on one occasion we see it nobly expressing itself in so many

13 And Joshua ^ublessed him, ^xand gave unto Caleb the son of Jephunneh, Hebron for an inheritance.

14 ^yHebron therefore became the inheritance of Caleb the son of Jephunneh the Kenezite unto this day; because that he ^zwholly followed the LORD God of Israel.

15 And ^athe name of Hebron before was Kirjath-arba; *which Arba was* a great man among the Anakims. ^bAnd the land had rest from war.

^u ch. 22. 6.   x ch. 10. 37, and 15. 13.   Judg. 1. 20.   See ch. 21. 11, 12.   1 Chron. 6. 55, 56.   y ch. 21. 12.   z ver. 8, 9.   a Gen. 23. 2.   ch. 15. 13.   b ch. 11. 23.   a Num. 34. 3.

CHAPTER XV.

*T**HIS* then was the lot of the tribe of the children of Judah by their families; ^a *even*

words, when he says of Ephesus, 'A great and effectual door is opened unto me, and *many adversaries.*' The 'adversaries' were no doubt among the special inducements that prompted him to enter that field. It is cause of gratitude to God that there are such spirits still to be found in the world, and that as long as there shall be sons of Anak on earth to intimidate the fearful, there shall be also sons of Caleb to grapple with and destroy them.——¶ *If so be the Lord will be with me,* &c. Chal. 'Perhaps the Word of the Lord will be for my help.' The ardor of a bold native temperament is here moderated by the workings of a spirit of conscious unworthiness and of humble dependence on the Divine blessing. Caleb in these words virtually acknowledges that the battle is not to the strong nor the race to the swift, and that the favorable presence of God with us in our undertakings is all in all to our success. The expression is not to be understood as implying any doubt in his mind of God's readiness to assist him, but simply as a disclaimer of exclusive reliance on his own unaided prowess. It is the language of one who feels that an arm of flesh, even all the forces of Israel combined, without the blessing of heaven, would be powerless to accomplish the desired result.

13. *And Joshua blessed him.* That is, not only granted his request, but applauded his brave and enterprising spirit, and *implored the blessing of God* upon him in reference to his proposed undertaking.

15. *Kirjath-arba.* That is, *the city of Arba,* the name of an individual distinguished either for his remarkable bodily stature and strength, or his power and authority, or perhaps both, among the Anakims.——¶*And the land had rest from war.* There were no more *general* wars. The inhabitants of Canaan could make no longer any head against the power of Israel. Being disjointed and broken, they could no longer rally in such force as to make it necessary for the *whole* Israelitish body to go against them in a *general* campaign. This may be considered as the genuine sense of the expression, though it be admitted that there were afterwards *particular* wars, arising from the attempts of each tribe to expel the ancient inhabitants still remaining in their respective territories.

CHAPTER XV.

1. *This then was the lot,* &c. The account of the partition of the land

to the border of Edom, the ᵇ wilderness of Zin southward *was* the uttermost part of the south coast.

ᵇ Num. 33. 26.

which was commenced ch. 14. 1-5, was interrupted by the mention of Caleb's application to Joshua for Hebron as his inheritance, and that being dispatched, the writer here returns from the digression, and resumes the thread of his narrative respecting the allotment of the tribes. The manner in which the designed partition should be made, had already been settled by Divine appointment, Num. 26. 25, 'The land shall be divided by lot: according to the names of their fathers shall they inherit.' In obedience to this command Joshua now proceeds. On this part of the history it may be remarked, (1) That the business of casting lots on this occasion was undoubtedly conducted with great seriousness and solemnity, and with devout prayer to God, whose is the disposal of the lot, that he would overrule it all to his own glory and the accomplishment of his wise purposes. (2) That although an *exact* survey of the land was not taken till some time after this, ch. 18. 4, 5, yet some general view of it must have been obtained, and some rude draught have been spread before them, sufficient, at least, to have enabled them to divide the land into nine and a half portions, with more or less accuracy. (3) That the respective lots did not, at this time, so peremptorily and unchangeably determine the bounds of each tribe, that they could not subsequently be either contracted or enlarged, or otherwise altered; for it is evident from what follows, ch. 19. 9, that after Judah's lot was fixed, Simeon's was taken out of it. It would seem, in fact, that the first designation of the portions of the several tribes was quite vague and general, but that the limits of each were afterwards adjusted and settled by Joshua and the elders, with as much precision as the nature of the case would admit. (4) As to the *manner* in which the casting of lots took place on this occasion, though we are not expressly informed, yet the probability is, that after the land was geographically divided into the requisite number of portions, these portions properly labelled, or otherwise distinguished, were put into one urn or pot, and the names of the several tribes into another; that then Joshua, for example, put his hand into the vessel containing the names of the tribes, and took out one slip, while Eleazar took out one from the other vessel, in which the names of the portions were put; whereupon the *name* drawn and the *portion* drawn being read, it was at once determined what portion was to be appropriated to such a tribe; and so of the rest. It is probable, however, that this plan was adopted, *on the present occasion*, only in respect to the two large and principal tribes of Judah and Joseph, as they were now at Gilgal, and the division certainly was not completed till after they arrived at Shilo, ch. 18. 1, 2. In reference, therefore, to this mode of drawing out the lots from the bottom of the urns, the phraseology of a lot's 'coming up' or 'coming forth,' became established. ——¶ *The lot of the tribe of the children*

2 And their south border was from the shore of the salt sea, from the bay that looketh southward:

of Judah. By the special disposition of providence the lot of Judah came up first, in token of the pre-eminence of that tribe over the rest. This distinction hereby received the Divine sanction.——¶ *Even to the border of Edom.* The geography of the sacred writings presents many difficulties, occasioned by the many changes which the civil state of the promised land has undergone, especially for the last two thousand years. Many of the ancient towns and villages have had their names so totally changed, that their former appellations are no longer discernible; several lie buried under their own ruins; and others have been so long destroyed that not one vestige of them remains. On these accounts, it is very difficult to ascertain the situation of many of the places mentioned in this and the following chapters. Yet the ancient appellations of many of these localities may still be detected in modified forms under the modern names, and the sites of a greater number of them satisfactorily determined, than would at first seem practicable. This portion of the sacred story cannot of course be so interesting, or so profitable to the general reader as details of another character, and we shall not therefore enlarge upon it in our remarks, but as many of the places here mentioned are frequently alluded to in the subsequent history and the prophets, this enumeration is important, as enabling us oftentimes to determine their situation; and it need not to be observed that the *geography* of a country is of the utmost importance in illustrating its *history.*

The quaint remark of Henry, therefore, on this subject, is deserving of attention, that 'we are not to skip over these chapters of hard names, as useless and not to be regarded; where God has a mouth to speak and a hand to write, we should find an ear to hear and an eye to read.' As it respects the lot of Judah, as here marked out, it was bounded on the south by the wilderness of Sin and the southern coast of the Salt Sea; on the east by that sea, reaching to the place at which it receives the waters of the Jordan; on the north, by a line drawn nearly parallel to Jerusalem, across from the northern extremity of the Salt Sea to the south boundary of the Philistines and to the Mediterranean Sea; which sea was its western boundary, as far as the river of Egypt. Joshua is particular in giving the limits of this tribe, as being the first, the most numerous, the most important, that which was to furnish the *kings* of Judea, that in which *pure religion* was to be preserved, and that from which the Messiah was to spring. As this portion, however, contained nearly half the southern part of Canaan, it was afterwards found too extensive, and the possessions of Simeon and Dan were taken out of it.

2. *From the bay that looketh southward.* Heb. לשון *leshōn, the tongue,* i. e. a gulf, bay, or arm of the sea. The like phrase occurs Is. 11. 15, 'The Lord shall utterly destroy *the tongue* of the Egyptian Sea.' The southern extremity of the Dead Sea, as laid down in the best maps, answers in its form to this description.

3 And it went out to the south side ᶜto Maaleh-acrabbim, and passed along to Zin, and ascended up on the south side unto Kadesh-barnea, and passed along to Hezron, and went up to Adar, and fetched a compass to Karkaa:

4 *From thence* it passed ᵈtoward Azmon, and went out unto the river of Egypt; and the goings out of that coast were at the sea: this shall be your south coast.

5 And the east border *was* the salt sea, *even* unto the end of Jordan: and *their* border in the north quarter *was* from the bay of the sea, at the uttermost part of Jordan:

6 And the border went up to ᵉBeth-hogla, and passed along by the north of Beth-arabah; and the border went up ᶠto the stone of Bohan the son of Reuben:

7 And the border went up toward Debir from ᵍthe valley of Achor, and so northward looking toward Gilgal, that *is* before the going up to Adummim, which *is* on the south side of the river: and the border passed toward the waters of En-shemesh, and the goings out thereof were at ʰEnrogel:

8 And the border went up ⁱby the valley of the son of Hinnom,

ᶜ Num. 34. 4. ᵈ Num. 34. 5. ᵉ ch. 18. 19. ᶠ ch. 18. 17. ᵍ ch. 7. 26.
ʰ 2 Sam. 17. 17. 1 Kings 1. 9. ⁱ ch. 18. 16.
2 Kings 23. 10. Jer. 19. 2. 6.

The term among us is generally applied to a *jutting promontory* of land.

3. *Maaleh-acrabbim.* Or, Heb. 'the ascent of (the mount of) scorpions;' probably so called from the multitude of those animals found there. Com. Num. 34. 4.——¶ *Kadesh-Barnea.* Called En-mishpat, Gen. 14. 7. It was on the edge of the wilderness of Paran, and about twenty-four miles from Hebron. Here Miriam, the sister of Moses and Aaron, died; and here Moses and Aaron rebelled against the Lord; whence the place was called Meribah-Kadesh, or *contention of Kadesh.*

5. *Unto the end of Jordan.* The mouth of Jordan; the place where it discharges itself into the Dead Sea.

6. *Beth-arabah.* Heb. 'house of solitude;' perhaps so called from the loneliness and dreariness of the place. ——¶ *The stone of Bohan.* A Reubenite, and probably a distinguished commander of the forces of that tribe which came over the Jordan. It is not unlikely that he died in the camp at Gilgal, and was buried not far off, under the stone here alluded to.

7. *En-shemesh.* Heb. 'fountain of the sun;' a place eastward of Jerusalem, on the confines of Judah and Benjamin. Some conjecture that it was a fountain dedicated by the Canaanites to the sun.——¶ *En-rogel.* Heb. 'fountain of the fuller;' perhaps from its water having afforded special conveniences to those that exercised the craft of fullers. It is supposed by some to have been the same as the Pool of Siloam; by others placed further down the valley, near the south-east of Jerusalem, and not far from what is now called the *Fountain of the Blessed Virgin.*

8. *The valley of the son of Hinnom.* A valley in the vicinity of Jerusalem, lying probably on the south of mount

B. C. 1444.] CHAPTER XV. 159

unto the south side of the [k] Jebusite; the same is Jerusalem: and the border went up to the top of the mountain that *lieth* before the valley of Hinnom westward, which *is* at the end [l] of the valley of the giants northward:

9 And the border was drawn from the top of the hill unto [m] the fountain of the water of Nephtoah, and went out to the cities of mount Ephron; and the border was drawn [n] to Baalah, which *is* [o] Kirjath-jearim:

10 And the border compassed from Baalah westward unto mount Seir, and passed along unto the side of mount Jearim (which *is* Chesalon) on the north side, and went down to Beth-shemesh, and passed on to [p] Timnah:

11 And the border went out unto the side of [q] Ekron northward: and the border was drawn

[k] ch. 18. 28. Judg. 1. 21, and 19. 10. [l] ch. 18. 16. [m] ch. 18. 15. [p] 1 Chron. 13. 6. [o] Judg. 18. 12. [p] Gen. 38. 13. Judg. 14. 1. [q] ch. 19. 43.

Zion, and consequently environing the ancient city on the south side. Who this Hinnom was, or why it was called his valley, is not known. This valley, or, more properly speaking, ravine, is only about one hundred and fifty feet in breadth, and is stated to have been in ancient times exceedingly verdant and shaded with trees. But from the inhuman practices of the Hebrews, in sacrificing their infants at a place in it called Tophet, the whole valley was denounced by Jehovah, and polluted by Josiah, by ordure and dead men's bones and every kind of filth from the city. After the captivity, the Jews regarded this spot with abhorrence, on account of the abominations which had been practised there, and following the example of Josiah, threw into it the carcases of animals and the dead bodies of malefactors, and every species of refuse. To prevent the pestilence which such a mass would occasion, if left to putrify, constant fires were kept up in the valley, in order to consume what was thrown into it. It became therefore a striking type of *Hell*, or that part of *Hades* where they supposed the souls of wicked men were punished in eternal fire. Under this idea, it was often called *Gehenna of fire;* the name 'Gehenna' being formed from the Heb. גיא הנם *Gë-hinnom, valley of Hinnom.* See Barnes' Notes on Mat. 6. 22.—¶ *Valley of the giants.* Or, Heb. רפאים *rephâim, of the Rephaim;* on which word see on Gen. 6. 4; Deut. 2. 7, 11. This valley lay about three miles to the southwest of Jerusalem, and appears to have been so called from its ancient gigantic inhabitants. It was the theatre of several signal victories obtained by David over the Philistines, and was also famed for its fertility and its excellent crops of corn. Is. 17. 5. The road from Jerusalem, says Maundrell, passes through this valley, and in it are pointed out to the traveller the ruined tower of Simeon, the Greek monastery of Elias, and the tomb of Rachel. The valley itself is now only partially cultivated, and even those parts which are sown with corn yield but a comparatively poor and scanty crop. 'He turneth a fruitful land into barrenness for

160   JOSHUA.   [B. C. 1444.

to Shicron, and passed along to mount Baalah, and went out unto Jabneel; and the goings out of the border were at the sea.

12 And the west border *was* ʳ to the great sea, and the coast *thereof*: this *is* the coast of the children of Judah round about, according to their families.

13 ¶ ˢ And unto Caleb the son of Jephunneh he gave a part among the children of Judah, according to the commandment of the Lord to Joshua, *even*

ʳ ver. 47.   Num. 34 6, 7.   ˢ ch. 14. 13.
ᵗ ch. 14. 15.

‘the city of Arba the father of Anak, which *city is* Hebron.

14 And Caleb drove thence ᵘ the three sons of Anak, ˣ Sheshai, and Ahiman, and Talmai, the children of Anak.

15 And ʸ he went up thence to the inhabitants of Debir: and the name of Debir before *was* Kirjath-sepher.

16 ¶ ᶻ And Caleb said, He that smiteth Kirjath-sepher, and taketh it, to him will I give Achsah my daughter to wife.

ᵘ Judg. 1. 10, 20.   ˣ Num. 13. 22.   ʸ ch. 10, 38. Judg. 1. 11.   ᶻ Judg. 1. 12.

---

the wickedness of them that dwell therein.'

13. *And unto Caleb he gave.* Or Heb. 'had given.' The historian seems pleased with every occasion to make mention of Caleb, and to do him honor, because he honored the Lord by following him fully. Respecting this grant to Joshua, see notes on the preceding chapter, v. 6-15.

14. *Drove thence the sons of Anak.* This is doubtless mentioned here to show, that the confidence he had before expressed of success in this affair, through the presence of God with him, did not deceive him. The event answered all his expectations; and it is here put on record at once to the praise of Caleb, to the glory of God, who never disappoints those that trust in him, and for the encouragement of believers in all ages. On the sense of the phrase 'drove out,' see on Judg. 1. 10.

15. *Debir—Kirjath-sepher.* These names, the former signifying *a word* or *oracle*, the latter, *the city of a book*, have led some commentators to suppose that this city was a seat of learning, or a repository of the records of the ancient inhabitants. It is not indeed probable that writings and *books*, in our sense of the words, were very common among the Canaanites; but some method of recording events and a sort of learning was doubtless cultivated in those regions.

16. *And Caleb said, He that smiteth*, &c. We cannot think so ill of Caleb, as to suppose that this proposition proceeded either from cowardice or sloth. He did not invite another to achieve a difficult and dangerous exploit because he shrunk from it himself. He had already evinced too much valor to allow of the supposition. But his generous spirit would not permit him to monopolise all the glory of these victories. He would give occasion to some of his younger brethren to signalise their prowess also; and to strengthen the inducement, he makes a proffer of his daughter in marriage to the successful combatant. Such an achievement would be presumptive evidence that the man was worthy of her, and one

B. C. 1444.] CHAPTER XV. 161

17 And ^a Othniel the ^b son of Kenaz, the brother of Caleb, took it: and he gave him Achsah his daughter to wife.

18 ^c And it came to pass, as she came *unto him*, that she moved him to ask of her father a field: and ^d she lighted off *her*

a Judg. 1. 13, and 3. 9. b Num. 32. 12. ch. 14 6.

c Judg. 1. 14. d Gen. 24. 64. 1 Sam. 25. 23.

who was likely to deserve well of his country. So Saul, in like manner, promised his daughter in marriage to him who should kill Goliath, 1 Sam. 17. 25. Fathers, in ancient times, appear to have had nearly an absolute power in the disposal of their daughters in marriage, as we learn from the case of Laban, and numerous other instances mentioned in the Scriptures. Caleb, however, could no doubt safely presume upon his daughter's preference coinciding with his, especially when such recommendations existed as were supposed in the very nature of the case. Deeds of valor have seldom failed, in any age of the world, to prove a powerful passport to the female heart, although it is to be hoped that the force of this attraction will diminish, as the influence of a religion of peace prevails in the world.

17. *Othniel, the son of Kenaz, the brother of Caleb, took it.* It was Kenaz, and not Othniel, who was the brother, and, as appears from Judg. 1. 13, the younger brother of Caleb; otherwise the marriage would have been unlawful, or at least of questionable propriety. It is not at all improbable, that Othniel previously entertained an affection for Achsah, so that he could not brook the thought that any one else should do more to win her favor, than he himself would. This prompted him unhesitatingly to take up the gage which Caleb had thrown down. The result proved that he was worthy both of the work and the wages; for he became afterwards a deliverer and a judge in Israel, the first single person who presided in their affairs, after the death of Joshua. 'It is good for those, who are setting out in the world, to begin betimes with that which is great and good; that, excelling in service when they are young, they may excel in honor when they are old.' *Henry.*

18. *As she came* unto him. Or, Heb. ' in her going;' i. e. in going from her father's house to live with her husband.——¶ *She moved him to ask.* Gr. 'she took counsel with him, saying, I will ask.' Being on the point of leaving the paternal roof, she seized the opportunity, when a parent's heart would naturally be tender and yielding, to persuade her husband to solicit an additional boon of her father. He readily consented to the request being made, but seems to have preferred that it should come from herself rather than him, as he would do nothing that would appear like taking advantage of Caleb's favorable disposition towards his son-in-law. Accordingly the petition was made by Achsah, who, in order to manifest more respect and reverence for her father, alighted off the animal on which she rode, and addressed him in the most suppliant posture. On this eastern mode of expressing respect, see 'Illustrations of Scripture,' p. 32, 282.

19. *Give me a blessing.* Do me an

14*

ass; and Caleb said unto her, What wouldest thou?

19 Who answered, Give me a ᵉblessing; for thou hast given me a south land, give me also springs of water: and he gave her the upper springs, and the nether springs.

20 This *is* the inheritance of the tribe of the children of Judah according to their families.

21 And the uttermost cities of the tribe of the children of Judah toward the coast of Edom southward were Kabzeel, and Eder, and Jagur.

22 And Kinah, and Dimonah, and Adadah,

23 And Kedesh, and Hazor, and Ithnan,

24 Ziph, and Telem, and Bealoth,

25 And Hazor, Hadattah, and Kerioth, *and* Hezron, which *is* Hazor,

26 Amam, and Shema, and Moladah,

27 And Hazar-gaddah, and Heshmon, and Beth-palet,

28 And Hazar-shual, and Beersheba, and Bizjothjah,

29 Baalah, and Iim, and Azem,

e Gen. 33. 11.

---

act of kindness, grant me a special favor, as a gift is sometimes called *a blessing*, Gen. 33. 11; 2 Kings 5. 15; 2 Cor. 9. 5. Or, she calls this *a blessing*, because it would add much to the comfort of her settlement, and she was sure, since she married not only with her father's consent, but in obedience to his command, he would not deny her his blessing.——¶ *Hast given me a south land.* Which by lying exposed to the burning rays of the sun, and to the sultry south winds, was comparatively ill-watered and barren.——¶ *Give me also springs of water.* By which she meant not simply gushing springs of water, but the field or fields in which they were situated, v. 18. Chald. 'Give me a place moistened with water.' If the fields belonged to one, and the springs to another, she would of course be little benefited by the possession.——¶ *He gave her the upper springs and the nether springs.* Both higher and lower ground; tracts of hill and dale well watered. An allusion of practical bearing is sometimes made to this, when we pray for spiritual and heavenly blessings, which relate to our souls as blessings of the upper springs, and those that relate to the body and the life that now is, as blessings of the nether springs. From this story we may learn, (1) That a moderate desire for the comforts and conveniences of this life is no breach of the commandment, 'Thou shalt not covet.' (2) That mutual consultation and joint agreement between husbands and wives, as touching the things they shall seek pertaining to the common good of themselves and their families, is the surest omen of success. (3) That parents should never think that lost which is bestowed upon their children, for their advantage. They forget themselves and their relations, who grudge their children what is convenient for them, when they can easily part with it.

20. *This is the inheritance,* &c. He now returns to the description of Judah's inheritance, from the digression made concerning Caleb and his family, in the preceding verses.

30 And Eltolad, and Chesil, and Hormah,

31 And ᶠ Ziklag, and Madmannah, and Sansannah,

32 And Lebaoth, and Shilhim, and Ain, and Rimmon: all the cities *are* twenty and nine, with their villages:

33 *And* in the valley, ᵍ Eshtaol, and Zoreah, and Ashnah,

34 And Zanoah, and En-gannim, Tappuah, and Enam,

35 Jarmuth, and Adullam, Socoh, and Azekah,

36 And Sharaim, and Adithaim, and Gederah, and Gederothaim; fourteen cities with their villages:

37 Zenan, and Hadashah, and Migdal-gad,

38 And Dilean, and Mizpeh, ʰ and Joktheel,

39 Lachish, and Bozkath, and Eglon,

40 And Cabbon, and Lahmam, and Kithlish,

41 And Gederoth, Beth-dagon, and Naamah, and Makkedah; sixteen cities with their villages:

42 Libnah, and Ether, and Ashan,

43 And Jiphtah, and Ashnah, and Nezib,

44 And Keilah, and Achzib, and Mareshah; nine cities with their villages:

45 Ekron, with her towns and her villages:

46 From Ekron even unto the sea, all that *lay* near Ashdod, with their villages:

47 Ashdod, with her towns and her villages; Gaza, with her towns and her villages, unto ⁱ the river of Egypt, and ᵏ the great sea, and the border *thereof*:

48 ¶ And in the mountains, Shamir, and Jattir, and Socoh,

49 And Dannah, and Kirjath-sannah, which *is* Debir,

50 And Anab, and Eshtemoh, and Anim,

51 ˡ And Goshen, and Holon, and Giloh; eleven cities with their villages:

52 Arab, and Dumah, and Eshean,

53 And Janum, and Beth-tappuah, and Aphekah,

54 And Humtah, and ᵐ Kirjath-arba (which *is* Hebron) and Zior; nine cities with their villages:

55 Maon, Carmel, and Ziph, and Juttah,

56 And Jezreel, and Jokdeam, and Zanoah,

57 Cain, Gibeah, and Timnah; ten cities with their villages:

58 Halhul, Beth-zur, and Gedor,

---

f 1 Sam. 27. 6. g Num. 13. 23. h 2 Kings 14. 7. i ver. 4. k Num. 34. 6. l ch. 10. 41, and 11. 16. m ch. 14. 15, and ver. 13.

---

32. *All the cities are twenty and nine.* But upon an exact computation there appears to be *thirty-eight.* The reason of the discrepancy doubtless is, either that nine of them were afterwards allotted to Simeon, or, as many of them are expressed by *compound* terms, translators may have combined what should be separated, and in one or two instances have formed the names of *cities* out of *epithets.*

59 And Maarath, and Beth-anoth, and Eltekon; six cities with their villages:

60 ⁿ Kirjath-baal (which *is* Kirjath-jearim) and Rabbah; two cities with their villages:

61 In the wilderness, Beth-arabah, Middin, and Secacah,

62 And Nibshan, and the city of Salt, and En-gedi; six cities with their villages.

63 ¶ As for the Jebusites, the inhabitants of Jerusalem, ᵒ the children of Judah could not drive them out: ᵖ but the Jebusites dwell with the children of Judah at Jerusalem unto this day.

CHAPTER XVI.

AND the lot of the children of Joseph fell from Jordan by Jericho, unto the water of Jericho, on the east, to the wilderness that goeth up from Jericho throughout mount Beth-el,

2 And goeth out from Beth-el to ᵃ Luz, and passeth along unto the borders of Archi to Ataroth,

3 And goeth down westward to the coast of Japhleti, ᵇ unto the coast of Beth-horon the nether, and to ᶜ Gezer: and the goings out thereof are at the sea.

4 ᵈ So the children of Joseph, Manasseh and Ephraim, took their inheritance.

5 ¶ And the border of the children of Ephraim according to their families was *thus*: even the border of their inheritance on the east side was ᵉ Ataroth-

ⁿ ch. 18. 14.   ᵒ See Judg. 1. 8, 21.   2 Sam. 5. 6.   ᵖ Judg. 1. 21.

ᵃ ch. 18. 13.   Judg. 1. 26.   ᵇ ch. 18. 13.   2 Chron. 8. 5.   ᶜ 1 Chron. 7. 28.   1 Kings 9. 15.   ᵈ ch. 17. 4.   ᵉ ch. 18. 13.

---

63. *The Jebusites—the children of Judah could not drive them out.* Joshua had before taken the *king* of Jerusalem, but not the city. The part from which the Jebusites could not be dislodged was more particularly the stronghold of Zion, falling within the lot of Benjamin, which was not finally reduced till the time of David, 2 Sam. 5. 6-10. As precisely the same thing is said of the children of Benjamin, Judg. 1. 21, which is here said of the children of Judah, the inference is inevitable that part of Jerusalem was in the lot of Judah, and part in the lot of Benjamin. The inability of Judah to expel these Jebusites was owing solely to their own remissness and unbelief. If they had attempted it with vigor and resolution, if they had all had the undaunted spirit of Caleb, there is no reason to doubt that God would have been present with them to crown their efforts with success.

CHAPTER XVI.

1. *The children of Joseph.* Ephraim and the half tribe of Manasseh. This portion, which was not one, but divided and distinct, lay in the very heart of Canaan, extending from the Jordan on the east, to the Mediterranean on the west. See Map. *Fell.* Heb. יצא *yëtzë, came out, went forth;* i. e. out of the vessel or urn from which it was drawn.——¶ *Unto the water of Jericho.* The fountain in the immediate vicinity of Jericho, whose waters were healed by Elisha, as related 2 Kings 2. 19-22.——¶ *Mount Bethel.* That is, the

addar, ^f unto Beth-horon the upper;

6 And the border went out toward the sea to ^g Michmethah on the north side; and the border went about eastward unto Taanath-shiloh, and passed by it on the east to Janohah;

7 And it went down from Janohah to Ataroth, ^h and to Naarath, and came to Jericho, and went out at Jordan.

8 The border went out from Tappuah westward unto the ⁱ river Kanah; and the goings out thereof were at the sea. This *is* the inheritance of the tribe of the children of Ephraim by their families.

9 And ^k the separate cities for the children of Ephraim *were* among the inheritance of the children of Manasseh, all the cities with their villages.

10 ^l And they drave not out the Canaanites that dwelt in Gezer: but the Canaanites dwell among the Ephraimites unto this day, and serve under tribute.

CHAPTER XVII.

THERE was also a lot for the tribe of Manasseh; for

---

f 2 Chron. 8. 5. g ch. 17. 7. h 1 Chron. 7. 28. i ch. 17. 9.

k ch. 17. 9. l Judg. I. 29. See 1 Kings 9. 16.

---

mount upon or near which mount Bethel was situated. There was no mountain so called.

10. *Drave not out the Canaanites.* Yet they so far prevailed against them as to subject them to tribute; which shows that with proper exertions they *might* have extirpated them entirely, and that they were inexcusable for not having done so. The remarks of Josephus undoubtedly furnish the true clue to their remissness. 'After this, the Israelites grew effeminate as to fighting any more against their enemies, but applied themselves to the cultivation of the land, which producing them great plenty and riches, they neglected the regular disposition of their settlement, and indulged themselves in luxury and pleasures.' 'The Benjamites, to whom belonged Jerusalem, permitted its inhabitants to pay tribute; the rest of the tribes, imitating Benjamin, did the same; and contenting themselves with the tributes that were paid them, permitted the Canaanites to live in peace.' Ant. B. V. ch. 2. § 5, 7. So it may be suggested that Christians are in danger of putting their own, or the sins of others *under tribute*, i. e. making them a source of worldly profit, instead of vigorously aiming to eradicate them utterly. It is a serious question, whether the gains of Christian venders of ardent spirits are not derived from this source. Is it not *taking tribute of the Canaanites?*

CHAPTER XVII.

1. *Also a lot for the tribe of Manasseh.* It was important to note this, to show, that although Jacob, in his blessing, Gen. 48. 19, 20, did, in a measure, set Ephraim before Manasseh, yet it was not to prejudice his rights of primogeniture. Ephraim, indeed, was to be more numerous and powerful than Manasseh, yet Manasseh was the first-born, and was to have his distinct inheritance, in-

he *was* the ᵃ first-born of Joseph; *to wit*, for ᵇMachir the first-born of Manasseh, the father of Gilead: because he was a man of war, therefore he had ᶜGilead and Bashan.

2 There was also *a lot* for ᵈthe rest of the children of Manasseh by their families; ᵉfor the children of Abiezer, and for the children of Helek, ᶠand for the children of Asriel, and for the children of Shechem, ᵍand for the children of Hepher, and for the children of Shemida: these *were* the male children of Manasseh the son of Joseph by their families.

ᵃ Gen. 41. 51, and 46. 20, and 48. 18. ᵇ Gen. 50 23. Num. 26. 29, and 32. 39, 40. 1 Chron. 7. 14. ᶜ Deut. 3. 15. ᵈ Num. 26. 29-32. ᵉ 1 Chron. 7. 18. Num. 26. 30. ᶠ Num. 26. 31. ᵍ Num. 26. 32.

3 ¶ But ʰZelophehad, the son of Hepher, the son of Gilead, the son of Machir, the son of Manasseh, had no sons, but daughters: and these *are* the names of his daughters, Mahlah, and Noah, Hoglah, Milcah, and Tirzah.

4 And they came near before ⁱEleazar the priest, and before Joshua the son of Nun, and before the princes, saying, ᵏThe LORD commanded Moses to give us an inheritance among our brethren: therefore according to the commandment of the LORD he gave them an inheritance among the brethren of their father.

5 And there fell ten portions

ʰ Num. 26. 33. and 27. 1, and 36. 2. ⁱ ch. 14 1. ᵏ Num. 27. 6, 7.

---

stead of being incorporated with his brother in possession.——¶ *Machir.* The name of the only son of Manasseh, but here as well as Judg. 5. 14, put for his posterity. Indeed, throughout this description of the boundaries of the tribes, the names of fathers stand for their descendants. ——¶ *The first-born of Manasseh.* Meaning his *only* son. It is a scriptural usage to denominate an *only* son the *first born.* See Matt. 1. 24, 25. ——¶ *The father of Gilead.* Although it is true, as expressly affirmed Num. 26. 29, and 27. 1, that Machir was the father of a son named Gilead, yet it is certain that this latter name, when used with the article in Heb. as here, is almost invariably applied to the *country* so called, and which received its denomination, in the time of Jacob, from the incident mentioned Gen. 31. 48. It can scarcely be doubted, therefore, that the phrase 'father of Gilead,' is here properly to be understood of Machir, and that he is so called just as in 1 Chron. 2. 24, 45, 49, 50, Asher is called 'father of Tekoa,' Maon 'father of Beth-zur,' Sheva, 'father of Gibea,' and Shabal 'father of Kirjath-jearim;' all the names of places. The reason of Machir, or rather his posterity, being so called, is immediately stated—because, being a warlike and valiant race, they had conquered Gilead and Bashan, therefore that region was allotted them.

2. *The male children of Manasseh.* This is mentioned merely to prepare the way for the ensuing digression, concerning the *daughters* of Zelophehad.

3. *But Zelophehad the son of Hepher*, &c. See Notes on Num. 26. 33, 27. 1.

to Manasseh, besides the land of Gilead and Bashan, which were on the other side Jordan; 6 Because the daughters of Manasseh had an inheritance among his sons: and the rest of Manasseh's sons had the land of Gilead.

7 ¶ And the coast of Manasseh was from Asher to ¹Michmethah, that *lieth* before Shechem; and the border went along on the right hand unto the inhabitants of En-tappuah.

8 *Now* Manasseh had the land of Tappuah: but ᵐTappuah on the border of Manasseh *belonged* to the children of Ephraim: 9 And the coast descended ⁿunto the river Kanah, southward of the river.. ºThese cities of Ephraim *are* among the cities of Manasseh: the coast of Manasseh also *was* on the north side of the river, and the outgoings of it were at the sea: 10 Southward *it was* Ephraim's, and northward *it was* Manasseh's, and the sea in his border; and·they met together in Asher on the north, and in Issachar on the east.

11 ᵖAnd Manasseh had in Issachar and in Asher, ᑫBeth-shean and her towns, and Ibleam and her towns, and the inhabitants of Dor and her towns, and the inhabitants of Endor and her towns, and the inhabitants of Taanach and her towns, and the inhabitants of Megiddo and her towns, *even* three countries.

12 Yet ʳthe children of Manasseh could not drive out the

l ch. 16. 6.   ᵐ ch. 16. 8.   ⁿ ch. 16. 8.   º ch. 16. 9.   p 1 Chron. 7. 29.   q 1 Sam. 31. 10. 1 Kings 4. 12.   r Judg. 1. 27, 28.

---

11. *Beth-shean and her towns.* Heb. בנותיה *benothëhâh, and her daughters.* Beth-shean, or Beth-san, the Scythopolis of the Greek and Roman writers, was situated in the plain of Jordan, at the east end of the great plain of Jezreel, and not far from the sea of Galilee. It is now called *Bisan,* eight hours, or twenty-four miles from Tiberias, and described, by Dr. Richardson, as a collection of miserable hovels, containing about two hundred inhabitants. But the interesting ruins in its vicinity point out to the traveller its former grandeur and importance.——¶ *And the inhabitants.* The phraseology is remarkable, implying that they *had* or *possessed* not the places only, but also the people; that is, that having spared them, contrary to the Divine command, they reduced them to the condition of dependants and menials, and *served themselves of them.*

12. *The children of Manasseh could not drive out,* &c. Their inability was wholly of the moral kind. They *could* not do it, because they were not *disposed* to do it, just as it is said of Joseph's brethren, Gen. 37. 4, that 'they *could not* speak peaceably unto him,' so strong was their personal dislike to him. The love of ease, the prospect of gain, and, perhaps, the feelings of humanity, accompanied by a gradual declension of faith and zeal, prevailed over the motives which should have prompted them to action, and so rendered them *unable* to effect the object. But an inability, arising from this source, was obviously inexcusable, on the same

inhabitants of those cities; but the Canaanites would dwell in that land.

13 Yet it came to pass, when the children of Israel were waxen strong, that they put the Canaanites to ˢtribute; but did not utterly drive them out.

ˢ ch. 16. 10.

14 ‘And the children of Joseph spake unto Joshua, saying, Why hast thou given me *but* ᵘ one lot and one portion to inherit, seeing I *am* ˣ a great people, forasmuch as the Lᴏʀᴅ hath blessed me hitherto?

ᵗ ch. 16. 4. ᵘ Gen. 48. 22. ˣ Gen. 48.19. Num. 26. 34, 37.

---

grounds that a drunkard's inability to master his propensity for strong drink is inexcusable. In like manner, the 'cannot' of the impenitent sinner, in regard to the performance of his duty, is equally inexcusable. ——¶ *The Canaanites would dwell in that land.* Heb. רוֹאֵל לָשֶׁבֶת *yoël làshebeth, willed to dwell.* A very remarkable expression, indicative of the obstinate determination of the Canaanites to retain possession of the country, and carrying with it a severe reflection upon the supineness, cowardice, and unbelief of the Israelites. The present version, 'would,' gives a very exact idea of the import of the original, which signifies *to will, to determine*, especially as the result of *complacency, content*, or *satisfaction* in any thing. It implies here, that the Canaanites resolved to *act their own will* in remaining, that they would do *as they pleased* about it. Alas! how often is it the case that our innate lusts, those hidden enemies of the heart, obtain such an advantage over us, that they may be conceived as uttering the same language! Long accustomed to toleration and forbearance, they at length spurn control, and domineer in the most absolute manner. As if they held their place and power by prescription, they seem determined not to be dispossessed, and lord it with all the airs of despotic masters over their too easy and obsequious subjects. But such a base subjection as this, always costs the Christian dear, if, indeed, he be a Christian over whom it is exercised. He may decline a vigorous contest now when the victory is comparatively easy, but he must prepare for the combat by and by, and must count upon tenfold difficulty in achieving a conquest. If he succeeds at all, he will barely escape with his life. Interest, duty, safety, all combine, therefore, to require of the believer the most determined and unremitting efforts to obtain and preserve a decided ascendency over the inbred corruptions of his nature.

13. *Yet it came to pass*, &c. This might better be rendered 'and,' or 'for it came to pass,' as the words are not intended to express an *opposition* to the leading sense of the preceding verse, but rather to point to the *reason* of the failure of the Israelites to expel their enemies: viz. because they found it more agreeable to put them under tribute, though in direct disobedience of the divine injunction, Deut. 20. 16.

14. *The children of Joseph.* That is, both the tribes of Ephraim and Manasseh conjointly. They speak, however, according to common usage in the Hebrew, as if they were but

15 And Joshua answered them, If thou be a great people, *then* get thee up to the wood-*country*, and cut down for thyself there in the land of the Periz- zites and of the ᵛ giants, if mount Ephraim be too narrow for thee. 16 And the children of Joseph said, The hill is not enough for us: and all the Canaanites that

ᵛ Gen. 14. 5, and 15. 20.

one person.——¶ *One lot and one portion.* It is not easy to determine whether they complain of having received but one lot, when they considered themselves entitled to two, as being two distinct tribes, or that the district assigned to them was so small as to be no more than sufficient for one tribe of ordinary dimensions. They complain, however, of the narrowness of their bounds, and plead that their great numbers should constitute a claim for a larger portion. ——¶ *Forasmuch as the Lord hath blessed me hitherto.* Increased, multiplied me. On this sense of the word 'bless,' see on Gen. 1. 22.

15. *If thou be a great people.* Joshua takes them at their word, and makes their alleged greatness an argument of their being the better able by their own energy and industry to make up any deficiency in their lot. The complete expulsion of the Canaanites from their territories would be a *virtual enlargement* of their bounds, and to this they ought to hold themselves obliged by the command and the promise of Jehovah. He intimates, if we mistake not, that their lot was in itself sufficiently extensive for their purposes, *would they but make it all available*, which he now enjoins it upon them to do. 'Many wish for larger possessions who do not cultivate and make the best of what they have; and think they should have more talents given them, when they do not trade with those with which they are intrusted.' *Henry.*——¶ *Get thee up to the wood-*country. That is, to the mountainous parts which are covered with wood. We suppose he still has in view certain parts of the tract which had not been expressly assigned, but which were, at present, possessed by the Perizzites and Rephaim, a gigantic and formidable race, whom they seem to have been backward to encounter.——¶ *Cut down for thyself.* That is, prepare a place for thyself. They were to combine the labors of the axe with those of the sword, in obtaining and fitting up for themselves a suitable possession. It is, however, to be remarked, that the original word here rendered 'cut down' is applied, Ezek. 23. 47, to *dispatching with the sword*, and that it is not, therefore, absolutely certain that it refers solely to the cutting down the trees of a forest. It may mean cutting down enemies in war. Probably the genuine idea is, *making a clearance for themselves*, whether by felling the forests, or by cutting off the giants, or both. It is worthy of notice, that the original word is from the same root with ברא *bârâ, to create,* Gen. 1. 1, and which we there endeavored to show, implied a process of *re-forming*, or *renovating*, just as the transforming an uninhabited woodland tract into cultivated fields, or populous towns, *renovates* or *re-creates* a country.

16. *The hill is not enough for us.*

15

dwell in the land of the valley have ʸchariots of iron, *both they* who *are* of Beth-shean and her towns, and *they* who *are* ᶻof the valley of Jezreel.

17 And Joshua spake unto the house of Joseph, *even* to Ephraim and to Manasseh, saying,

y Judg. 1. 19, and 4. 3.

Thou *art* a great people, and hast great power: thou shalt not have one lot *only:*

18 But the mountain shall be thine; for it *is* a wood, and thou shalt cut it down: and the outgoings of it shall be thine: for thou shalt drive out the Canaan-

z ch. 19. 18. 1 Kings 4. 12.

Heb. לא ימצא לנו *lo yimmâtzë lânu, shall not be found for us.* That is, perhaps, is unattainable by us, cannot be mastered. The grounds of their apprehension, they proceed to state in what follows.——¶ *And all the Canaanites,* &c. Rather, *for* all the Canaanites, &c. It would be impossible, they thought, to make themselves masters of the mountains, so long as their enemies, with their iron chariots, commanded all the adjacent valleys. Such a formidable defence would effectually preclude all access. ——¶*Chariots of iron.* Not chariots made wholly of iron, but armed with it; chariots with long scythes fastened to their axle-trees, as described above, ch. 11. 4.

17. *Thou shalt not have one lot* only. Thou shalt not be restricted to what *thou callest* one lot; it is in fact a much larger territory; and thou doest wrong to call it by so diminutive a title. Only possess the whole, and great and powerful as thou art, thou wilt find no reason to complain of too contracted bounds.

18. *But the mountain shall be thine.* The same mountainous or hilly tract of which he had spoken before. Seeing that their request proceeded only from pusillanimity and want of faith, he insists upon his first suggestion. He would have them quit themselves like men, and take possession of the fine wooded hills to which he referred before. There was no reason why they should ask any thing more. And as to the Canaanites and their chariots of iron, what were they when set in opposition to the almighty arm of Israel's God? They were not to fear for a moment but that they should drive them out, terrible as they were.——¶ *The outgoings of it shall be thine.* Meaning, probably, the passages and valleys leading to it; q. d. ' Clear away the wood, occupy the mountain, and you shall soon be able to command all the defiles, all the avenues of approach, and no enemy can make head against you.' Otherwise, the meaning may be, The mountainous tract, *in all the extent of its boundaries,* shall be thine. This is sometimes the sense of 'outgoings.' We may learn from this petition of the sons of Joseph, (1) How prone men are to be discontented with their lot. A dissatisfied mind, a disposition to murmur, envy, and covet, rather than to be content, thankful, and liberal, is, alas! too often characteristic of those who are really highly favored of Heaven, would they but survey their blessings in all their length and breadth, and extract the most out of them that they are capable of yielding. (2) Our complaints of comforts withheld are often no more than testimonies of our own su-

ites, ¹ though they have iron chariots, *and* though they *be* strong.

CHAPTER XVIII.

AND the whole congregation of the children of Israel assembled together ᵃ at Shiloh,

¹ Deut. 20.

and ᵇ set up the tabernacle of the congregation there: and the land was subdued before them.

2 And there remained among the children of Israel seven tribes, which had not yet received their inheritance.

ᵃ ch. 19. 51, and 21. 2, and 22. 9. Jer. 7. 12.
ᵇ Judg. 18. 31. 1 Sam. 1. 3, 24, and 4. 3, 4.

---

pineness, negligence, and fear of the cross. From an ignoble fear that our enemies are too many, or too mighty for us, and that we can do nothing, we sit down and attempt nothing: and yet we complain of providential allotments. Thus it is that 'the foolishness of man perverteth his way, and (yet) his heart fretteth against the Lord.'

CHAPTER XVIII.

1. *The whole congregation—assembled at Shiloh.* The withdrawment of the tribes of Judah, Ephraim, and Manasseh, to take possession of their respective lots, would sensibly diminish the body of the people encamped around the tabernacle at Gilgal, and make it inconvenient as a place of resort to those who were becoming settled at a distance. The expediency, therefore, of removing the tabernacle itself to a more central position was obvious, though the step, it may be presumed, would not be taken without divine direction, for God expressly retained to himself the prerogative of 'choosing the place where he should cause his name to dwell,' Deut. 12. 11. Shiloh accordingly was selected for this purpose. The name of this city is the same as that by which Jacob predicted the Messiah, 49. 10, and some commentators suppose that it was first called Shiloh on this occasion, when selected for the resting-place of the ark, and the observance of those institutions which pointed to Christ, the great Peacemaker between heaven and earth. It was situated in the tribe of Ephraim, in the very centre of Canaan, about twenty miles north of Jerusalem, twelve north of Bethel, and ten south of Shechem. It was therefore the most convenient location possible for all the tribes, and as Joshua was himself of the tribe of Ephraim, he, as chief magistrate of the nation, would always have a ready access to the sanctuary, when the God of Israel was to be consulted. In this place the ark and the tabernacle remained for upwards of three hundred and fifty years, till taken by the Philistines, in the time of Eli, 1 Sam. 4. 1-11. It was afterwards removed to Nob, and finally, in the reign of David, to Jerusalem.——¶ *And the land was subdued before them.* Or, Heb. '*for* the land was subdued,' intimating to the reader, how it happened that they were enabled to avail themselves of this favorable location. They were freed from the molestation of their enemies. The Canaanites were so far subdued that they offered no resistance or impediment to the occupation of the spot.

2. *Seven tribes which had not yet received their inheritance.* The rea-

3 And Joshua said unto the children of Israel, ^c How long are ye slack to go to possess the land which the Lord God of your fathers hath given you?

c Judg. 18. 9.

sons of this delay are unknown. The probability is, that the original survey, on which the division thus far made was founded, was so imperfect, that the remaining tribes were unwilling to have it made the basis of their respective allotments. This is to be inferred from the fact that Judah's portion was soon found to be too large, as Joseph's had already been found too small. The dissatisfaction expressed had led therefore to a temporary suspension of the work, till a new and more exact survey could be made. Add to this, that they appear to have become tired of the war. Their former conquests had enriched them with spoil, they were enjoying the ample provisions which had been treasured up for the use of the former inhabitants, and they became self-indulgent, slothful, and dilatory. They were now living at ease in the midst of their brethren; the regions that yet remained to be divided were remote from the station around which they were clustered, and if they went to take possession of them, they must break up their present connexions, drive their flocks and herds, and convey their wives and children to strange places, and undergo new hardships and trials. Besides this, great numbers of the Canaanites still remained in the unappropriated districts, and these, they knew, could not be expelled but at the expense of great effort, fatigue and peril. Their hearts accordingly sunk within them at the prospect. They knew the work was to be done—they wished it *were* done—but still they had not spirit to undertake it. 'The soul of the sluggard desireth and hath nothing.' What a striking picture of the too common apathy and sluggishness of the candidate for the heavenly inheritance! How frequently is he diverted from present duties and debarred from present comforts, by giving way to slothful or timorous apprehensions of the difficulties that beset his path. Forty years after this time, the tribe of Dan had to fight for their inheritance, and it was four hundred years before the Jebusites were driven from Jerusalem. Had all the tribes proceeded with united vigor to fulfil the divine command in its utmost extent, they would not so long have been annoyed by their remaining enemies, as 'scourges in their sides, and thorns in their eyes.' And who does not find that corruptions gather strength by indulgence, and that graces decay for want of exercise? Therefore let us look to ourselves, that we lose not the things that we have wrought.

3. *How long are ye slack to go to possess the land*, &c. This is surely the language of rebuke, and implies that there had been a criminal remissness, among the tribes, in regard to this matter, the probable source of which is explained in the remarks on the preceding verse. It is true, indeed, that they could not well be enjoined to enter immediately, to rush, as it were, upon their inheritances, for the particular assignments were first to be made to each, but the point of the censure is directed *to*

B. C. 1444.] CHAPTER XVIII. 173

4 Give out from among you three men for *each* tribe: and I will send them, and they shall rise, and go through the land, and describe it according to the inheritance of them, and they shall come *again* to me.

5 And they shall divide it into seven parts: ^d Judah shall abide in their coast on the south, and ^e the house of Joseph shall abide in their coast on the north.

6 Ye shall therefore describe

d ch. 15. 1. e ch. 16. 1, 4.

their indifference in this respect. They manifested no interest in, they were taking no steps towards having the requisite survey and division made. This was the essence of their offence. So, in reproving the impenitent for his neglecting to work out his own salvation with fear and trembling, and in pressing upon him the faithful discharge of every Christian duty, it is still to be understood that his *first*, his *immediate* business is to become reconciled to God, by unfeigned repentance; and thus to secure a *title* to eternal life. When this is done, his great concern in life is, like that of the Israelites in Canaan, to labor to *enter into possession* of his eternal inheritance.

4. *Give out from among you.* Heb. הבו לכם *hâbu lâkem, give ye for yourselves;* i. e. appoint, select, ordain. ¶ *Three men of* each *tribe.* Of each of the seven tribes that yet remained to be provided for, making twenty-one in all. ¶ *Go through the land.* Accompanied, perhaps, by a military guard, to prevent the surveyors from being cut off by straggling parties of the Canaanites. Others suppose the Canaanites were supernaturally intimidated and restrained from attacking them. ¶ *Describe it.* See on v. 9. ¶ *According to the inheritance of them.* Heb. לפי נחלתם *lepi nahalâthâm, according to the mouth of their inheritance;* i. e., probably, to the *value*

of their inheritance, or the country which they were to inherit; not of their *particular* inheritances, for these were afterwards to be assigned them by lot, but of the country in general which was to constitute their inheritance. This is frequently the sense of the Heb. term פי *pi, mouth*, as may be seen by consulting Ex. 12. 4; 16. 18; Gen. 43. 7; Prov. 12. 8. The words of Josephus, in his account of this affair, give, as we conceive, very nearly the precise import of the original. 'He also gave them a charge to *estimate* the measure of that part of the land that was most fruitful, and what was not so good.' Again, 'Joshua thought the land for the tribes should be divided by *estimation of its goodness*, rather than the largeness of its measure; it often happening that one acre of some sorts of land was equivalent to a thousand other acres.' Ant. B. V., ch. 1. § 21. Joshua's instructions, therefore, required the commissioners to have a special eye to the intrinsic value of the different parts of the country, as being more or less fertile and eligible.

5. *And they shall divide it.* Or, Heb. התהלכו *hithhalleku, divide ye it.* ¶ *Judah shall abide in their coast.* In their district, in their region. Heb. 'shall stand upon his border.' The meaning undoubtedly is, that in this survey they were not to take into consideration the tribe of Judah, which was in the south, nor

the land *into* seven parts, and bring *the description* hither to me, ᶠ that I may cast lots for you here before the Lord our God.

7 ᵍBut the Levites have no part among you; for the priesthood of the Lord *is* their inheritance. ʰ And Gad, and Reuben, and half the tribe of Manasseh, have received their heritance beyond Jordan on the east, which Moses the servant of the Lord gave them.

8 ¶ And the men arose, and went away: and Joshua charged them that went to describe the land, saying, Go, and walk through the land, and describe it, and come again to me, that I may here cast lots for you before the Lord in Shiloh.

9 And the men went and passed through the land, and described it by cities into seven parts in a book, and came *again* to Joshua to the host at Shiloh.

10 ¶ And Joshua cast lots for them in Shiloh before the Lord: and there Joshua divided the land unto the children of Israel according to their divisions.

11 ¶ And the lot of the tribe of the children of Benjamin came up according to their

---

f ch. 14. 2, and ver. 10. g ch. 13. 33.
h ch. 13. 8.

---

the tribes of Ephraim and Manasseh, which were on the north of where they now were, but were carefully to divide the remaining territory which was not occupied by these tribes into seven equal parts. The tribes of Judah and Joseph had been already provided for; let them *stand* by themselves. The terms *north* and *south* are here used relatively to Shiloh, rather than to the actual position of these two tribes.

6. *Before the Lord our God.* Before the ark or tabernacle, over which the symbol of the divine presence rested. See on ch. 3. 11. The transaction was a solemn one, and he would have it so performed as that the tribes should look upon their possessions, as established to them by divine authority. The pious heart ever delights to look upon God as 'determining the bounds of our habitations.'

7. *The Levites have no part among you.* See on ch. 13. 14.

8. *And Joshua charged.* Rather, 'Joshua had charged,' as we find mentioned, v. 6. These words and the remaining part of the verse should be included in a parenthesis.

9. *Described it in a book.* Laid it down on a map or chart, accompanied, perhaps, with a verbal description of the leading features of the country. This is the earliest instance of land-surveying on record. The art was perhaps learned from the Egyptians; for their fields being annually overflowed by the Nile, and the land-marks swept away, they would be compelled frequently to resurvey them, in order to adjust their limits.——¶ *Described it by cities.* Setting down the most remarkable cities, with their towns and villages, their distances from each other, and the territories adjacent.——¶ *And came again to Joshua.* According to Josephus, at the end of seven months.

10. *According to their divisions.* According to their respective apportionments.

families: and the coast of their lot came forth between the children of Judah and the children of Joseph.

12 ⁱAnd their border on the north side was from Jordan; and the border went up to the side of Jericho on the north side, and went up through the mountains westward; and the goings out thereof were at the wilderness of Beth-aven.

13 And the border went over from thence toward Luz, to the side of Luz (ᵏwhich *is* Beth-el) southward; and the border descended to Ataroth-adar, near the hill that *lieth* on the south side ˡof the nether Beth-horon.

14 And the border was drawn *thence*, and compassed the corner of the sea southward, from the hill that *lieth* before Beth-horon southward; and the goings out thereof were at ᵐKirjath-baal (which *is* Kirjath-jearim) a city of the children of Judah. This *was* the west quarter.

15 And the south quarter *was* from the end of Kirjath-jearim, and the border went out on the west, and went out to ⁿthe well of waters of Nephtoah:

16 And the border came down to the end of the mountain that *lieth* before °the valley of the son of Hinnom, *and* which *is* in the valley of the giants on the north, and descended to the valley of Hinnom, to the side of Jebusi on the south, and descended to ᵖEn-rogel,

17 And was drawn from the north, and went forth to En-shemesh, and went forth toward Geliloth, which *is* over against the going up of Adummim, and descended to ᵠthe stone of Bohan the son of Reuben,

18 And passed along toward the side over against ʳArabah northward, and went down unto Arabah:

19 And the border passed along to the side of Beth-hoglah northward: and the out-goings of the border were at the north bay of the salt-sea at the south end of Jordan. This *was* the south coast.

20 And Jordan was the border of it on the east side. This *was* the inheritance of the children of Benjamin, by the coasts thereof round about, according to their families.

21 Now the cities of the tribe

ⁱ See ch. 16. 1. ᵏ Gen. 28. 19. Judg. 1. 23. ˡ ch. 16. 3. ᵐ ch. 15. 9. ⁿ ch. 15. 9. ° ch. 15. 8. ᵖ ch. 15. 7. ᵠ ch. 15. 6. ʳ ch. 15. 6.

---

11. *And the lot—came up.* That is, came forth from the urn or vessel in which the lots were deposited. And so by an easy metaphor it is said immediately after, that 'the coast came forth,' because the lot on which it depended came forth. In like manner it is said, Levit. 16. 9, 'The goat upon which the Lord's lot *fell*, (Heb. upon which the Lord's lot *came up*.')

—¶ *Between the children of Judah and the children of Joseph.* See on Deut. 33. 12. The prediction of Moses in regard to the lot of Benjamin was remarkably fulfilled, as may be seen in the Note on Deut. 33. 12.

of the children of Benjamin according to their families, were Jericho, and Beth-hoglah, and the valley of Keziz,

22 And Beth-arabah, and Zemaraim, and Beth-el,

23 And Avim, and Parah, and Ophrah,

24 And Chephar-haammonai, and Ophni, and Gaba; twelve cities with their villages:

25 Gibeon, and Ramah, and Beeroth,

26 And Mizpeh, and Chephirah, and Mozah,

27 And Rekem, and Irpeel, and Taralah,

28 And Zelah, Eleph, and ᵃJebusi, (which *is* Jerusalem) Gibeath, *and* Kirjath; fourteen cities with their villages. This *is* the inheritance of the children of Benjamin according to their families.

CHAPTER XIX.

AND the second lot came forth to Simeon, *even for* the tribe of the children of Simeon according to their families: ᵃand their inheritance was within the inheritance of the children of Judah.

ᵃ ch. 15. 8. ᵃ ver. 9.

CHAPTER XIX.

1. *The second lot came forth.* Out of the urn. See on ch. 18. 11.—— ¶ *For the tribe of the children of Simeon.* Exegetical of the preceding word 'Simeon,' showing that the names of *persons* are employed, as we have often elsewhere remarked, in a collective sense for the political bodies, the tribes, kingdoms, or countries of which they are the founders.—— ¶ *Their inheritance was within the inheritance of the children of Judah.* It would seem that the first rude survey had led to an erroneous impression of the extent of the country. They had supposed it to be much larger than it really was. Under this impression they had assigned a large territory to Judah, taking it for granted that the lots of the other tribes would be in the same proportion. But upon closer examination it was found that at that rate of assignment the land would not hold out, and some of the tribes must be very much scanted or left wholly destitute of their just inheritance.

The obvious expedient was to take a part of the territory of Judah and allot it to Simeon. The inheritance of this tribe therefore is said to have fallen *within* the inheritance of Judah, because it was included within the original limits of the latter tribe, and is elsewhere seldom or never spoken of as a *distinct district*. In this arrangement the providence of God is to be especially noted, as Jacob, in the spirit of prophecy, had foretold that Simeon and Levi should be 'divided in Jacob, and scattered in Israel.' Gen. 49. 7. This was accordingly most literally fulfilled in the manner in which these tribes were now disposed of. Levi was 'scattered' throughout all the land, not having received any distinct inheritance, but only certain 'cities to dwell in;' and Simeon, as we here learn, was 'divided,' or dispersed over the territories of Judah instead of having one of their own. This arrangement brought them into confederacy with the tribe of Judah, Judg. 1 3, and afterwards was the

B. C. 1444.] CHAPTER XIX. 177

2 And ᵇ they had in their inheritance, Beer-sheba, and Sheba, and Moladah,

3 And Hazar-shual, and Balah, and Azem,

4 And Eltolad, and Bethul, and Hormah,

5 And Ziklag, and Beth-marcaboth, and Hazar-susah,

6 And Beth-lebaoth, and Sharuhen; thirteen cities and their villages:

7 Ain, Remmon, and Ether, and Ashan; four cities and their villages:

8 And all the villages that *were* round about these cities to Baalath-beer, Ramath of the south. This *is* the inheritance of the tribe of the children of Simeon according to their families.

9 Out of the portion of the children of Judah *was* the inheritance of the children of Simeon: for the part of the children of Judah was too much for them: ᶜ therefore the children of Simeon had their inheritance within the inheritance of them.

ᵇ 1 Chron. 4. 28.   ᶜ ver. 1.

---

occasion of the adherence of many of this tribe to the house of David at the time of the revolt of the ten tribes to Jeroboam. 2 Chron. 15. 9, 'Out of Simeon they fell to Asa in abundance.'

2. *Beersheba, Sheba.* Heb. 'Beersheba *and* (or *even*) Sheba.' That one and the same city is designated by both these names, is clear from the fact that otherwise there would have been fourteen cities instead of thirteen. Besides, in 1 Chron. 4. 28, where Simeon's cities are enumerated, the mention of Sheba is omitted as superfluous. As to the import of these names, see on Gen. 21. 31, 32. In the description of the lots of Judah and Benjamin, an account is given both of the limits by which they were bounded and of the cities contained in them. In that of Ephraim and Manasseh the boundaries are given, but not the cities. In this chapter Simeon and Dan are described by their cities only, and not by their borders, because they were small, and the former lay within the limits of another tribe. The rest have both their borders described, and their cities named.

9. *The part of the children of Judah was too much for them.* Too large in proportion to the other tribes, and too large for their actual necessities; although, as being the most numerous of all the tribes, it might justly claim a more extensive territory than any of the rest. Yet when it was found that they could not insist upon the original allotment without manifest injustice to the other tribes, the men of Judah submitted without a murmur to relinquish a part of their possession. They will take no advantage of an unintentional error by withholding that which equity and kindness would require them to give up. The same generous principle will operate in like manner with every good man. If he has chanced, through the inadvertency or mistake of another, to gain an undue advantage in a contract, he will cheerfully waive his right and make all the concessions which, in similar circumstances, he would wish to have made to himself. He

10 ¶ And the third lot came up for the children of Zebulun according to their families: and the border of their inheritance was unto Sarid:

11 ᵈ And their border went up toward the sea, and Maralah, and reached to Dabbasheth, and reached to the river that *is* ᵉbefore Jokneam,

12 And turned from Sarid eastward, toward the sun-rising, unto the border of Chisloth-tabor, and then goeth out to Dabereth, and goeth up to Japhia,

13. And from thence passeth on along on the east to Gittah-hepher, to Ittah-kazin, and goeth out to Remmon-methoar to Neah;

14 And the border compasseth it on the north side to Hannathon: and the out-goings thereof are in the valley of Jiphthah-el:

15 And Kattath, and Nahallal, and Shimron, and Idalah, and Beth-lehem; twelve cities with their villages.

16 This *is* the inheritance of the children of Zebulun according to their families, these cities with their villages.

17 ¶ *And* the fourth lot came out to Issachar, for the children of Issachar according to their families.

18 And their border was toward Jezreel, and Chesulloth, and Shunem,

19 And Hapharaim, and Shihon, and Anaharath,

20 And Rabbith, and Kishion, and Abez,

21 And Remeth, and En-gannim, and En-haddah, and Beth-pazzez;

22 And the coast reacheth to Tabor, and Shahazimah, and Beth-shemesh; and the out-goings of their border were at Jordan: sixteen cities with their villages.

23 This *is* the inheritance of the tribe of the children of Issachar according to their families, the cities and their villages

24 ¶ And the fifth lot came out for the tribe of the children of Asher according to their families.

25 And their border was Hel-

---

d Gen. 49. 13. e ch. 12. 22.

---

will, as the apostle enjoins, look upon the things of others, as well as upon his own.

10. *The third lot came up for the children of Zebulun.* Though Zebulun was younger than Issachar, yet both in the prophetic blessing of Jacob and of Moses he came before him, and in like manner he has the precedency here also in the allotment of his inheritance. Providence is wonderful in its correspondence with prophecy. The lot of this tribe was washed by the Mediterranean on the west, and by the sea of Galilee on the east, agreeably to Jacob's prediction, Gen. 49. 13, that Zebulun should be 'a haven of ships.'

15. *Beth-lehem.* A place lying at a great distance to the north of the Beth-lehem in Judah where our Lord was born.

25. *And their border.* The word 'border' or 'boundary' both here and in what follows, is not to be understood simply of the boundary line,

kath, and Hali, and Beten, and Achsaph,

26 And Alammelech, and Amad, and Misheal; and reacheth to Carmel westward, and to Shihor-libnath;

27 And turneth toward the sun-rising to Beth-dagon, and reacheth to Zebulun, and to the valley of Jiphthah-el toward the north side of Beth-emek and Neiel, and goeth out to Cabul on the left hand,

28 And Hebron, and Rehob, and Hammon, and Kanah, [f]*even* unto great Zidon;

29 And *then* the coast turneth to Namah, and to the strong city [g] Tyre; and the coast turneth to Hosah: and the out-goings thereof are at the sea from the coast to [h] Achzib:

30 Ummah also, and Aphek, and Rehob: twenty and two cities with their villages.

f ch. 11. 8. Judg. 1. 31.   g 2 Sam. 5. 11.
h Gen. 38. 5.   Judg. 1. 31.   Mic. 1. 14.

31 This *is* the inheritance of the tribe of the children of Asher according to their families, these cities with their villages.

32 ¶ The sixth lot came out to the children of Naphtali, *even* for the children of Naphtali according to their families.

33 And their coast was from Heleph, from Allon to Zaanannim, and Adami, Nekeb, and Jabneel, unto Lakum; and the out-goings thereof were at Jordan:

34 And *then* [i] the coast turneth westward to Aznoth-tabor, and goeth out from thence to Hukkok, and reacheth to Zebulun on the south side, and reacheth to Asher on the west side, and to Judah upon Jordan toward the sun-rising.

35 And the fenced cities *are* Ziddim, Zer, and Hammath, Rakkath, and Cinneroth,

i Deut. 33. 23.

---

but also of all the towns and lands which it embraces. It might be rendered, 'district' or 'territory.'

30. *Twenty and two cities.* The above enumeration gives us nearly thirty cities instead of twenty-two, but probably several are mentioned which were only frontier towns, sometimes reckoned as belonging to one tribe, and sometimes to another, or perhaps some of the appendant *villages* are named, as well as the *towns*.

34. *To Judah upon Jordan.* How this is to be understood is not clear. It is certain that the tribe of Naphtali did not border on the east nor in any other direction, upon Judah, for there were several tribes that lay between them. Both tribes, however, were bounded by the Jordan on the east, and they might be considered as in some sort conjoined by the easy communication with each other by means of that river. This we deem the only plausible interpretation of the passage, and thus understood it goes strikingly to illustrate the obscure prediction of Moses, Deut. 33. 23, that Naphtali should 'possess the west and the south,' i. e. that although his settlement should be in the west or northwest, yet by means of the navigation of the Jordan, he should avail himself of the advantages of traffic with all the southern section of the land.

36 And Adamah, and Ramah, and Hazor,

37 And Kedesh, and Edrei, and En-hazor,

38 And Iron, and Migdal-el, Horem, and Beth-anath, and Beth-shemesh; nineteen cities with their villages.

39 This *is* the inheritance of the tribe of the children of Naphtali according to their families, the cities and their villages.

40 ¶ *And* the seventh lot came out for the tribe of the children of Dan according to their families.

41 And the coast of their inheritance was Zorah, and Eshtaol, and Ir-shemesh,

42 And ʲShaalabbin, and Ajalon, and Jethlath,

43 And Elon, and Thimnathah, and Ekron,

44 And Eltekeh, and Gibbethon, and Baalath,

45 And Jehud, and Bene-berak, and Gath-rimmon,

46 And Me-jarkon, and Rakkon, with the border before ᵏJapho.

47 And ˡthe coast of the children of Dan went out *too little* for them: therefore the children of Dan went up to fight against Leshem, and took it, and smote it with the edge of the sword, and possessed it, and dwelt therein, and called Leshem, ᵐDan, after the name of Dan their father.

48 This *is* the inheritance of the tribe of the children of Dan according to their families, these cities with their villages.

49 ¶ When they had made an end of dividing the land for inheritance by their coasts, the children of Israel gave an inheritance to Joshua the son of Nun among them:

ʲ Judg. 1. 35.   ᵏ Acts 9. 36. ˡ Judg. 18. ᵐ Judg. 18. 29.

---

47. *The coast of the children of Dan went out* too little *for them.* Heb. יצא מהם *yëtzë mëhem, went out from them;* i. e. out of their hands, out of their possession. A similar usage of the Heb. verb occurs Lev. 25. 28–33, where the lands in the year of the jubilee are said to 'go out;' i. e. out of the hands of the present possessor, to the original owner. The meaning here undoubtedly is, that the Danites, being closely pressed upon by their powerful neighbors the Philistines, were forced in considerable numbers to abandon their allotted possessions. In consequence of having their original portion thus wrested out of their hands, they were induced to seek another in a distant quarter of the land, and made an inroad accordingly upon Leshem, lying at the foot of mount Lebanon and near the sources of the river Jordan. This event, which occurred some time after the death of Joshua, and is more fully recorded, Judg. 18. 1–29, is touched upon here both to complete what is said of the inheritance of the Danites, and to intimate how it happened, that a part of the tribe were afterwards found inhabiting a district of the country so remote from their original possessions. This addition to the narrative was perhaps made by Phineas.

49. *The children of Israel gave an*

50 According to the word of the LORD they gave him the city which he asked, *even* ⁿ Timnath-serah in mount Ephraim: and he built the city, and dwelt therein.

51 ᵖ These *are* the inheritances which Eleazer the priest, and Joshua the son of Nun, and the heads of the fathers of the tribes of the children of Israel, divided

ⁿ ch. 24. 30.   ᵒ 1 Chron. 7. 24.   ᵖ Num. 34. 17.   ch. 14. 1.

for an inheritance by lot ᑫ in Shiloh before the LORD, at the door of the tabernacle of the congregation. So they made an end of dividing the country.

CHAPTER XX.

THE LORD also spake unto Joshua, saying,

2 Speak to the children of Israel, saying, ᵃ Appoint out for you cities of refuge, whereof I

ᑫ ch. 18. 1, 10.   ᵃ Exod. 21. 13.   Numb. 35. 6, 11, 14.   Deut 19. 2, 9.

---

inheritance to Joshua. As it is said immediately afterwards, v. 50, that Joshua received his inheritance 'according to the word of the Lord,' it could be considered no otherwise the gift of the people, than as they cheerfully acquiesced in the assignment, and were glad of an opportunity of thus testifying, by their hearty concurrence, their affection for their venerable leader and their interest in his comfortable settlement in his old age. On his part, he evinced a striking moderation and disinterestedness, and proposed a noble example to all in public places, in making no provision for himself till he saw all the tribes fixed in their respective inheritances. This was acting in the true spirit of a public servant—to prefer the general welfare to his private convenience, ease, or emolument. So the servants of Christ, while they fully appreciate and ardently covet an inheritance in the Canaan above, will deem it soon enough to *enter* upon it when they have done all in their power towards bringing others to partake of the same glorious possession.

50. *According to the word of the Lord.* According to the promise of the Lord; made probably at the same time that a particular inheritance was promised to Caleb. This is to be inferred from Caleb's words, ch. 14. 6, who in speaking to Joshua says, 'Thou knowest the things that the Lord said unto Moses the man of God concerning *me* and *thee* in Kadesh-barnea.' As Joshua had, on the occasion referred to, evinced equal courage and fidelity with Caleb, it is reasonable to suppose that he received the same tokens of the divine approbation.——¶ *Timnath-serah.* Called *Timnath-heres*, Judg. 2. 9, where we learn that the name of the mountain on which it stood was *Gaash.* It was here that Joshua was buried, ch. 24. 30.——¶ *He built the city.* Repaired it, put it in order, perhaps enlarged and adorned it. In this sense Nebuchadnezzar is said, Dan. 4. 30, 'to have built Babylon.'

51. *These are the inheritances*, &c. This verse is inserted as a general conclusion to all that has been thus far said of the distribution of the land among the several tribes. The writer now turns to another subject.

CHAPTER XX.

2. *Appoint out for your cities of*

spake unto you by the hand of Moses:

3 That the slayer that killeth *any* person unawares *and* unwittingly may flee thither: and they shall be your refuge from the avenger of blood.

4 And when he that doth flee unto one of those cities shall stand at the entering of ᵇ the

b Ruth 4. 1. 2.

---

refuge. Heb. לכם תנו *tenu lâkem, give for yourselves.* No delinquency on the part of Joshua is to be inferred from this command, as if he had neglected, or were likely to neglect, a very important part of the arrangements designed to be carried into effect after the settlement of Israel in Canaan. He was well aware of the divine intention in this respect, and would doubtless have acted upon it, as well as upon every other order with which he was charged, but God saw fit to interpose to remind him that *now was the precise time*, when the tribes had just received their inheritances, and while they were yet together, to separate the cities of refuge for the uses for which they were intended, and respecting which such copious instructions had been before given, Num. 35. 11-34; Deut. 19. 2-10. To the notes on these passages the reader is referred for a fuller account of the nature and object of this institution. It was an essential appendage to the patriarchal system of government, as far as the avenging of blood was concerned. It has been already remarked, that the *nearest of kin* to a deceased person had not only the right of redeeming an inheritance that had been forfeited or alienated, but had also authority to slay on the spot the person who had slain his relative. But as a man might *casually* kill another against whom he had no ill will, and with whom he had no quarrel, and might thus be liable to lose his own life undeservedly, at the hands of the *avenger of blood*, these privileged cities were wisely and humanely appointed for the protection of those who had committed accidental homicide, till the cause could receive a judicial hearing from the magistrate. They had authority, according as, upon strict examination, they found him guilty or not of wilful murder, to deliver him up to the *avenger of blood*, or, after the lapse of a certain time, to grant him a discharge.—¶ *By the hand of Moses.* By the agency, by the ministry of Moses; by him as an organ of communication.

3. *The slayer that killeth any person.* Heb. נפש מכה *makkeh nëphesh, that smiteth* (i. e. fatally) *any soul.* On this frequent sense of the word 'soul,' see Note on Gen. 12. 5.—— ¶ *Unawares and unwittingly.* Heb. בשגגה *bishgâgàh, through ignorance, error, and mistake, and without knowledge.* The conditions are stated with the *utmost explicitness*, in words amounting almost to repetition, as is evidently proper where a matter of so much consequence as the life of a human being is concerned. In cases of *wilful* murder, no place whatever could afford protection. A man might be taken even from the temple, or the horns of the altar. Ex. 21. 14; 2 Kings 2. 31, 34.

4. *Shall stand at the entering of the gate.* The usual place of judicature among the people of the East.——

gate of the city, and shall declare his cause in the ears of the elders of that city, they shall take him into the city unto them, and give him a place, that he may dwell among them.

5 ᶜ And if the avenger of blood pursue after him, then they shall not deliver the slayer up into his hand; because he smote his neighbor unwittingly, and hated him not before-time.

6 And he shall dwell in that city, ᵈ until he stand before the congregation for judgment, *and* until the death of the high priest that shall be in those days: then shall the slayer return, and come unto his own city, and unto his own house, unto the city from whence he fled.

7 ¶ And they appointed ᵉ Kedesh in Galilee in mount Naphtali, and ᶠ Shechem in mount Ephraim, and ᵍ Kirjath-arba, (which *is* Hebron) in ʰ the mountain of Judah.

c Num. 35. 12.   d Num. 35. 12, 25.
e ch. 21. 32. 1 Chron. 6. 76.   f ch. 21. 21.
2 Chron. 10. 1.   g ch. 14. 15, and 21. 11, 13.
h Luke 1. 39.

¶ *Shall declare his cause.* Shall give a true, honest, and exact statement of all the circumstances under which the accident occurred.——¶ *They shall take him into the city.* Heb. אסף אתו *âsephu otho,* shall *gather him.* Provided they are satisfied, from his relation of the facts, that he is innocent.——¶ *That he may dwell among them.* It may be asked why, if the proper judges were satisfied of his innocence of the crime of wilful murder, he were not at once dismissed from their jurisdiction, and suffered to go at large as usual. The proper reply doubtless is, (1) That he might still be in danger from the enraged passions of the pursuer. (2) He was to await the issue of another trial, v. 6. (3) His detention was probably designed as somewhat of a punishment for the rashness or heedlessness to which the homicide was owing. Something of a penalty was to be paid for carelessness, as well as for crime.

6. *Until he stand before the congregation for judgment.* In order to a still greater security for the interests of justice, and to guard with the utmost vigilance against a wrong decision, another hearing seems to have been appointed, after a considerable interval, and before a larger court, whose verdict was to be final in the case. It is probable that the 'congregation' here spoken of was that of his own city, or of the people at large, who were also allowed to constitute a tribunal, and to sit in judgment on the case. Compare Notes on Num. 35. 25.——¶ *Until the death of the high priest.* See on Num. 35. 25.

7. *And they appointed.* Heb. יקדשו *yakdishu,* sanctified, *consecrated;* a term implying the peculiar *sacredness* which God would have attached in the minds of his people to this institution. Accordingly they are sometimes, though not perhaps by the sacred writers, called *sanctuaries.*——¶ *In mount Naphtali.* Or, Heb. 'in the mountain,' i. e. the mountainous region or district of Naphtali; and so in respect to the two other places mentioned. They were situated on high hills that they might be more conspicuous at a distance. It may also be remarked of

8 And on the other side Jordan by Jericho eastward, they assigned ⁱBezer in the wilderness upon the plain out of the tribe of Reuben, and ᵏRamoth in Gilead out of the tribe of Gad, and ˡGolan in Bashan out of the tribe of Manasseh.

9 ᵐThese were the cities appointed for all the children of Israel, and for the stranger that sojourneth among them, that whosoever killeth *any* person at unawares might flee thither, and not die by the hand of the avenger of blood, ⁿuntil he stood before the congregation.

CHAPTER XXI.

THEN came near the heads of the fathers of the Levites unto ᵃEleazar the priest, and unto Joshua the son of Nun, and unto the heads of the fathers of the tribes of the children of Israel;

2 And they spake unto them at ᵇShiloh in the land of Canaan, saying, ᶜThe LORD commanded by the hand of Moses to give us

---

ⁱ Deut. 4. 43. ch. 21. 36. 1 Chron. 6. 78.
ᵏ ch. 21. 38. 1 Kings 22. 3. ˡ ch. 21. 27.
ᵐ Num. 35. 15.

ⁿ ver. 6. ᵃ ch. 14. 1, and 17. 4. ᵇ ch. 18. 1. ᶜ Num. 35. 2.

---

these cities, (1) That they were located at convenient distances from each other for the benefit of the several tribes. So of those here mentioned, Kedesh was in the northern, Shechem in the central, and Hebron in the southern district of Canaan. (2) They were all Levitical cities; which appears to have been so ordered, that the cases of manslaughter might come under the cognizance of those who might be presumed to be most thoroughly versed in the law of God, and most competent to give judgment according to it, and who, moreover, would be less likely than any others to be swayed by private bias in their decisions. Compare Deut. 21. 5, where it is said of the priests, the sons of Levi, that 'by their word shall every controversy and every *stroke* be tried.' See also to the same purpose, Deut. 17. 8–13, and the Notes on Deut. 33. 9, 10.

8. *They assigned.* Or, 'had assigned,' for the assignment had been previously made by Moses, Deut. 4. 41–43; or the meaning may be, that they formally acknowledged, confirmed, and ratified the selection that Moses had before made of these cities.

9. *Until he stood before the congregation.* The judges and elders of the people, in trying civil and criminal causes, always *sat;* the persons who came for judgment, or who were tried, always *stood.* Hence the expressions so frequent in the Scripture, '*Standing* before the Lord, before the judges, before the elders,' &c.

CHAPTER XXI.

1. *The heads of the fathers of the Levites.* The most distinguished persons among the fathers, chiefs, or elders of the three families of Kohath, Gershom, and Merari, which constituted the body of the tribe of Levi. They here make their petition precisely at the time when it could be most conveniently granted, viz. just after the allotments had been made to the other tribes. Whether this was prior or subsequent to the designation of the cities of refuge, men-

cities to dwell in, with the suburbs thereof for our cattle.

3 And the children of Israel gave unto the Levites out of their inheritance, at the commandment of the LORD, these cities and their suburbs.

4 And the lot came out for the families of the Kohathites: and ᵈ the children of Aaron the priest, *which were* of the Levites, ᵉ had by lot out of the tribe of Judah, and out of the tribe of Simeon, and out of the tribe of Benjamin, thirteen cities.

d ver. 8. 19.   e See ch. 24. 33.

---

tioned in the foregoing chapter, it is not possible to determine.

3. *The children of Israel gave unto the Levites.* They cheerfully obeyed the divine command. They gave them cities out of their several inheritances, without any fear of being impoverished by the appropriation. Nor will men ever find themselves sufferers in their temporal interests, in consequence of a liberal allowance to the ministers of the sanctuary. These cities were assigned by lot, that it might fully appear that God designed the Levites their *habitations*, as he designed the others their *inheritances*. The result of this arrangement would naturally be, that the Levites would be dispersed in every part of the land, to instruct the people in the knowledge of the divine law, to edify them by their example, to restrain them from idolatry, and prompt them to a constant adherence to the worship of Jehovah, the only true God. Thus the prophetic sentence of the patriarch, Gen. 49. 7, that they should be 'divided in Jacob, and scattered in Israel,' though originally carrying with it a punitive import, was through the special mercy of heaven converted to a blessing to themselves and to the nation.
—¶ *These cities.* Referring to those which are enumerated in the sequel of this chapter.

4. *And the lot came out.* It would seem that a certain number of cities were previously designated and set apart *en masse*, as the habitations of the Levites, and that the *particular appropriation* of them to the several families and their branches was then determined by lot.——¶ *The children of Aaron the priest.* All the Kohathites were children of Aaron, in being lineally descended from him, but they were not all *priests;* whereas the phrase 'children of Aaron' here is but another name for the *priests*, his successors in office; and these had their allotment of cities in the tribes of Judah, Simeon, and Benjamin; the rest, who were merely Levites and not priests, had their lot, as appears from v. 5, in the tribes of Ephraim, Dan, and the half-tribe of Manasseh. The providence of God in this assignment is very remarkable, as in consequence of it the *priestly* part of Aaron's posterity, who were the stated ministers of the sanctuary, the seat of which was afterwards to be fixed at Jerusalem, had their location nearest to that city, so that they were always conveniently situated with reference to the work to which they were appointed.——
¶ *Thirteen cities.* This was a large proportion for the *present* number of priests, which was small, but in view of the prospective increase of this body, and their future wants, it was no more than was requisite.

5 And ᶠthe rest of the children of Kohath *had* by lot out of the families of the tribe of Ephraim, and out of the tribe of Dan, and out of the half tribe of Manasseh, ten cities.

6 And ᵍthe children of Gershon *had* by lot out of the families of the tribe of Issachar, and out of the tribe of Asher, and out of the tribe of Naphtali, and out of the half-tribe of Manasseh in Bashan, thirteen cities.

7 ʰThe children of Merari by their families *had* out of the tribe of Reuben, and out of the tribe of Gad, and out of the tribe of Zebulun, twelve cities.

8 ⁱAnd the children of Israel gave by lot unto the Levites these cities with their suburbs, ᵏas the Lord commanded by the hand of Moses.

9 ¶ And they gave out of the tribe of the children of Judah, and out of the tribe of the children of Simeon, these cities which are *here* mentioned by name,

10 ˡWhich the children of Aaron, *being* of the families of the Kohathites, *who were* of the children of Levi, had: for theirs was the first lot.

11 ᵐAnd they gave them the city of Arba the father of ⁿAnak (which *city is* Hebron) ᵒin the hill-*country* of Judah, with the suburbs thereof round about it.

f ver. 20, &c. g ver. 27, &c. h ver. 34, &c. i ver. 3. k Num. 35. 2. l ver. 4. m 1 Chron. 6. 55. Gen. 23. 2. n ch. 15. 13, 14. o ch. 20. 7. Luke 1. 39.

As to the nature of the tenure by which the Levites held these appropriated cities, the probability is that they had no other property in them than merely the right to certain places of habitation, which they might let or sell, but always with the right of perpetual redemption; and with the understanding that they were to return to them in the year of jubilee. But on this head see Notes on Lev. 25. 32, 33.

5. *Out of the tribe of Dan,* &c., *ten cities.* A less number than was given out of the tribes above-mentioned, because their inheritance was less. The law by which the appropriation was to be regulated is contained Num. 35. 8, 'And the cities which ye shall give shall be the possession of Israel; from them that have many (cities), ye shall give many; but from them that have few, ye shall give few; every one shall give of his cities unto the Levites, according to his inheritance which he inheriteth.' It may be remarked, that there is no evidence that the priests were bound to live in these and in no other cities. When the tabernacle was at Nob, both the priests and Levites dwelt there, 1 Sam. 21. 1-7; and when the worship of God was established at Jerusalem, multitudes both of priests and Levites resided there, though it was no Levitical city; as did the *courses* of the priests afterwards at Jericho. This was a circumstance which Moses had foreseen, and for which he had provided, Deut. 18. 6, &c. So, on the other hand, persons belonging to the other tribes were not precluded from living in the Levitical cities; as for instance Gibeah of Benjamin, which is here made a Levitical city, v. 17, was always

[B. C. 1444.] CHAPTER XXI. 187

12 But P the fields of the city, and the villages thereof, gave they to Caleb, the son of Jephunneh for his possession.

13 ¶ Thus q they gave to the children of Aaron the priest, r Hebron with her suburbs, *to be* a city of refuge for the slayer; s and Libnah with her suburbs,

14 And t Jattir with her suburbs, u and Eshtemoa with her suburbs,

15 And x Holon with her suburbs, y and Debir with her suburbs,

16 And z Ain with her suburbs, a and Juttah with her suburbs, *and* b Beth-shemesh with her suburbs; nine cities out of those two tribes.

17 And out of the tribe of Benjamin, c Gibeon with her suburbs, d Geba with her suburbs.

18 Anathoth with her suburbs, and e Almon with her suburbs; four cities.

19 All the cities of the children of Aaron, the priests, *were* thirteen cities with their suburbs.

20 ¶ f And the families of the children of Kohath, the Levites which remained of the children of Kohath, even they had the cities of their lot out of the tribe of Ephraim.

21 For they gave them g Shechem with her suburbs in mount Ephraim, *to be* a city of refuge for the slayer; and Gezer with her suburbs,

22 And Kibzaim with her suburbs, and Beth-horon with her suburbs; four cities.

23 And out of the tribe of Dan, Eltekeh with her suburbs, Gibbethon with her suburbs,

24 Aijalon with her suburbs, Gathrimmon with her suburbs; four cities.

25 And out of the half tribe of Manasseh, Tanach with her suburbs, and Gath-rimmon with her suburbs; two cities.

26 All the cities *were* ten with their suburbs, for the families of

p ch. 14. 14. 1 Chron. 6. 5. q 1 Chron. 6. 57, &c. r ch. 15. 54, and 20. 7. s ch. 15. 42. t ch 15. 48. u ch. 15. 50. x 1 Chron. 6. 58. ch. 15. 51. y ch. 15. 49. z 1 Chron. 6. 59. ch. 15. 42. a ch. 15. 55. b ch. 15. 10. c ch. 18. 25. d ch. 18. 24. e See ch. 24. 33. f ver. 5. 1 Chron. 6. 66. g ch. 20. 7.

peopled by the Benjamites, as appears from Judg. 19.

12. *The fields of the city—gave they to Caleb.* As it would not necessarily involve the exclusion of himself or his family from a residence in the city, he probably gave it to the priests in order to set an example to his brethren of cheerfully contributing to the maintenance of religion. See on ch. 14. 6-15.

25. *Tanach with her suburbs, and Gath-rimmon.* In the parallel passage, 1 Chron. 6. 70, Aner and Bileam are mentioned instead of the above. A careful examination of the two catalogues will discover several other discrepancies of the same kind, which are probably owing to the fact, either that some of the cities were called by different names, or that their names in process of time were changed. Others conjecture that some of the cities here enumerated being at this time in possession of the Canaanites, and not easily to

the children of Kohath that remaineth.

27 ¶ ʰAnd unto the children of Gershon, of the families of the Levites, out of the *other* half-tribe of Manasseh *they gave* ⁱGolan in Bashan with her suburbs, *to be* a city of refuge for the slayer, and Beeshterah with her suburbs; two cities.

28 And out of the tribe of Issachar, Kishon with her suburbs, Dabareh with her suburbs,

29 Jarmuth with her suburbs, Engannim with her suburbs; four cities.

30 And out of the tribe of Asher, Mishal with her suburbs, Abdon with her suburbs,

31 Helkath with her suburbs, and Rehob with her suburbs; four cities.

32 And out of the tribe of Naphtali, ᵏKedesh in Galilee with her suburbs, *to be* a city of refuge for the slayer; and Hammoth-dor with her suburbs, and Kartan with her suburbs; three cities.

33 All the cities of the Gershonites, according to their families, *were* thirteen cities with their suburbs.

34 ¶ ˡAnd unto the families of the children of Merari, the rest of the Levites, out of the tribe of Zebulun, Jokneam with her suburbs, and Kartah with her suburbs,

35 Dimnah with her suburbs, Nahalal with her suburbs; four cities.

36 And out of the tribe of Reuben, ᵐBezer with her suburbs, and Jahazah with her suburbs,

37 Kedemoth with her suburbs, and Mephaath with her suburbs; four cities.

38 And out of the tribe of Gad, ⁿRamoth in Gilead with her suburbs, *to be* a city of refuge for the slayer; and Mahanaim with her suburbs,

39 Heshbon with her suburbs, Jazer with her suburbs; four cities in all.

40 So all the cities for the children of Merari by their families, which were remaining of the families of the Levites, were *by* their lot twelve cities.

41 ºAll the cities of the Levites within the possession of the children of Israel *were* forty and eight cities with their suburbs.

42 These cities were every one with their suburbs round

h ver. 6. 1 Chron. 6. 71. i ch. 20. 8.
k ch. 20. 7. l ver. 7. See 1 Chron. 6. 77.
m ch. 20. 8. n ch. 20. 8. o Num. 35. 7

---

be taken out of their hands, others were given them in their stead.

41. *All the cities—were forty and eight cities, with their suburbs.* This was in exact accordance with the direction given by Moses several years before, as we learn from Num. 35. 7. This order of Moses is a direct demonstration that it was given under divine inspiration, as otherwise, how could he possibly have known that so many cities could be assigned to the Levites, without unduly encroaching on the limits of the other tribes?

42. *These cities were every one with*

B. C. 1444.] CHAPTER XXII. 189

about them. Thus *were* all these cities.

43 ¶ And the LORD gave unto Israel ᵖall the land which he sware to give unto their fathers: and they possessed it, and dwelt therein.

44 ᵟ And the LORD gave them rest round about, according to all that he sware unto their fathers: and ʳthere stood not a

p Gen. 13. 15, and 15. 18, and 26. 3, and 28. 4, 13. q ch. 11. 23, and 22. 4.

man of all their enemies before them; the LORD delivered all their enemies into their hand.

45 ˢThere failed not aught of any good thing which the LORD had spoken unto the house of Israel; all came to pass.

CHAPTER XXII.

THEN Joshua called the Reubenites, and the Gad-

r Deut. 7. 24. s ch. 23. 14.

their suburbs round about them. Heb. 'these cities were city, city, and suburbs round about them.' That is, they each and every one had suburbs attached to them; by which is meant the adjacent territory to the extent of two thousand cubits on every side; of which see Num. 35. 5.

43. *And the Lord gave unto Israel all the land,* &c. The foregoing history is here wound up by a suitable acknowledgment of the faithfulness of God, in the performance of all his promises. The Canaanites, it is true, were yet in possession of some parts of the country, but they were so far subdued, that they gave them no serious molestation, and they were enabled to sit down in their possessions in the enjoyment of comparative rest and quiet. They had as much of the land in *actual* possession as they could occupy; and as they increased God enabled them, according to his promise, Ex. 23. 30, to carry forward the work of extermination, and obtain further room for their settlement. All the assurances given to Joshua, ch. 1. 5, of a successful tide of victories during his life, were accomplished, and as to the subsequent annoyance and occasional prevalence of

their enemies, it was owing solely to the supineness and infidelity of Israel. So long as they were obedient, they were uniformly triumphant and prosperous. See notes on ch. 1. 5. 'The inviolable truth of God's promise, and the performance of it to the utmost, is what all the saints have been ready to bear their testimony to; and if in any thing it has seemed to come short, they have been as ready to own that they themselves must bear all the blame.' *Henry.* 'In due season all the promises of God will be accomplished to his true people; and their believing hope, and patient waiting and self-denying obedience, will terminate in joyful songs of triumph, and thankful celebrations of his faithfulness, love, and power. Then it will be universally acknowledged that there hath not failed ought of any good thing which the Lord had spoken: nay, that he has exceeded their largest expectations, and made them more than conquerors, and brought them to their delightful rest and inheritance. May none of us at that season be found among his enemies, "who shall be destroyed for ever."' *Scott.*

ites, and the half-tribe of Manasseh,

2 And said unto them, Ye have kept ᵃall that Moses the servant of the Lord commanded you, ᵇand have obeyed my voice in all that I commanded you:

3 Ye have not left your brethren these many days unto this day, but have kept the charge of the commandment of the Lord your God.

4 And now the Lord your God hath given rest unto your brethren, as he promised them: therefore now return ye, and get you unto your tents, *and* unto the land of your possession, ᶜwhich Moses the servant of the Lord gave you on the other side Jordan.

5 But ᵈtake diligent heed to do the commandment and the law, which Moses the servant of the

ᵃ Numb. 32. 20.   Deut. 3. 18.   ᵇ ch. 1. 16, 17.

ᶜ Num. 32. 33.   Deut. 29. 8.   ch. 13. 8.
ᵈ Deut. 6. 6, 17, and 11. 22.

CHAPTER XXII.

1. *Then Joshua called*, &c. The war being now, for the present at least, concluded, and their services no longer required.

3. *Ye have not left your brethren these many days unto this day.* Probably for the space of seven years; for the people were occupied for this period of time in subduing the land. Yet it is very possible that in the intervals of action, and when the rest of the army had retired into winter-quarters, some of them at least may have visited their families across the Jordan, or been relieved by other detachments, though we have no clear intimation that this was the fact. Certain it is that these two tribes and a half had always their quota of men, originally amounting to 40,000, in readiness at their respective posts, for any service to which they might be called; and after so long a delay we can easily imagine how ardently they must have longed for the period of their release, when they could return to their peaceful homes to be met with a joyful welcome by their wives and children. But like faithful soldiers they await the full close of the war and an honorable discharge. Had they departed sooner they would have been recalled as fugitives or branded as cowards; now they retire with blessings and applause. So though our home in heaven be ever so attractive, we are required to remain contentedly on earth till our warfare be accomplished, and instead of anticipating our removal, to wait for a due discharge at the hands of our divine Leader.

4. *Get you unto your tents.* To your settled habitations, frequently called tents in the scriptures. 2 Sam. 18. 17; Hos. 9. 6; Mal. 2. 12. It is probable, however, that they still retained somewhat of the nomade habits of their ancestors, and that tents were by no means uncommon among them.

5. *Take diligent heed*, &c. Joshua thinks it not enough merely to dismiss them with the commendations which their zeal and fidelity had so richly merited, but in the spirit of a true servant of God, adds to his encomiums the most pious counsels and exhortations. It is not simply a general admonition relative to their religious duties, in which case one

LORD charged you, ᵉ to love the LORD your God, and to walk in all his ways, and to keep his commandments, and to cleave unto him, and to serve him with all your heart, and with all your soul.

6 So Joshua ᶠblessed them,

ᵉ Deut. 10. 12.

and sent them away; and they went unto their tents.

7 ¶ Now to the *one* half of the tribe of Manasseh, Moses had given *possession* in Bashan: but unto the *other* half thereof gave Joshua among their breth-

ᶠ Gen. 47. 7. Exod. 39. 43. ch. 14. 13. 2 Sam. 6. 18. Luke 24. 50. ᵍ ch. 17. 5.

---

or two brief intimations would have sufficed, but the expressions are remarkably varied and accumulated, to show in the most forcible manner the unspeakable importance to every child of man of a life of devoted obedience. They were to give the most diligent heed to themselves to see that the *love of God*, as the great ruling principle of action, was deeply seated in their hearts; this must be evinced by the *universality* of their obedience, extending to every divine precept, and still further illustrated by the *constancy, humility, resolution*, and *affection* which were to characterize their walk. Counsel like this can never be unseasonable or superfluous. Even the most established Christian, whose progress in holiness has hitherto been most exemplary, cannot deem himself beyond the need of similar exhortations. As long as he abides in the flesh he needs to be 'put in remembrance of these things, though he knows them, and be established in the present truth.' Especially does he need these kindly monitions when settled down, or about to be settled down, in a state of peace and prosperity; for such a state is one of peculiar danger to his spiritual interests. These disbanded soldiers of Israel were now returning to the bosom of their families, and the peace-

ful prosecution of their worldly business. They needed, therefore, to be reminded of the danger, of which Moses had long before warned them, of forgetting the Lord their God while enjoying 'houses which they built not, wells which they digged not, and vineyards which they planted not.' A constant mindfulness of God accordingly was the great object of Joshua's solicitude for his departing brethren, and in his example we see the spirit of a Christian parent or guardian, and what kind of counsel he will be most anxious to impart to the children of his charge when about to retire from his immediate control and enter upon the wide stage of action in the world.

6. *So Joshua blessed them.* Spake respectfully of their faithful services, wished them every spiritual and temporal good, and prayed earnestly to God to protect and prosper them. They undoubtedly returned with all convenient expedition. It had been a long absence, and the meeting was no doubt proportionably happy. Here below, business, journeys, voyages, and other casualties are continually separating the dearest relatives; but they are glad to get home in peace. How much happier for the Christian pilgrim, when his warfare of life is accomplished, and receiving the divine blessing, to cross

JOSHUA. [B. C. 1444.

ren on this side Jordan westward. And when Joshua sent them away also unto their tents, then he blessed them,

8 And he spake unto them, saying, Return with much riches unto your tents, and with very much cattle, with silver, and with gold, and with brass, and with iron, and with very much raiment: ʰdivide the spoil of your enemies with your brethren.

9 ¶ And the children of Reuben, and the children of Gad, and the half-tribe of Manasseh returned, and departed from the

ʰ Num. 31. 27. 1 Sam. 30. 14.

children of Israel out of Shiloh, which *is* in the land of Canaan, to go unto ⁱthe country of Gilead, to the land of their possession, whereof they were possessed, according to the word of the Lord by the hand of Moses.

10 ¶ And when they came unto the borders of Jordan, that *are* in the land of Canaan, the children of Reuben, and the children of Gad, and the half-tribe of Manasseh built there an altar by Jordan, a great altar to see to.

11 ¶ And the children of Is-

ⁱ Num. 32. 1, 26, 29.

Jordan, and meet his brethren in glory, the family of God!

7. *To the one half of the tribe of Manasseh, &c.* This appears to come in here as a parenthesis, intimating the reason why the tribe was divided into two parts. Moses had before assigned one half of them their lot on the other side Jordan.

8. *Divide the spoil of your enemies with your brethren.* Your brethren that have remained on the other side of the Jordan, protecting your families, flocks, and goods. It is not implied, however, that those who remained at home were to have an *equal* share of the spoil, as this would have been manifestly unjust from their superior numbers and inferior claims. See on Num. 31. 27.

10. *The borders of Jordan.* Heb. גְּלִילוֹת *geliloth*, properly the *windings, meanderings* made by the Jordan in its course, sometimes assuming almost a *circular* form, in accordance with the sense of the original term, which is used in some ca-

ses to signify a *ring*. The altar was doubtless erected on the *eastern* side of the Jordan, but it might have been situated upon a projecting tongue or promontory of land, that extended into the borders of Canaan proper. The reader will observe, moreover, that the word 'are,' being printed in Italics, does not occur in the original, so that we may as properly render it 'is,' and understand the relative 'that' of the river Jordan.——

¶ *A great altar to see to.* Very conspicuous. Heb. 'an altar great to the sight.' A vast mass of earth, stones, &c., elevated to a commanding height and visible at a great distance; intended merely as a memorial to all future ages that they belonged to the tribes of Israel, and that they were worshippers of Israel's God, but made in imitation of the altar of burnt-offering at the tabernacle. Their motive in this was an apprehension that at some future period they might be disowned by their brethren on account of their not hav-

rael ᵏheard say, Behold, the children of Reuben, and the children of Gad, and the half-tribe of Manasseh, have built an altar over against the land of Canaan, in the borders of Jordan, at the passage of the children of Israel.

12 And when the children of Israel heard *of it*, ¹the whole congregation of the children of Israel gathered themselves to-

ᵏ Deut. 13. 12, &c. Judg. 20. 12. ¹ Judg. 20. 1.

ing their inheritance in the land of Canaan proper.

11. *Have built an altar over against the land of Canaan.* This may be deemed conclusive proof that the site of the altar was on the *east* of the Jordan, in the inheritance of the two tribes and a half, and not on the *west*. There would have been no cause of suspecting it designed for sacrifice, had it been built on the Canaan side of Jordan.

12. *The whole congregation—gathered themselves together.* Not perhaps in their own persons, but by their representatives the elders, who transacted all affairs of this nature in the name and behalf of the people.——¶ *To go up to war against them.* The case was one that laid a just ground for suspicion. Having no conception of an altar being erected for any purpose but that of sacrifice, the other tribes naturally regarded it as an act of rebellion against God, and determined instantly to go and punish the supposed apostates. By an express command, Ex. 20. 24 : Lev. 17. 8, 9 : Deut. 12. 5–13, the nation had been prohibited from worshipping God except at one altar, and for what other than a religious purpose could this structure have been reared ? They moreover felt themselves impelled to this course by the tenor of the law, Deut. 13. 7–13, requiring the most summary judgment to be executed upon the individuals or cities that should be found setting up an idolatrous worship. Their zeal for the Lord of hosts under this impression was very commendable. Though these trans-Jordanic tribes are their own brethren, bone of their bone, companions with them in tribulation in the wilderness, and their generous allies in the wars of Canaan, yet if they revolt from the true God and turn to the service of idols, or openly make a breach in the unity of his worship they are determined to treat them no longer as brethren, but as enemies who were to be cut off as unsparingly as the Canaanites themselves. Their holy jealousy, therefore, in these circumstances was no more than a proper expression of their intense concern for the glory of God and the honor of his institutions. But their zeal was tempered with the meekness of wisdom, and before proceeding to extremities they determined to send an embassy to inquire into the facts, and if their suspicions were confirmed, to see whether they could not be prevailed upon by milder methods to abandon their wicked enterprise and return to their allegiance to the God of Israel. Instead of saying that the case was too clear to admit of doubt, or too gross to allow of apology, they evidently go on the presumption that they *may* have been mistaken in their construction of the affair, and that at any rate it

gether at Shiloh, to go up to war against them.

13 And the children of Israel ᵐ sent unto the children of Reuben, and to the children of Gad, and to the half-tribe of Manasseh into the land of Gilead, ⁿ Phinehas the son of Eleazar the priest,

14 And with him ten princes, of each chief house a prince throughout all the tribes of Israel; and ° each *one* was a head of the house of their fathers among the thousands of Israel.

15 ¶ And they came unto the children of Reuben, and to the children of Gad, and to the half-tribe of Manasseh, unto the land of Gilead, and they spake with them, saying,

16 Thus saith the whole congregation of the LORD, What trespass *is* this that ye have committed against the God of Israel, to turn away this day from following the LORD, in that ye

ᵐ Deut. 13. 14. Judg. 20. 12. ⁿ Exod. 6. 25. Num. 25. 7.

° Num. 1. 4.

---

was proper that they should not condemn their brethren unheard, but should give them the opportunity of justifying themselves in the measure if it were possible. According to the wise man's direction they will 'upon good advice make war.' A noble example of moderation, forbearance, and charity, shines forth in this conduct. How many an unhappy strife might be prevented by similar precaution, by simply staying to inquire calmly into that which constitutes the avowed matter of offence! How often would a few words of candid explanation smother in embryo the most angry controversies, violent quarrels, and embittered persecutions! By barely adopting the prudent conduct of Israel on this occasion, individuals, families, churches, and communities, might, in a thousand instances, be saved a world of jealousy, enmity, discord, war and bloodshed.

13, 14. *Phineas—and with him ten princes.* Persons of age, experience, and approved discretion, possessing weight of character in the congregation, and likely to be influenced more by the dictates of cool judgment than of hasty passion, were very properly selected to act in behalf of the people on this occasion. The ardent temperament of younger men could not so safely be trusted on such a trying emergency.

16. *What trespass is this*, &c. Without acquitting the ten tribes of the charge of somewhat of an undue precipitancy in taking up their unfavorable impressions, the matter in question was one on which they were justified in feeling strongly and acting promptly. As it now appeared, it was a step fraught with the most momentous consequences to the whole body of Israel. Repeated occasions had arisen wherein the sin of individuals had been visited upon the entire nation. The iniquity of Achan had not long since caused the defeat of Israel's hosts, together with the loss of six and thirty men; and not very long before the connexion of many with the Midianitish women had brought destruction on twenty-four thousand Israelites in one day.

have builded you an altar, ᵖ that ye might rebel this day against the Lord?

17 *Is* the iniquity ᑫ of Peor too little for us, from which we are not cleansed until this day, although there was a plague in the congregation of the Lord,

18 But that ye must turn away this day from following the

Lord? and it will be, *seeing* ye rebel to-day against the Lord, that to-morrow ʳ he will be wroth with the whole congregation of Israel

19 Notwithstanding, if the land of your possession *be* unclean, *then* pass ye over unto the land of the possession of the Lord, ˢ wherein the Lord's tabernacle

p Lev. 17. 8, 9. Deut. 12. 13, 14. q Num. 25. 3, 4. Deut. 4. 3.

r Num. 16. 22. s ch. 18. 1.

What then could be expected, but that, if those who had erected the altar should go unpunished, God would punish all the other tribes as partners in their guilt? And if formerly one man's sin wrought so much indignation, what would be the consequences of the apostasy of two tribes and a half? To avert so terrible an evil, therefore, they felt to be their bounden duty at all events, and in order to this nothing could be more effectual than plainly reminding them of the sad effects of past transgression. 'It is good to recollect and improve those instances of the wrath of God which have fallen out in our own time, and of which we ourselves have been eye-witnesses. The remembrance of great sins committed formerly, should engage us to stand upon our guard against the least occasions and beginnings of sin; for the way of sin is down-hill' *Henry.*

17. *Is the iniquity of Peor too little for us?* The iniquity of our worshipping Peor. Num. 25. 3; Deut. 4. 3. Does this sin seem so small to us that we cannot be content with that, but must go on adding iniquity to iniquity?——¶ *From which we are not cleansed until this day.* That is, of

which we have not ceased to suffer the consequences to this day. The wrath of God was indeed so far appeased on that occasion by the zeal of Phineas, that he stayed the farther ravages of the plague, yet the shame, the disgrace, the infamy of that transaction still remained, and more than this, some tokens of the divine displeasure still continued to linger among the congregation. As we see from the case of David, men may repent of a heinous transgression and be graciously freed from the guilt of it, while at the same time they may continue to suffer from its evil consequences even to the close of life. In the present instance, however, the words may perhaps imply that some measure of that corrupt leaven still remained among them, that the infection was not wholly cured, and that though suppressed for the present, it was still secretly working, and was liable to break out again with fresh violence, as is also intimated in the words of Joshua, ch. 24. 23.

19. *If the land of your possession be unclean.* If you have any prejudice against the land of your inheritance; if you think it not equally with ours under the divine favor

dwelleth, and take possession among us: but rebel not against the LORD, nor rebel against us, in building you an altar besides the altar of the LORD our God.

20 'Did not Achan the son of Zerah commit a trespass in the accursed thing, and wrath fell

t ch. 7, 1, 5.

on all the congregation of Israel? and that man perished not alone in his iniquity.

21 ¶ Then the children of Reuben, and the children of Gad, and the half-tribe of Manasseh answered, and said unto the heads of the thousands of Israel,

---

and protection. They imagined that the two tribes and a half might think their land less holy for the want of an altar and such tokens of the divine presence as pertained to the tabernacle. An opinion was generally prevalent among the ancients, that those countries, in which there was no place set apart for the worship of God, were unhallowed and unclean. The proposal displayed a very generous and disinterested spirit, a willingness to make sacrifices in order to preserve purity, and consequently peace. Rather than they should set up a separate altar from a groundless dissatisfaction with their inheritance, they would cheerfully welcome them back to the other side of the Jordan, 'where the Lord's tabernacle dwelt,' though they should straiten themselves by so doing. But what was a little inconvenience to themselves when such an evil was to be averted, and such a good secured? How kind, how conciliating, how self-denying, how eager for accommodation, is the spirit of true piety!——¶ *But rebel not against the Lord.* Implying that a deliberate departure from the instituted mode of worship is nothing short of downright rebellion against the God of heaven. Compare with this the parallel expression of Samuel relative to the conduct of Saul, 1 Sam.

15. 13.——¶ *Besides the altar of the Lord our God.* In addition to it.

20. *And that man perisheth not alone in his iniquity.* The idea expressed in these words of our common translation is unquestionably conveyed by the original; still it is not an exact version. The literal rendering of the Heb. is, 'and he, one man, did not perish in his iniquity.' That is, though he were but a single individual, and it might have been supposed that his death would have been the winding up of his existence in every respect, yet in reality such was his relation to the whole people as a sinner, such the connexion between his offence and the punishment of the whole nation, that in one sense he may be said to have survived his own death. He still lived in the fearful effects of his transgression, as visited upon the entire congregation. His life and his crime did not terminate together. A strikingly analogous passage occurs Num. 27. 3.

21. *Then the children of Reuben—answered.* If we find somewhat to blame in each of the opposite parties; in the one, an undue precipitation in building the altar, and in the other, an undue hastiness in ascribing it to wrong intentions, we yet behold very much to admire in both. When the accusers found themselves mistaken, they did not shift their ground, and

B. C. 1444.] CHAPTER XXII. 197

22 The LORD ᵘ God of gods, the LORD God of gods, he ˣ knoweth, and Israel he shall know; if *it be* in rebellion, or if in transgression against the LORD, (save us not this day,)

u Deut. 10. 17. x 1 Kings 8. 39. Job 10. 7, and 23. 10. Ps. 44. 21, and 139. 1, 2. Jer. 12. 3. 2 Cor. 11. 11, 31.

23 That we have built us an altar to turn from following the LORD, or if to offer thereon burnt-offering, or meat-offering, or if to offer peace-offerings thereon, let the LORD himself ʸ require *it;*

y Deut. 18. 19. 1 Sam. 20. 16.

condemn their brethren for imprudence; nor when the accused had evinced their innocence, did they upbraid their accusers with hasty, rash, or unjust surmises. Aware that the measure was easily susceptible of the interpretation their brethren had put upon it, they took their reproofs, severe as they were, in good part, and instead of angry retorts or recriminations, gave them the soft answer which turneth away wrath, and by a candid and honest declaration of their real intentions, at once set themselves right in the opinion of their brethren.

22. *The Lord God of gods.* The original words אֵל אֱלֹהִים יהוה *El Elohim Yehovah,* are exceedingly emphatic, and cannot be easily translated. They are the three principal names by which the supreme God was known among the Hebrews, and may be rendered 'The strong God, Elohim Jehovah,' which is nearly the version of Luther, 'Der starke Gott, der Herr,' *the strong God, the Lord.* q. d. 'that almighty and omniscient Jehovah, whom we as well as you acknowledge and adore as the God of gods, infinitely superior to all that are called gods—to him we appeal as knowing our innocency, and that we would shudder at the thought of forsaking or dividing his worship.' By this solemn appeal they would convince their brethren that their religious faith was unchanged, and their future conduct, they also intimate, should satisfy all Israel that with clean hands and an upright heart they had engaged in this undertaking. Where there is evidence of a deep and heart-felt reverence for God, there is the best security for pure intentions and a blameless course of conduct.—— ¶ *Save us not this day.* Let God the Judge cause us to perish by the sword of our enemies or of our brethren, if either in principle or practice we have knowingly departed from him. It is a sudden apostrophe to God, prompted by strong emotion and frequently occurring in speeches of a very earnest and vehement character, and highly expressive of conscious integrity.

23. *Let the Lord himself require it.* Requite it. Let him call us to account for it and punish us as the offence may deserve, as the word 're-quite,' often signifies. See on Gen. 9. 5; Deut. 18. 19; 1 Sam. 20. 16. The trans-Jordanic tribes were accused of erecting an altar prohibited by the law, and that with the design of apostatizing from the true religion. They in their answer imply that the law is not violated except by altars intended for sacrifice; but such was not theirs, as they show by specifying the three principal uses of the

17*

24 And if we have not *rather* done it for fear of *this* thing, saying, In time to come your children might speak unto our children, saying, What have ye to do with the Lord God of Israel?

25 For the Lord hath made Jordan a border between us and you, ye children of Reuben and children of Gad; ye have no part in the Lord. So shall your children make our children cease from fearing the Lord.

26 Therefore we said, Let us now prepare to build us an al-

---

divinely appointed altar, and denying that they contemplated either of these uses in erecting theirs.

24. *For fear of this thing.* What this thing was they immediately go on to state. They were apprehensive of certain consequences resulting from their local separation from their brethren, which are fully detailed in the ensuing verses. The original word for 'fear' denotes a great perplexity and solicitude of mind bordering upon actual distress. It occurs Prov. 12. 25, where it signifies *affliction.* The amount of their answer is, that they were actuated by motives directly the reverse of those attributed to them.——¶ *In time to come.* Heb. ' to-morrow.' See note on ch. 4. 6.

25. *So shall your children make our children cease from fearing the Lord.* The danger to which they allude was not immediate, but prospective. There was little probability of their being disowned by their brethren of the present generation, but their children might be looked upon in after ages as having no interest in the God of Israel, or his instituted worship. The consequence would be, that, being cut off from public ordinances, the life and power of religion would die out from among them, they would become reckless of their duty and allegiance to God, wickedness would abound, and they would sink to a state of comparative heathenism. This was a prospect of which they could not endure to think. It was a state of things to be by all means averted; and though it would perhaps have been better to have consulted Joshua, or rather to have taken counsel of the Lord, respecting this measure before they carried it into execution, yet this solicitude for the spiritual welfare of their posterity cannot be too highly praised. Nothing weighs more deeply on the truly pious heart, than the transmission to the latest generations of those inestimable religious privileges, which have been the comfort and blessing of their fathers. If the outward institutions of piety are wanting in any community, the very existence of piety itself is endangered, and where that is the case, the judgments instead of the mercies of heaven will descend, as the inheritance of posterity. Yet, alas! how much more anxious are thousands to entail upon their descendants ample worldly possessions, even at the hazard of all their better interests, than to perpetuate among them those invaluable means of grace which take hold on eternal life! God forbid that we should ever be willing that our children should dwell in splendid mansions, or revel in accumulated riches, on which 'Ichabod' is written!

B. C. 1444.] CHAPTER XXII. 199

tar, not for burnt-offering, nor for sacrifice:

27 But *that* it *may be* ᶻa witness between us, and you, and our generations after us, that we might ᵃdo the service of the LORD before him with our burnt-offerings, and with our sacrifices, and with our peace-offerings; that your children may not say to our children in time to come, Ye have no part in the LORD.

28 Therefore said we, that it shall be, when they should *so* say to us or to our generations in time to come, that we may say *again*, Behold the pattern of the altar of the LORD, which our fathers made, not for burnt-offerings, nor for sacrifices; but it *is* a witness between us and you.

29 God forbid that we should

ᶻ Gen. 31. 48. ch. 24. 27. ver. 34. ᵃ Deut. 12. 5, 6, 11, 12, 17, 18, 26, 27.

rebel against the LORD, and turn this day from following the LORD, ᵇto build an altar for burnt-offerings, for meat-offerings, or for sacrifices, besides the altar of the LORD our God that *is* before his tabernacle.

30 ¶ And when Phinehas the priest, and the princes of the congregation, and heads of the thousands of Israel which *were* with him, heard the words that the children of Reuben, and the children of Gad, and the children of Manasseh spake, it pleased them.

31 And Phinehas the son of Eleazar the priest said unto the children of Reuben, and to the children of Gad, and to the children of Manasseh, This day we perceive that the LORD *is* ᶜamong us, because ye have not

ᵇ Deut. 12. 13, 14. ᶜ Lev. 26. 11, 12. 2 Chron. 15. 2.

27. *That it may be a witness.* An indelible monument and assurance that we are as truly the Lord's people as yourselves, and entitled to share unto perpetuity in the same distinguishing services and privileges.

28. *Say to us, or to our generations in time to come.* Rather according to the well-known Heb. idiom, 'say to us, *even* to our generations.' It is evident that their fears concerned their offspring, and not themselves. ——¶ *That we may say* again. That is, that our posterity, who shall be then living may say. See on ch. 4. 23.——¶ *Behold the pattern.* Rather the copy; the exact representation and resemblance. This they would have regarded as a sign, a memorial,

that they both acknowledged and served the same God, and both made use of one and the same altar.

31. *This day we perceive that the Lord is among us.* Rendered in the Targum of Jonathan, 'This day we know that the majesty of the Lord dwelleth among us, because ye have not committed this prevarication against the Word of the Lord, and thus ye have delivered the children of Israel from the hand of the Word of the Lord.' The sense undoubtedly is, that the happy issue of the affair proved conclusively that God was among them by his preventing goodness. Had their motives been less pure and conscientious than they were, the result would have been unquestionably far more

committed this trespass against the Lord: now ye have delivered the children of Israel out of the hand of the Lord.

32 ¶ And Phinehas the son of Eleazar the priest, and the princes, returned from the children of Reuben, and from the children of Gad, out of the land of Gilead, unto the land of Canaan, to the children of Israel, and brought them word again.

33 And the thing pleased the children of Israel; and the children of Israel [d] blessed God, and did not intend to go up against them in battle, to destroy the land wherein the children of Reuben and Gad dwelt.

34 And the children of Reuben and the children of Gad called the altar [e] *Ed:* for it *shall be* a witness between us that the Lord *is* God.

d 1 Chron. 29. 20. Neh. 8. 6. Dan. 2. 19. Luke 2. 28. e ch. 24. 27.

---

disastrous. But as all unhappy consequences had been avoided, the inference was inevitable that God was that day in the midst of them, that he had approved the spirit and motives in which the step originated, and, accordingly, would not suffer a well meant design to be productive of the injurious and mournful effects which they at one time apprehended. The obvious lesson taught by the passage is, that pure and pious motives in our conduct secure the presence of God with us, and consequently an exemption from the evils and disasters that would be sure to follow a contrary course. 'When a man's ways please the Lord, even his enemies shall be at peace with him.' How delightful to recognize the hand of a gracious Providence overruling the most untoward events and brightening the darkest prospects, in reference to his humble servants, who are aiming to walk in his fear! How desirable to afford to others the evidence that God is with us, and smiling upon us by the happy and prosperous results of all our undertakings!——¶ *Ye have delivered the children of Israel out of the hand of the Lord.* As it is a sinful and perverse deportment that delivers us *into* the hand of God for punishment, so it is only repentance and a corresponding humble and conscientious walk, that will deliver us *out of* his hand. The effect of our example on the public welfare should operate at once to deter us from transgression, and engage us in the practice of every moral virtue.

32. *Brought them word again.* Made a full and faithful report of the whole transaction upon their return to their brethren.

33. *Did not intend to go up.* Heb. 'said not to go up.' So 2 Sam. 21. 16, 'And Ishbi-benob—thought to have slain David;' Heb. 'said to have slain;' i. e. purposed, intended. They renounced the intention of going up. They had at first intended it, but the statements of their delegates convinced them there was no necessity for it, and they accordingly abandoned the idea entirely.——¶ *To destroy the land.* To lay waste, to ravage, to make desolate the land.

34. *Called the altar* Ed. It is remarkable that the last word in this clause, 'Ed,' *a witness*, is not found

CHAPTER XXIII.

AND it came to pass, a long time after that the LORD ᵃ had given rest unto Israel from all their enemies round about, that Joshua ᵇ waxed old *and* stricken in age.

2 And Joshua ᶜ called for all Israel, *and* for their elders, and for their heads, and for their

ᵃ ch. 21. 44, and 22. 4. ᵇ ch. 13. 1. ᶜ Deut. 31. 28. ch. 24. 1. 1 Chron. 28. 1.

---

in the original, at least in the common copies, though others are said to contain it, and it occurs in the Arabic and Syriac versions. Our translators have properly supplied it in Italics, as it is the word which the sense evidently requires. How it comes to be lacking in the common editions of the Heb. it is impossible to determine. This altar, upon which there was probably an inscription, was henceforth to be a witness of the relation in which they stood to God and to Israel, and of their concurrence with the rest of the tribes in the great fundamental truth, that 'the Lord he is God,' he and no other, and that he was to be worshipped in no other way, and at no other place, than he had himself prescribed. It was, moreover, a witness to posterity of their care to transmit their religion pure and unimpaired to them, and would be a witness against them, if ever they should forsake God and turn to idolatry.—From the incidents above related we may gather, (1) That the best meant things may afford cause of suspicion; as those are sometimes suspected of aiming to effect a breach in the unity of the church, who are most diligently laboring to heal her divisions, and to preserve to posterity the purity of her doctrines and worship. (2) It can do our brethren no injury to be jealous over them with a godly jealousy, even when we may be mistaken in our fears. (3) Nothing will so soon kindle the zeal of a faithful and devoted spirit, as the symptoms of apostasy from God in others, because to such an one nothing is so dear as his glory. (4) Rising corruptions and dangerous errors should, in the spirit of meekness, be resisted as soon as broached, lest the evil leaven, being permitted to spread, should leaven the whole mass. (5) The testimony of a good conscience is the most effectual support against the heaviest accusations.

CHAPTER XXIII.

1. *A long time after,* &c. This is supposed to have been in the last or one hundred and tenth year of Joshua's life, about thirteen or fourteen years after the conquest of Canaan, and seven after the division of the land among the tribes.——¶ *Old and stricken in years.* Heb. זקן בא בימים *zâkên bâ bayâmim,* old (and) *come, or gone, into days.*

2. *Called for all Israel,* and *for their elders,* &c. Or, Heb. 'called for all Israel, *even* for their elders,' &c. clearly indicating that by 'all Israel,' is not meant the whole body of the nation assembled in their own persons, but their elders, heads, judges, &c., convened and acting representatively in the name of the people. They could easily communicate the substance of the charge in their several districts, so that all

judges, and for their officers, and said unto them, I am old *and* stricken in age :

3 And ye have seen all that the LORD your God hath done unto all these nations because of you ; for the ^d LORD your God *is* he that hath fought for you.

4 Behold, ^e I have divided unto you by lot these nations that remain, to be an inheritance for your tribes, from Jordan, with all the nations that I have cut

^d Exod 14. 14. ch. 10. 14, 42

^e ch. 13. 2, 6, and 18. 10.

Israel could hear. This appears to have been the usual method of conducting the great and important affairs of the nation. See on Num. 16. 1. Whether this assembly was held at Timnath-serah, where Joshua dwelt, or at Shiloh, where the ark was, it is not possible to determine. From the solemn object of the meeting we should infer that the latter was the place.

3. *Ye have seen,* &c. Joshua here speaks with characteristic modesty and humility. The scope of his address is to engage the covenant people, and their seed after them, to persevere in upholding the true faith and worship of the God of Israel. In order to this, he begins by putting them in mind of the divine interpositions in their behalf. He appeals to what their own eyes had seen, but so as at once to abase himself and exalt the Most High. He does not say, 'Ye have seen what I have done, or what you have done, but what God himself has done.' They were mere instruments in his hand. It was no doubt natural for the Israelites to look upon their veteran general, who had led them on from conquest to conquest, with the most profound respect, and to say, 'Had we not had such a commander, we had never succeeded so remarkably in obtaining possession of this goodly land.' But Joshua will leave them no ground for such reflections. He will not divide the glory of their success with God. He shows them that their enemies had been defeated, not by his prowess or theirs, but solely because the Lord their God had fought for them. The battle was the Lord's, and not his, and He was entitled to all the glory. This sentiment is strikingly reiterated by the Psalmist, Ps. 44. 3, ' For they got not the land in possession by their own sword, neither did their own arm save them ; but thy right hand, and thine arm, and the light of thy countenance, because thou hadst a favor unto them.' The leader of Israel, in these words, speaks the language of every pious heart, in view of every species of worldly success and prosperity.

4. *I have divided unto you by lot.* Heb. הפלתי לכם *hippalti lâkem, I have caused to fall unto you.——* ¶ *Those nations that remain.* That remain yet unconquered ; where 'nations' stands for the land, or country which they occupied ; as on the contrary, 'land' often stands for 'nation,' or 'people.' Remnants of the devoted Canaanites still lingered about the country, though their armies had long since been broken to pieces, and they were disabled from making any effectual head against Israel.

5. *And drive them from out—and ye*

B. C. 1427.] CHAPTER XXIII. 203

off, even unto the great sea westward.

5 And the LORD your God, [f] he shall expel them from before you, and drive them from out of your sight; and ye shall possess their land, [g] as the LORD your God hath promised unto you.

6 [h] Be ye therefore very courageous to keep and to do all that is written in the book of the law of Moses, [i] that ye turn not aside therefrom *to* the right hand or *to* the left;

7 That ye [k] come not among these nations, these that remain among you; neither [l] make mention of the name of their gods, nor cause to swear *by them*, neither serve them, nor bow yourselves unto them:

---

[f] Exod. 23. 30, and 33. 2, and 34. 11. Deut. 11. 23. ch. 13. 6. [g] Num. 33. 53. [h] ch. 1. 7.

[i] Deut. 5. 32, and 28. 14. [k] Exod. 23. 33. Deut. 7. 2, 3. Prov. 4. 14. Ephes. 5. 11. [l] Exod. 23. 13. Ps. 16. 4. Jer. 5. 7. Zeph. 1. 5. Num. 32. 38.

---

shall possess. The same Heb. word, ירש *yârash*, is here used to signify, *to expel from an inheritance*, and to *succeed* those thus expelled. Ye shall *disinherit* them from before you, and ye shall *inherit* the land in their stead.

6. *Be ye therefore very courageous to keep and to do.* See observations on ch. 1. 7–9.

7. *That ye come not among these nations.* That ye have no familiar intercourse, nor form intimate connexions with them; which could not be done without contracting some measure of the defilement which their idolatries and iniquities had brought upon them. 'Evil communications corrupt good manners.' The prohibition, as appears from v. 12, is pointed especially at intermarriages with their heathen neighbors. ——¶ *Neither make mention of the name of their gods.* Or, Heb. תזכירו *tazkirû, cause to be remembered.* Instead of showing the least respect to their idols, they were to endeavor, on the contrary, to bury the remembrance of them in perpetual oblivion; let their very names be forgotten. So David says of false gods, Ps. 16. 4, 'Their names will I not take up into my lips.' On the same principle, God says, Hos. 2. 16, 17, 'At that day thou shalt call me Ishi; and shall call me no more Baali. For I will take away the names of Baalim out of her mouth, and they shall *no more be remembered* by their name.' Though Baali and Ishi signify the same thing, yet as the former was the appropriated name of idols, he would have it no longer employed, even in reference to himself. The habitual mention of the names of idols would go gradually to diminish the abhorrence in which they were bound to hold them, and eventually to introduce the custom of swearing by them in common discourse. This would infallibly tend to the general prevalence, if not to the formal establishment of idolatrous practices among them. In like manner it may be seriously questioned, whether the paintings, statues, and poems, which abound in Christian countries, replete with allusions to the detestable heathen mythology, have not a most pernicious effect in lessening a just abhorrence of the Greek and Roman idolatry, and thus subserving the

JOSHUA. [B. C. 1427.

8 But ᵐcleave unto the Lord your God, as ye have done unto this day.

9 ⁿFor the Lord hath driven out from before you great nations and strong: but *as for* you, ᵒno man hath been able to stand before you unto this day.

10 ᵖOne man of you shall chase a thousand: for the Lord your God, he *it is* that fighteth for you, ᵍas he hath promised you.

11 ʳTake good heed therefore unto yourselves, that ye love the Lord your God.

ᵐ Deut. 10. 20, and 11. 22, and 13. 4. ch. 22. 5. ⁿ Deut. 11. 23. ᵒ ch. 1. 5.

ᵖ Lev. 26. 8. Deut. 32. 30. Judg. 3. 31, and 15. 15. 2 Sam. 23. 8. ᵍ Exod. 14. 14, and 23. 27. Deut. 3. 22. ʳ ch. 22. 5.

---

cause of scepticism, infidelity, and vice.——¶ *Nor cause to swear* by them. To swear by any god was virtually to acknowledge him as a witness and avenger in the case of the violation of contracts, and so in effect a suitable object of religious worship. It is implied that they were not to make any covenants with idolaters, because in confirming their covenants they would swear by their idols. 'Let no Israelite be a party to any transaction which should involve such a consequence. Neither swear by them yourselves, nor cause others by your procurement to do it.' By neglecting these slighter occasions of idolatry they might be imperceptibly betrayed into it, and led along by degrees, till they had finally reached its highest step, which was serving false gods, and bowing down to them, in direct transgression of the letter of the second commandment.

8. *Cleave unto the Lord your God,* &c. Delight in him, depend upon him, devote yourselves to his glory, and continue to do so unto the end, as you have done unto this day; ever since arriving in Canaan. For since that time, though there might have been many things more or less amiss among them, yet the nation at large had behaved much better than they did in the wilderness, and had not been guilty of any open or gross apostasy from God, but had followed him with exemplary fidelity.

9. *For the Lord hath driven out.* Or, as the original will admit of being rendered, 'and the Lord will drive out,' &c., and so the whole verse may be rendered in the future instead of the past, in which case it will connect more easily and naturally with the verse ensuing.——¶ *No man hath been able to stand before you.* That is, when it actually came to an issue. Some of the ancient inhabitants did indeed yet remain unconquered, but in every engagement the Israelites came off victorious. In this sense no man had been able to stand before them. Wherever an enemy had been encountered he had been overcome.

11. *Take good heed therefore unto yourselves.* Intimating the condition on which the foregoing promise should be made good to them. Let not the assurance of the divine favor, presence, and protection, tend to relax your diligence, or weaken the sense of obligation to love and serve him; on the contrary, let it operate as an additional motive to the most intense affection and devotedness towards your heavenly benefactor. As the temptations arising from the

12 Else if ye do in any wise ⁸go back, and cleave unto the remnant of these nations, *even* these that remain among you, and shall ᵗmake marriages with them, and go in unto them, and they to you:

13 Know for a certainty that ᵘthe LORD your God will no more drive out *any of* these na-

ˢ Heb. 10. 38, 39. 2 Pet. 2. 20, 21. ᵗ Deut. 7. 3. ᵘ Judg. 2. 3.

tions from before you: ˣ but they shall be snares and traps unto you, and scourges in your sides, and thorns in your eyes, until ye perish from off this good land which the LORD your God hath given you.

14 And behold, this day ʸI am going the way of all the

ˣ Exod. 23. 33. Num. 33. 55. Deut. 7. 16. 1 Kings 11. 4. ʸ 1 Kings 2. 2. Heb. 9. 27.

presence of your corrupt neighbors, and your own peace and prosperity, are greater than they were in the wilderness, it will require greater watchfulness and diligence to keep yourselves continually approved in the sight of heaven.

13. *Know for a certainty.* Heb. ידוע תדעו *yâdoa tidu, knowing thou shalt know.*——¶ *They shall be snares and traps unto you.* You will be caught by their wiles; their baits and allurements will seduce you into crime, into a participation of their vile impieties; and as a consequence of this, taking advantage of your weakness, they will vex and harass, torment and oppress you, and as willing though unconscious instruments in the hand of a chastising providence, will be as continual goads, spurs, or scourges in your sides, or as annoying thorns in your eyes. They will kill or drive away your cattle, burn or steal your harvests, lay waste your vineyards, alarm or plunder your houses, and in a thousand ways be a perpetual source of trouble. Nay, so completely shall they at length obtain the ascendency, that your respective conditions shall be reversed; instead of exterminating *them* from the bounds of Canaan,

you shall *yourselves* fall before them, or be utterly driven from your inheritance, from the 'good land' which the Lord himself hath given. What could tend more powerfully to arm their spirits against the forbidden alliances than the prospect of such calamities as these?——¶ *Scourges in your sides, and thorns in your eyes.* 'What!' says a wife to her angry husband, 'am I a thorn in your eyes?' 'Alas! alas! he has seen another; I am now a thorn in his eyes.' 'Were I not a thorn in his eyes, his anger would not burn so long.' 'My old friend Tamban never looks at my house now, because it gives him thorns to his eyes.' *Roberts.*

14. *Going the way of all the earth.* About to die, to go into the grave. To die is in a sense to go a journey, a journey to our long home; it is the way of all the earth, the way that all mankind must go sooner or later. Joshua felt himself near his end, and he would have his people look upon him and listen to him as a dying man, that so his words might sink the deeper into their hearts. He would spend his last breath in taking them to witness that God had been punctiliously faithful to every promise, and in solemnly assuring them that

earth; and ye know in all your hearts and in all your souls, that ᶻ not one thing hath failed of all the good things which the Lord your God spake concerning you; all are come to pass unto you, *and* not one thing hath failed thereof.

15 ᵃ Therefore it shall come to pass, *that* as all good things are come upon you, which the Lord your God promised you; so shall the Lord bring upon you ᵇ all evil things, until he have destroyed you from off this good

z ch. 21. 45.   Luke 21. 33.   a Deut. 28. 63.
b Lev. 26. 16.   Deut. 28. 15, 16, &c.

land which the Lord your God hath given you.

16 When ye have transgressed the covenant of the Lord your God, which he commanded you, and have gone and served other gods, and bowed yourselves to them; then shall the anger of the Lord be kindled against you, and ye shall perish quickly from off the good land which he hath given unto you.

CHAPTER XXIV.

AND Joshua gathered all the tribes of Israel to ᵃ She-

a Gen. 35. 4.

---

every threatening, however fearful, would receive an equally certain and exact accomplishment.——¶ *Ye know—that not one thing hath failed,* &c. The same appeal which is here made by Joshua to Israel after sixty years' experience, may be made to every believer that ever lived. We may bring forth every promise from the Bible, and then search the annals of the world, and inquire of every creature in it, and one single instance will be sought in vain of God's violating or forgetting a promise. The accomplishment may have been delayed or brought to pass in a way that was not expected, but the whole world may be challenged to impeach his veracity, or contradict the assertion that ' *all* which he hath promised is come to pass: not one thing hath failed thereof.' But let it not be forgotten that the veracity of God is as much pledged for the execution of his threatenings, as for the performance of his promises. The one is a proof of the other. Yet among the world of the impenitent where is there a mind divested of the floating impression, that mercy will in some way interpose to stay the outgoings of wrath? How many, alas! are now experiencing in hell what they would not believe on earth! The subsequent history of the chosen people abundantly shows that both the apostasy here deprecated and the threatenings here denounced did actually take place. Let then every Christian fear as he reads, ' If God spared not the natural branches, take heed lest he spare not thee.' The worldly, carnal, sensual Christian has no more right to expect indulgence from the justice of God than the disobedient Jew.

CHAPTER XXIV.

1. *Gathered all the tribes.* That is, the heads, elders, and chief men of the tribes. though not them exclusively. See on ch. 23 2. Joshua probably found his life prolonged beyond his expectation, and, like Peter in his old age, thinking it meet ' as long as he was in this tabernacle'

chem, and ᵇ called for the elders of Israel, and for their heads and for their judges, and for their

ᵇ ch. 23. 2.

to do his utmost towards 'putting' and keeping his people 'in remembrance' of the great things of their duty, embraces one more opportunity of convening the tribes by their representatives, and giving them a solemn parting charge. The pious servants of God may be disabled through age and infirmities from continuing their personal exertions, but they will never relax their zeal in the service of their divine Master; and what they want in effective labors, they will endeavor to supply by stimulating and confirming the zeal of others. As Moses, at an advanced age, renewed the covenant in the plains of Moab which had been first entered into at Horeb forty years before, so Joshua on this occasion imitates his example, and makes it his last labor to engage the tribes of Israel once more to give themselves up to God, in a perpetual covenant. Thus the good effects of his influence would remain when he himself was taken from them. 'We must never think our work for God done till our life is done; and if he lengthen out our days beyond what we thought, we must conclude it is because he has some further service for us to do.' *Henry*.——¶ *To Shechem*. As it is immediately added that 'they presented themselves before God,' the natural inference would be that this transaction took place in the presence of the ark and the tabernacle, the usual *meeting-place* of God and his people, which were now, as far as we know, at Shiloh instead of Shechem. This has occasioned some difficulty to commentators, especially as the Greek of the Sept. has Σηλω, *Shilo*, both here and v. 25, though the Aldine and Complutensian editions have Συχεμ, *Sychem*, in both places, which leads us to suppose that the former reading is a designed alteration, made with a view to obviate an apprehended discrepancy in the original. At any rate, there is no sufficient ground for questioning the genuineness of the present Hebrew text. The two following solutions, therefore, may be proposed; either, (1) By Shechem here is meant not the city so called, but the territory adjacent, extending to the distance of several miles, within the limits of which it is conjectured that Shiloh stood. But this is less likely, as Shiloh was at least ten miles distant from Shechem, and if the meeting had been at Shiloh we can see no reason why it should not have been expressly so stated. Or, (2) that Shechem was really the place of the convocation, but that the tabernacle was for the present occasion transferred thither, as we learn Judg. 20. 1, 18; 1 Sam. 4. 3; 2 Sam. 15. 24, that it was sometimes on extraordinary emergencies temporarily removed. There were several reasons why Shechem should be considered the most suitable place for the assembling of the tribes on this occasion. It was a Levitical city, and nearer than Shiloh to Timnath-serah, Joshua's residence, whose age and infirmities might at this time have incapacitated him from travelling even a short distance from home. It was the place where the covenant was

officers; and they ᶜpresented themselves before God.

2 And Joshua said unto all the people, Thus saith the LORD God of Israel, ᵈYour fathers dwelt on the other side of the flood in old time, *even* Terah, the father of Abraham, and the

c 1 Sam. 10. 19.   d Gen. 11. 26, 31.

first made with Abraham ages before, Gen. 12. 6, 7, and so would be a peculiarly appropriate place for renewing that covenant, which was one end to be answered by their now coming together. It adds to the force of this reason, that it was in this immediate vicinity, between the two mounts Gerizim and Ebal, that Joshua had before, on their first entrance into Canaan, convened the nation for a similar object, ch. 8. 30–35. So that all the associations connected with the place would tend eminently to heighten the solemnity and impressiveness of the transaction in which they were about to engage. If, moreover, as from v. 32, many suppose it was on this occasion that the bones of Joseph, and perhaps of the other patriarchs, Acts 7. 15, 16, were deposited in the piece of ground which his father gave him near Shechem, it would constitute another strong reason for selecting this, in preference to Shilo, as the place of the present meeting. That such was the fact, however, whatever might have been the reasons, and whatever the imagined difficulties involved in the supposition, there can be no doubt as long as we adhere to the letter of the sacred record. ——¶ *Presented themselves before God.* As intimated above, the presumption is that this presentation of themselves was before the ark of the covenant and the tabernacle, the visible residence of God among his people, and now removed to Shechem to give additional solemnity to the proceedings of the assembly. This impression is confirmed by v. 26, where it is said that 'a great stone was set up there under an oak that was *by the sanctuary of the Lord;*' i. e. by the place where the sanctuary temporarily stood during the time of that convention. Yet the words do not *necessarily* demand this construction. The phrase 'before God,' or 'before the Lord,' is sometimes equivalent to *religiously, devoutly, as if under the inspection of the divine eye.* Thus Isaac, Gen. 27. 7, is said to have blessed Jacob, 'before the Lord,' i.e. as in his presence, in his name, in a very solemn and devout manner. So Jephthah is said, Judg. 11. 11, to have uttered all his words 'before the Lord;' in the same sense. See on ch. 4. 13.

2. *Joshua said unto all the people.* All the people now assembled, consisting mainly of the elders, chiefs, &c., v. 1, but in addition to them of such portions of the body of the people as found it convenient to attend. ——¶ *On the other side of the flood.* That is, on the other side of the river, the river Euphrates; so called by way of eminence. 'Flood' is an unfortunate rendering, as the original word is the common word for 'river,' and repeatedly and for the most part so translated in our established version.——¶ *In old time.* Heb. מעולם *mëolâm, from everlasting;* i. e. from an indefinite period of remote antiquity; as the same term often sig-

father of Nachor: and ᵉthey served other gods.

3 And ᶠI took your father Abraham from the other side of the flood, and led him throughout all the land of Canaan, and

multiplied his seed, and ᵍgave him Isaac.

4 And I gave unto Isaac ʰJacob and Esau: and I gave unto ⁱEsau mount Seir, to possess it;

ᵉ Gen. 31. 53. ᶠ Gen. 12. 1. Acts 7. 2, 3. ᵍ Gen. 21. 2, 3. Ps. 127. 3. ʰ Gen. 25. 24, 25, 26. ⁱ Gen. 36. 8. Deut. 2. 5.

---

nifies an indefinite period of time future.——¶ *Served other gods.* From this it seems clear that Abraham's grandfather and father, and perhaps himself in the first instance, worshipped the idols of the country in which they lived. By this, however, we are probably not to understand that they had no knowledge of, or reverence for, the true God, but that they did not render to him that *exclusive* worship which was his due. In fact, we may conclude them to have been in much the same condition as Laban, who at a subsequent period represented that part of the family which remained beyond the Euphrates, and who certainly reverenced Jehovah, but who also had idols which he called his gods, and the loss of which filled him with vexation and anger. The partial idolatry of their ancestors, however, was humiliating to Israel. Even Abraham, the father of their nation, in whom they gloried, and who was subsequently so highly honored of God, was born and bred up in the worship of false gods. This fact would cut off all vain-boasting in the worthiest of their ancestors, as far as native character or early conduct was concerned. The father of the faithful himself became what he was purely by the grace of God, and not in virtue of his own innate tendencies to good. Indeed his justification is expressly set forth by the apostle, Rom. 4. 5, as an instance of God's 'justifying the ungodly.'

3. *And I took your father Abraham,* &c. I exercised such an influence upon him as induced him to leave that land of idolators; I prompted him to go. Though no violence was employed, it implies that he would never have gone thence unless God had 'taken' him, unless by a divine impulse he had moved him to go. See on Gen. 2. 15, relative to God's 'taking' Adam and putting him into the garden of Eden. So it is the special grace of God that 'takes' a sinner out of a state of impenitence and unbelief, and puts him in the way to eternal life, the road to the heavenly Canaan, that better country where lies the inheritance of the saints.——¶ *Led him throughout all the land of Canaan.* Gave him my gracious guidance and protection during all his wanderings to and fro in that land of promise. ——¶ *Multiplied his seed, and gave him Isaac.* That is, multiplied his seed *by giving* him Isaac. As this 'multiplication,' however, could not be said to be accomplished merely by the birth of a single son, it is to be understood, not of Isaac alone, but of the long and spreading line of his posterity, among whom he enumerates Jacob and Esau, including their issue, in the next verse.

4. *I gave unto Esau mount Seir.* See on Gen. 36. 7, 8. In order that

ᵏ but Jacob and his children went down into Egypt.

5 ˡ I sent Moses also and Aaron, and ᵐ I plagued Egypt, according to that which I did among them: and afterward I brought you out.

6 And I ⁿ brought your fathers out of Egypt: and ᵒ ye came unto the sea; ᵖ and the Egyptians pursued after your fathers with chariots and horsemen unto the Red sea.

7 And when they ᑫ cried unto the Lord, ʳ he put darkness between you and the Egyptians, ˢ and brought the sea upon them, and covered them; and ᵗ your eyes have seen what I have done in Egypt: and ye dwelt in the wilderness ᵘ a long season.

8 And I brought you into the land of the Amorites, which dwelt on the other side Jordan; ˣ and they fought with you: and I gave them into your hand, that ye might possess their land; and I destroyed them from before you.

9 Then. ʸ Balak the son of Zip-

ᵏ Gen. 46. 1, 6. Acts 7. 15. ˡ Exod. 3. 10. ᵐ Exod. 7. and 8. and 9. and 10. and 12. ⁿ Exod. 12. 37, 51. ᵒ Exod. 14. 2. ᵖ Exod. 14. 9. ᑫ Exod. 14. 10. ʳ Exod. 14. 20. ˢ Exod. 14. 27, 28. ᵗ Deut. 4. 34, and 29. 2 ᵘ ch 5. 6. ˣ Num. 21. 21, 33. Deut. 2. 32, and 3. 1. ʸ Judg. 11. 25.

---

the land of Canaan, by the removal of Esau, might be reserved entire to Jacob and his posterity.——¶ *But Jacob and his children went down into Egypt.* Where they suffered a long and grievous bondage, the particulars of which the speaker does not deem it necessary to recite.

5. *According to that which I did among them.* Heb. עשׂיתי בקרבו *asithi bekirbo, which I did in the midst of him.* A peculiar phraseology, and not capable perhaps of being fully reached in any other language. It imples the *essential reality* of any thing compared with the outward *manifestation, sign,* or *expression* of it. Thus it is said of the butler and baker in prison, Gen. 40. 5, that they each dreamed a dream, ' according to the interpretation of his dream,' i. e. one of which the *event* answered to the *dream itself;* a dream capable of a sound interpretation, which Joseph gave, and which the actual fulfilment confirmed. So here the plagues of Egypt corresponded *in fact, in reality,* with all that had been predicted of them beforehand, with all that was recorded of them afterwards, and with all that struck the senses at the time of their actual occurrence. There was no *illusion* about them in any manner or degree. It was all *reality.*——¶ *Afterward I brought you out.* Spoken of the present generation, though strictly true only of their fathers. Of the *usus loquendi* here involved, see note on ch. 4. 23. So also in the ensuing verses, where the reader will notice that the words *your fathers* and *ye, them* and *you,* are remarkably interchanged.

6. *Came unto the sea.* The Red Sea, as is afterwards expressed.

7. *Brought the sea upon them—covered them.* Heb. ' brought 'he sea upon him—covered him.' Spoken of, according to usual analogy, as one man.——¶ *Dwelt in the wilderness a long season.* A mild term for their being condemned to wander for forty years in the wilderness as a punishment for their sins.

B. C. 1427.] CHAPTER XXIV. 211

por, king of Moab, arose and warred against Israel, and ᶻ sent and called Balaam the son of Beor to curse you:

10 ᵃ But I would not hearken unto Balaam; ᵇ therefore he blessed you still: so I delivered you out of his hand.

11 And ᶜ ye went over Jordan, and came unto Jericho: and ᵈ the men of Jericho fought against you, the Amorites, and the Perizzites, and the Canaanites, and the Hittites, and the Girgashites, the Hivites, and the Jebusites, and I delivered them into your hand.

12 And ᵉ I sent the hornet before you, which drave them out from before you, *even* the two

ᶻ Num. 22. 5. Deut. 23. 4.   ᵃ Deut. 23. 5.
ᵇ Num. 23. 11, 20, and 24. 10.   ᶜ ch. 3. 14, 17, and 4. 10, 11, 12.
ᵈ ch. 6. 1, and 10. 1, and 11. 1.   ᵉ Exod. 23. 28. Deut. 7. 20.

9. *Then Balak—arose and warred against Israel.* From the previous history, Num. 23. and 24. and also from Judg. 11. 25, it would appear that Balak did not at any time *actually engage* in conflict with Israel. He is said, therefore, in this place to have 'warred' against them because he *intended* it, because he cherished a *hostile purpose*, and concerted his schemes and made his preparations accordingly. The Scripture idiom often speaks of men as doing what they fully design and endeavor to do, and it is a very slight stretch of language to denominate him a warring enemy who has all the will and lacks only the opportunity to become so. See Gen. 37. 21; Ezek. 24. 13; Mat. 5. 28; John 10. 32, 33. A similar phraseology occurs in v. 11, in reference to the men of Jericho, which is perhaps to be explained on the same principle.

10. *I would not hearken unto Balaam.* Would not comply with his secret wish and purpose, nor allow him to curse to you; would not fall in with or favor the ruling desire of his heart.——¶ *Delivered you out of his hand.* Out of the hand of Balak, and all the wicked machinations which he had set on foot against you.

11. *The men of Jericho fought against you.* Heb. 'the masters or lords of Jericho.' This is understood by many expositors of the rulers or magistrates of Jericho; but as the ensuing words, 'the Amorites, the Perizzites,' &c , seem to stand in immediate apposition with ' men,' or masters, we take it that *they* are meant by the term, and are called 'masters' of Jericho from the fact that that city belonged to an extensive confederacy composed of the various neighboring nations here specified, of whom it is obviously true that they 'fought' against Israel, and were signally delivered into their hand. If, however, the phrase be understood of the *citizens*, or *chief men* of the city of Jericho, though they did not actually meet Israel in the field, yet they may be said to have fought against them, inasmuch as they *stood upon the defensive, and opposed* them by *shutting their gates,* and probably in making what resistance they could after an entrance had been gained into the city. See on v. 9.

12. *I sent the hornet before you.* Understood by some literally of the insect so called, by others figuratively of the anxieties, perplexities, and

kings of the Amorites; *but* ᶠnot with thy sword, nor with thy bow.

13 And I have given you a land for which ye did not labor, and ᵍ cities which ye built not, and ye dwell in them; of the vineyards and olive-yards which ye planted not do ye eat.

14 ¶ ʰ Now therefore fear the Lord, and serve him in ⁱ sincerity and in truth; and put away the gods which your fathers

ᶠ Ps. 44. 3, 6. ᵍ Deut. 6. 10, 11. ch. 11. 13. ʰ Deut. 10. 12. 1 Sam. 12. 24. ⁱ Gen. 17. 1, and 20. 5. Deut. 18. 13. Ps. 119. 1. 2 Cor. 1. 12. Eph. 6. 24. ᵏ ver. 2, 23. Lev. 17. 7. Ezek. 20 18.

---

pungent terrors which invaded the minds of the Canaanites on the reported approach of the hosts of Israel. For further remarks on the subject, see on Ex. 23. 28, and 'Illustrations of the Scriptures,' p. 66. The writer of the apocryphal book entitled 'The Wisdom of Solomon,' seems to have taken the words as literally true. ch. 12. 8–10, 'Nevertheless, thou didst send wasps, forerunners of thine host, to destroy them by little and little. Not that thou wast unable to bring the ungodly under the hand of the righteous in battle, or to destroy them at once with cruel beasts, or with one rough word: But executing thy judgments by little and little thou gavest them place of repentance, not being ignorant that they were a naughty generation, and that their malice was bred in them, and that their cogitation would never be changed.'—— ¶ *Not with thy sword, nor with thy bow*. Not that these implements were not made use of in their wars, but that they would have used them in vain unless God, by his secret or open judgments, had previously smitten and paralysed the power of the enemy. See the passage before quoted from Ps. 44. 3.

13. *For which ye did not labor*. Heb. לא יגעת *lo yâgatâ, thou didst not labor*. The whole body of the nation addressed collectively as one person.——¶ *Of the vineyards and olive-yards—do you eat*. That is, of their fruits; a usage of speech of not uncommon occurrence. Thus Gen. 3. 11, 'Hast thou eaten of the tree, whereof,' &c., i. e. of the fruit of the tree. So also Rev. 2. 7, 'I will give to him to eat of the tree of life.'

14. *Now therefore fear the Lord*, &c. The address of Joshua to Israel has thus far been occupied with a recital of the leading events of their national history, events going to show, in the most striking manner, the interposition of the divine hand in their behalf. He would thus lay a foundation for that deep sense of obligation and obedience, which he aims in the remainder of his discourse to impress upon their minds. From this point, therefore, he begins a practical application of the various facts he had before enumerated, turning the whole into a powerful appeal to the consciences and the hearts of his hearers.——¶ *Serve him in sincerity and in truth*. In uprightness, in integrity; not in pretence and outward semblance only, but in reality and in truth. Do not serve or worship other gods in private, while in public, in the eyes of men, you maintain the form of the worship of the true God.——¶ *Put away the gods which your fathers*

CHAPTER XXIV.

served on the other side of the flood, and ¹ in Egypt; and serve ye the LORD.

15 And if it seem evil unto you to serve the LORD, ᵐ choose you this day whom ye will serve, whether ⁿ the gods which your fathers served that *were* on the other side of the flood, or ᵒ the gods of the Amorites in

1 Ezek. 20. 7, 8, and 23. 3. m Ruth 1. 15. 1 Kings 18. 21. Ezek. 20. 39. John 6. 67.   n ver. 14.   o Exod. 23. 24, 32. 33, and 34. 15. Deut. 13. 7, and 29. 18. Judges 6. 10.

served, &c. From the general character of this generation, as evinced by their conduct, and from the commendation bestowed upon them by Joshua, ch. 23. 8, it is difficult to conceive that the positive practice of idolatry was now fairly chargeable upon them. If the secret sin of Achan, in stealing certain forbidden articles at the siege of Jericho, brought such fearful tokens of wrath upon the congregation, have we not reason to suppose that the act of paying divine honors to idols, however hidden from human observation, would have incurred, at least, an equal measure of divine indignation. And if such a sin were actually prevalent among them, how is it to be accounted for that Joshua had not warned them against it before? But perhaps the words of Joshua, in just construction, do not necessarily force upon us such a sense. The phrase, ' Put away the gods,' &c., may mean simply, *keep away, renounce, repudiate, have nothing to do with,* being equivalent to a charge to *preserve themselves pure* from a contagion to which they were peculiarly liable. We prefer, therefore, to understand the expression of a *vigorous and determined purpose of mind* to which the speaker exhorts the chosen people, while at the same time we cannot deny that there may have been in solitary instances some lingering relics of actual idolatry which Joshua would effectually extinguish by this solemn mandate. But that the offence was now prevalent to any considerable extent among the people, we have no idea. Not but that there was sufficient corruption in their natures for such a propensity to live and act upon, but the tenor of the narrative does not, we conceive, justify the supposition in respect to them at this time. We are warranted, however, in drawing from Joshua's words the practical inference, that God requires the heart in his worship, without which there is no acceptable service; and that that is still an idol, to which our affections cleave more than they do to God himself.——¶ *In Egypt.* This fact is nowhere else expressly asserted respecting the Israelites in Egypt, although Ezek. 23. 3, 8, and Acts, 7. 42, 43, go strongly in confirmation of Joshua's words. Considering the idolatrous tendencies of human nature, it is not surprising that they should have suffered themselves to become infected with an evil so every where rife around them, and it was, perhaps, in part owing to this that their sufferings were so aggravated and embittered in that 'house of bondage.'

15. *If it seem evil in your eyes.* Unjust, unreasonable, or attended with too many inconveniences.——¶ *Choose ye this day whom ye will serve.* Not implying that it was pre-

whose land ye dwell: ᵖbut as for me and my house, we will serve the Lord.

p Gen. 18. 19.

viously a matter of indifference, whether they served God or no, or that they were really at liberty to refuse his service if they saw fit. He adopts this rhetorical mode of speech, in order to impress upon them more forcibly a sense of their duty, and the utter absurdity, as well as impiety, of devoting themselves to any other than the true God. It is a striking way of bringing the matter to an issue. His aim is to bring them to a decided stand; to a free, intelligent, firm, and lasting choice of God as their portion. In effecting this he makes use of a style of address which evidently implies that the service of idols compared with the service of God is so irrational, absurd, and brutish, that no man in the calm exercise of his understanding could hesitate which to choose. If reason and conscience could but be allowed to speak, they would not fail to speak on the side of God. A similar course, having the same object in view, was pursued by Elijah, 1 Kings 18. 21, who 'came unto all the people, and said, How long halt ye between two opinions?. If the Lord be God, follow him; but if Baal, then follow him.' The grand inference to be drawn from this mode of address is,—that the service of God is matter of voluntary choice, and that it is his will that we should all seriously and solemnly make this choice. He would have us weigh the matter well, compare the respective claims of his service and the service of sin and the world, and if our candid judgment, as it surely will, pronounces on the side of that which is good, and true, and right, and saving, to resolve at once to embrace it, and adhere to it with a constancy stronger than death. As the evidences in favor of religion are so clear and indisputable, and its infinite advantages so obvious, the man who declines making the choice here enjoined must be considered as deliberately preferring Satan to Christ, death to life, hell to heaven. He who *acknowledges* the paramount claims of God and his Gospel, and yet does not *act* accordingly, does not sincerely and solemnly *choose* his service, as that better part which cannot be taken from him, must stand self-condemned both here and hereafter.——¶ *As for me and my house, we will serve the Lord.* Ye may act your pleasure in this matter, but whatever may be *your* election, *I* am decided as to my own course. As far as myself and my household are concerned, the question whom we shall serve is settled. Whatever halting or wavering there may be in other cases, there is none in mine. This declaration of their venerated leader, while devoid of the least air of dictation, and apparently leaving them the most unrestrained liberty of choice, was in fact the most powerful argument he could have used to influence their minds in the direction he wished. For the force of example is in proportion to the depth of respect and estimation in which an individual is held, and he could not fail to perceive that the reverence with which he was regarded would give to his example a weight and authority almost amounting to

B. C. 1427.] CHAPTER XXIV. 215

16 And the people answered, and said, God forbid that we should forsake the LORD, to serve other gods;

17 For the LORD our God, he *it is* that brought us up, and our fathers, out of the land of Egypt, from the house of bondage, and

---

absolute law. Gratitude for his services, confidence in his wisdom, and love for his person would all combine to make his conduct a pattern for theirs; and how blessed is it when those who possess these immense advantages for exerting a salutary influence on others, are disposed, like Joshua, to make it available to the salvation of their fellow-men! This noble resolutio nof the captain of Israel obviously suggests the following reflections; (1) The service of God is nothing below the most distinguished of men. It is no diminution of their greatness, no disparagement of their rank, reputation, or honor, to be decidedly pious, and to be openly and avowedly so. On the contrary, it heightens every other distinction, and makes all honor still more honorable. (2) In regard to the great interests of religion and the soul, we are to be concerned for others, particularly our households, as well as for ourselves. It should be our earnest aim to unite our families, our wives, children, and servants, those that come under our special care and influence, with us in every pious resolution and labor. Heads of households should feel not only *anxiety*, but *deep responsibility*, in respect to those thus entrusted to their charge. (3) Those that lead and rule in other things should be first in the service of God, and go before in every good work. (4) We should resolve to do right and to do good, whatever others may do. Though others may desert the cause of God, we should stand by it at all hazards, whatever charge of singularity or expression of popular odium it may bring upon us. 'Those that are bound for heaven must be willing to swim against the stream, and must not do as the *most* do, but as the *best* do.' *Henry.*

16. *The people answered and said, God forbid,* &c. Joshua has the pleasure of finding the people ready from their hearts to concur with him in his pious resolution. By an emphatic expression, denoting the greatest dread and detestation imaginable, they show that they startle at the thought of apostatizing from God, as if it would imply their being utterly lost to justice, gratitude, honor, and every generous feeling. At the same time, they give such substantial reasons for their choice, as to show that it was not purely out of compliment to Joshua, highly as they esteemed him, that they made it, but from a full conviction of its intrinsic reasonableness and equity. They professedly and justly found their obligations, first on the consideration of the great and merciful things which God had done for them, in bringing them out of Egypt through the wilderness into Canaan, where they were now planted in peace; and, secondly, of the relation in which they stood to God as a covenant people. 'He is our God;' he has graciously engaged himself by promise to us, and we have bound ourselves by solemn vow to him. Woe to us if we prove false and treacherous to our plighted faith.

which did those great signs in our sight, and preserved us in all the way wherein we went, and among all the people through whom we passed:

18 And the Lord drave out from before us all the people, even the Amorites which dwelt in the land: *therefore* will we

^q Matt. 6. 24. ^r Lev. 19. 2. 1 Sam. 6. 20.

also serve the Lord; for he *is* our God.

19 And Joshua said unto the people, ^q Ye cannot serve the Lord: for he *is* a ^rholy God: he *is* ^sa jealous God; ^the will not forgive your transgressions, nor your sins.

Ps. 99. 5, 9. Isa. 5. 16. ^s Exod. 20. 5. ^t Exod. 23. 21.

---

19. *Ye cannot serve the Lord*, &c. It cannot be supposed for a moment that Joshua intended to deter the people from the service of God by representing it as impracticable or dangerous. On the contrary, his design is to enlist them more sincerely and steadfastly in it, but his knowledge of the weakness and corruption of our fallen nature, prompted him to do this in a manner that savors of discouragement and repulsiveness. Finding them now animated by a glowing zeal, forward and abundant in their professions, and unconsciously prone to trust to their own strength, Joshua, in these words, designs to administer a wholesome check to their ardor, by setting impressively before them the holy and sin-avenging character of the God with whom they had to do, and the fearful consequences of disobedience and apostasy. This would beat them off from that overweening self-confidence which they were so prone to indulge. It would convince them that it was no light and easy matter to persevere in the strict observance of the divine precepts, and thus they would be more cautious, circumspect, and humble in their professions, and go forward in their walk with more awe upon their spirits, and a more trembling sense of their dependence on a higher power than their own. This Joshua well knew was the only frame of mind which could be trusted to for permanent and happy results, and he therefore aims to have their present lively zeal based upon the only foundation that would ensure its continuance. He would have them count the cost of the engagements into which they proposed to enter, and be fully aware of the temptations, tribulations, conflicts and self-denials which they would involve; and above all would have their inmost souls pervaded by *a deep and awful reverence of God*, the essential principle of all true religion. In like manner, it deserves very serious deliberation whether there is not danger of representing the sincere service of God as a matter of very little difficulty, provided only there be evidence of a *present vigorous resolution*, and whether it be not better in such cases wisely to repress, chasten, and even dampen the warmth of present zeal by considerations like those which Joshua now pressed upon the children of Israel. The same infallible authority which assures us that the yoke of Christ is easy and his burden light, assures us also that the gate is strait, and the way narrow, that leads to life, and that there is need of *striving* as well as

B. C. 1427.]   CHAPTER XXIV.   217

20 ᵘ If ye forsake the LORD, and serve strange gods, ˣ then he will turn and do you hurt, and consume you, after that he hath done you good.

21 And the people said unto Joshua, Nay; but we will serve the LORD.

u 1 Chron. 28. 9. 2 Chron. 15. 2. Ezra 8. 22. Isa. 1. 28, and 65. 11, 12. Jer. 17. 13.
x ch. 23. 15. Isa. 63. 10. Acts 7. 42.

---

seeking to enter in. Certain it is, that great wisdom is requisite in every spiritual guide in digging deep and laying the foundations sure of a life of consistent, uniform, and devoted piety. Nor are we of opinion that the policy of such eminent servants of God, as Moses, Joshua, Samuel, Peter, and Paul, will ever be out of date in the church. The more the sinner despairs of his own sufficiency, the better security will he give for his ultimate stability and perseverance in the faith.—— ¶ *He is an holy God.* Heb. אלהים קדשים *elohim kedoshim, he is holy Gods;* the adjective being plural as well as the substantive. The expression is remarkable and contrary to usual analogy, but whether carrying with it any special implication in regard to the divine nature, it is perhaps impossible to say. We imagine, on the whole, that to a Hebrew ear the phrase would merely convey the idea of more emphasis, solemnity, and awfulness in respect to the attribute here affirmed of Jehovah.—— ¶ *He is a jealous God.* As he has no equal, so neither can he suffer a rival. To pay to idols that worship which he alone deserves, or even to associate them with the homage which is paid to him, is to contest with him, to take from a part of that perfect holiness which constitutes his glory, and is what the Scriptures call *profaning* his holy name.—— ¶ *Will not forgive.* Or, Heb. לא ישא *lo yissà, will not bear, will not tolerate.*

The meaning is, not that God was implacable, or that he would not show mercy to the penitent, however great their sins, but that *they* could not offend against him with impunity, that he would certainly punish their transgressions. However it might be with others, *they* would be sure to be visited for their iniquities.

20. *Strange gods.* Heb. אלהי נכר *elohë nëkâr, gods of the stranger or foreigner.*—— ¶ *Then he will turn,* &c. Not in himself or in his dispositions towards his creatures, for we are elsewhere told that with him there is 'no variableness nor the least shadow of turning.' But the character of his dispensations, the course of his providence towards them should be entirely changed, in view of the change in their conduct towards him. He would henceforward be as severe and vindictive, as he had before been kind and gracious.—— ¶ *Consume you, after that he hath done you good.* Nothing so embitters the judgments of God, as the reflection that they have been incurred after the experience of his tender mercies. The fact that we have made him to repent of his past kindnesses to us, and forget all the good he had wrought in our behalf, barbs and envenoms the arrow of remorse beyond the power of language to describe.

21. *We will serve the Lord.* This shows that they understood the words of Joshua to imply no moral inability on their side, and notwithstanding his statement of difficulties, and the

19

22 And Joshua said unto the people, Ye *are* witnesses against yourselves that ʸ ye have chosen you the LORD, to serve him. And they said, *We are* witnesses.

23 Now therefore ᶻ put away (*said he*) the strange gods which *are* among you, and incline your heart unto the LORD God of Israel.

24 And the people said unto Joshua, the LORD our God will we serve, and his voice will we obey.

25 So Joshua ᵃ made a covenant with the people that day, and set them a statute and an ordinance ᵇ in Shechem.

y Ps. 119. 173. z ver. 14. Gen. 35. 2. Judg. 10. 16. 1 Sam. 7. 3.

a Exod. 15. 25. 2 Kings 11. 17. b ver. 26.

---

seeming discouragements which he throws in their way, but which are really intended to quicken and invigorate their resolutions, they declare a firm and fixed purpose of obedience. In so saying they did virtually confirm and ratify by their own express consent the covenant which Joshua would now impose upon them, and by voluntarily engaging, as he intimated would be the case, to be witnesses against themselves, provided they turned aside from God, they did in effect affix their name and seal to that solemn covenant, and bind themselves under fearful sanctions to its faithful observance. Thus we have a sacred renewal, an authentic confirmation, of the covenant into which their fathers had entered with God, as their King, Ex. 12 and 24, which after this they could no more infringe, without being guilty in the highest degree of perjury.

23. *Put away the strange gods*, &c. See above on v. 14. Rabbi Levi, son of Gerson, a Jewish commentator, remarks upon this passage, that Joshua 'says this to them, in order that if their hearts had been enticed by any of the idolatries of the people of that land, they should *put away the pernicious thoughts* that were in them.' Augustin is of the same opinion in relation to the true meaning of the passage.

25. *Joshua made a covenant.* Heb. יכרת ברית *yikrōth berith, cut a covenant;* alluding to the *sacrifice* usually offered on such occasions. But whether the ordinary rites were performed at this time is uncertain. The use of this term does not perhaps necessarily imply that they were. The ceremonies usual in *forming* and in *renewing* a covenant might not have been the same.—— ¶ *Set them a statute and an ordinance.* That is, as some suppose, on renewing the covenant he formed the whole into a statute and ordinance which was promulgated for all Israel to receive and obey. Both they and their posterity were to regard it in the light of a binding enactment, having all the force of a divine ordinance. Otherwise the phrase, 'he set them a statute,' &c., may mean that he declared or propounded to them, he set before them, the sum and substance of the Mosaic statutes, which their covenant obliged them to observe. But from what is said in the next verse of his writing these words in the book of the law, we think the former the most correct interpretation.

26. *Wrote these words in the book*

B. C. 1427.] CHAPTER XXIV. 219

26 ¶ And Joshua ^c wrote these words in the book of the law of God, and took ^d a great stone, and ^e set it up there ^f under an oak that *was* by the sanctuary of the LORD.

27 And Joshua said unto all the people, Behold, this stone shall be ^g a witness unto us: for ^h it hath heard all the words of the LORD which he spake unto us: it shall be therefore a witness unto you, lest ye deny your God.

c Deut. 31. 24. d Judg. 9. 6. e Gen. 28. 18. ch. 4. 3. f Gen. 35. 4.

g Gen. 31. 48, 52. Deut. 31. 19, 21, 26. ch. 22. 27, 28, 34. h Deut. 32. 1.

of the law of God. He made a record of the transaction, particularly of the solemn engagements of the people, and inserted it on some blank space of the great roll on which the sacred canon was originally inscribed. There it was written, that their obligation to obedience by the divine precept and by their own promise, might remain on record together. It would thus, as intimated in v. 25, from its very position, serve more effectually as 'a statute and an ordinance,' and be in fact an everlasting witness against them in case they should prove unfaithful to the compact, for it was probably transcribed from thence into all the other copies of the law which were multiplied in after ages for the benefit of the nation.——¶ *Took a great stone, and set it up there under an oak.* To insure still more effectually the memory of this solemn transaction, Joshua reared a pillar of stone on the spot, according to the custom of ancient times, Gen. 28. 18; Deut. 27. 2, as an enduring monument of the event which had now occurred. Whether the stone contained an inscription defining the purpose of its erection, is not certain, though not improbable. The 'oak' here mentioned is supposed by some to have been the same with that under which Jacob buried the idols and images that were found in his family, Gen. 35. 4, but in Judg. 9. 6, the original term is translated 'plain,' and the place where the stone was set up is called 'the plain of the pillar.'——¶ *That was by the sanctuary of the Lord.* Near the place where the ark and the tabernacle now stood, during their temporary continuance at Shechem. See on v. 1.

27. *It hath heard all the words,* &c. A strong figure of speech, by which he tacitly upbraids the people with the hardness of their hearts, as if this stone had heard to as good purpose as some of them; and if they should forget what was now done, this stone would so far preserve the remembrance of it, as to reproach them for their stupidity and carelessness, and be a witness against them. Williams very appositely cites from Livy the following instance of a similar phraseology;—' The general of the Æqui informed the Roman ambassadors (sent to complain of a plundering excursion) that they might deliver their message to an oak which shaded his tent. On this one of the ambassadors, turning away, said: ' This *venerable oak* and all the gods *shall know* that you have violated the peace; they shall now *hear* our complaints; and may they soon *be witnesses,* when we revenge with our arms the violation of divine and hu-

28 So ⁱJoshua let the people depart, every man unto his inheritance.

29 ¶ ᵏ And it came to pass after these things, that Joshua the son of Nun the servant of the Lord died, *being* a hundred and ten years old.

30 And they buried him in the border of his inheritance in ˡTimnath-serah, which *is* in mount Ephraim, on the north side of the hill of Gaash.

31 And ᵐ Israel served the Lord all the days of Joshua, and all the days of the elders that overlived Joshua, and which

i Judg. 2. 6.   k Judg. 2. 8.   l chap. 19. 50. Judges 2. 9.   m Judges 2. 7.

---

man rights.' By a like usage of speech the sacred writers frequently call upon the *heavens* and the *earth* to hear their addresses to the people of Israel. Deut. 32. 1; Is. 1. 2.

28. *So Joshua let the people depart, every man to his own inheritance.* Heb. וישלח *yeshallâh, sent away, or dismissed.* This verse occurs in nearly the same words Judg. 2. 6, with the added clause, 'to possess the land;' i. e. that every one might manfully exert himself to expel the Canaanites and obtain the complete possession of his destined inheritance.—' In this affecting manner Joshua took his leave of Israel, went from this last and perhaps best source to God and them, and was speedily taken to his rest in heaven.' *Scott.*

29. *Joshua—died, being a hundred and ten years old.* Precisely the age of his renowned ancestor Joseph; yet he was not buried in the same place with him, but in his own inheritance, which seems to have been the general practice.—How long he lived after the entrance of Israel into Canaan we have no means of determining. Lightfoot thinks it was about seventeen years, but the Jewish chronologers generally fix it at twenty-seven or twenty-eight. There is no mention of any public mourning at his death, as there was for Moses and Aaron, and his only epitaph was, in effect, couched in the brief terms, 'THE SERVANT OF THE LORD.' This however comprehended the sum of the highest eulogiums that could be bestowed on his character. Though inferior in many respects to Moses, yet in this he was equal to him, that according as his work was in the sphere in which he was placed, he had approved himself a diligent, devoted, and faithful servant of the Most High; and no man need desire a more honorable testimonial to record his worth to his own or future generations.

30. *Buried him in the border of his inheritance in Timnath-serah.* In the compass, in the limits of his inheritance. See the remark on the import of the word 'border' in the note on ch. 19. 25. Of Timnath-serah, see on Judg. 2. 9.

31. *The elders that over-lived Joshua.* Heb. ' that prolonged their days after Joshua.' Intimating that the salutary influence of Joshua's exemplary life and character extended beyond the term of his natural existence, and served for a number of years to keep the people in a general course of obedience. Whether for good or for evil the effect of our example may be expected to live after us. This shows that this part of the

had ⁿ known all the works of the LORD that he had done for Israel.

32 ¶ And ᵒ the bones of Joseph, which the children of Israel brought up out of Egypt, buried they in Shechem, in a parcel of ground ᵖ which Jacob bought of the sons of Hamor the father of Shechem for a hundred pieces of silver ; and it became the inheritance of the children of Joseph.

33 And Eleazar the son of Aaron died ; and they buried him in a hill *that pertained to* ᑫ Phinehas his son, which was given him in mount Ephraim.

n Deut. 11. 2, and 31. 13. ᵒ Gen. 50. 25. Exod. 13. 19. ᵖ Gen. 33. 19.

q Exod. 6. 25. Judg. 20. 28.

---

book must have been written a considerable time after the death of Joshua. See on ch. 4. 9.——¶ *Which had known all the works of the Lord.* Who had been eye-witnesses of them, who had profoundly and devoutly regarded them ; who had not only seen them, but pondered upon them with those sentiments which they were calculated to excite. Such is the genuine import of ' known ' in this connexion.

32. *The bones of Joseph buried they in Shechem.* Joseph's death took place in Egypt about two hundred years before that of Joshua, and we learn, Gen. 50. 25 ; Ex. 13. 19, that prior to his decease he had given a strict charge that his bones should be conveyed away out of Egypt by his people when they themselves went up from thence. Accordingly they had carried these precious relics with them in all their wanderings through the wilderness, and never attempted to bury them till they were peaceably settled in the promised land. The act of sepulture, though here related *after* the account of the death of Joshua, undoubtedly took place *before* it, and not improbably at the time of the general convention at Shechem described in the present chapter. The occasion, at any rate, would seem to have been a very suitable one, for such a solemn ceremony, although it be true that a considerable long interval had now elapsed since the conquest and occupation of Canaan. If any one prefers to translate the original ' had buried,' instead, of ' buried,' implying that the circumstance took place some years before, when the children of Joseph first received their inheritance, which they would naturally be disposed at once to consecrate by depositing within it the remains of their venerated ancestor, we know of nothing to object against it.——¶ *Which Jacob bought,* &c. See on Gen. 33. 19.

33. *And Eleazar—died.* Probably about the same time with Joshua. ——¶ *In a hill* that pertained to *Phinehas.* As the cities assigned to the priests lay in the lots of Judah, Benjamin and Simeon, neither father nor son could properly *inherit* a portion located in Mount Ephraim. But such a portion might be *given* them there, and the probability is that the people voluntarily gave to the high priest a place of residence situated at a convenient distance from Joshua and the tabernacle, and that this was called the ' hill of Phinehas,' because he dwelt longer there than his father Eleazar had done.

www.ingramcontent.com/pod-product-compliance
Lightning Source LLC
Chambersburg PA
CBHW060605230426
43670CB00011B/1981